MATTER OF GLORY

MATTER OF GLORY

A NEW PREFACE TO PARADISE LOST

by

JOHN PETER RUMRICH

UNIVERSITY OF PITTSBURGH PRESS

Published by the University of Pittsburgh Press, Pittsburgh, Pa. 15260
Copyright © 1987, University of Pittsburgh Press
All rights reserved
Feffer and Simons, Inc., London
Manufactured in the United States of America

Library of Congress Cataloging-in-Publication Data

Rumrich, John Peter, 1954–
  Matter of glory.

  Includes index.
    1. Milton, John, 1608–1674. Paradise lost.
  2. Glory in literature. 3. Chaos (Christian theology)
  in literature. I. Title.
  PR3562.R86 1987   821'.4   87-40158
  ISBN 0-8229-3564-3

For
Julia M. Rumrich

In memory of
Guenther G. Rumrich
1911–1983

"I don't know what you mean by 'glory,'" Alice said.

Humpty Dumpty smiled contemptuously. "Of course you don't — till I tell you. I meant 'there's a nice knock-down argument for you!'"

"But 'Glory' doesn't mean 'a nice knock-down argument," Alice objected.

"When I use a word," Humpty Dumpty said, in rather a scornful tone, "it means just what I choose it to mean — neither more nor less."

"The question is," said Alice, "whether you can make words mean so many different things."

"The question is," said Humpty Dumpty, "which is to be master — that's all."

— Through the Looking Glass, *chapter 6*

CONTENTS

ACKNOWLEDGMENTS

M Y CHIEF INTELLECTUAL DEBT is to William Kerrigan, who taught me *Paradise Lost* and who, with the subtle yet incisive James Nohrnberg, presided over my Ph.D. dissertation. This work also benefits from the presence of other revered teachers: Paul Houser, Stanley Holberg, Thomas Berger, and Lester Beaurline.

In the last five years, this book has undergone a substantial metamorphosis of its own, and I am grateful to those who have helped me work this change. Generally, I have learned most from students, among whom three well represent others I must leave unnamed: Yue Xu, Bradley Knopp, and especially Michael Bauman, who not only assisted with research but also, as I was teaching him Milton, taught me theology. Various portions of this work have profited from the comments and valued advice of John Boyd, S.J., James Earl, Richard Giannone, Maurice Kelley, David Loewenstein, and Warwick Wadlington. As the reconstructed parts looked as if they might form a more perfect union, colleagues at the University of Texas offered the fruits of their experience and wisdom. Of them, Wayne Rebhorn and John Velz scrutinized the entire manuscript and responded in detail and with blessed candor. Leo Damrosch, a longtime teacher and friendly voice of sanity, took time to consider the penultimate draft and improved it by his advice. The unselfish Stephen Fallon offered the sincerest recognition of active engagement, and his objections unerringly identified weaknesses in my argument.

Some chapters have appeared elsewhere in less finished form, and I wish to express my appreciation to the journals where they appeared. The basis of chapter 4 occurred as "Milton's Concept of Substance," *English Language Notes* 19 (1982), pp. 218–33. Parts of chapters 1 and 3 comprised a single essay under the title of "Milton and the Meaning of Glory," *Milton Studies* 20 (1984), pp. 75–86. And much of chapter 10 was published as "Milton, Duns Scotus, and the Fall of Satan," *Journal of the History of Ideas* 46 (1985), pp. 33–49.

The University Research Institute of the University of Texas granted funds for the preparation of this manuscript. Ona Kay Stephenson typed it and set an example of accuracy and perseverance for me to follow. When circumstances had me in Beijing, China, without a typewriter available for final revisions, Bill Jaquess of IBM graciously lent the use of a machine that allowed me to meet my deadline.

Finally, sympathetic friends Ted H. Roberts and Deborah Firlit lent moral support during a difficult time, as have my sisters, brother, and Aunt Kathleen at all times. Though Jill Rumrich's contributions to this work go mostly unspoken, I wish publicly to thank her for being the toughest critic of my prose, especially of its every tendency toward pomp and prolixity. Such excess as remains I acknowledge mine, as I do the rest of this book's shortcomings and overdoings.

The great debts lie secure beyond my ability to express or even to recognize them. And I have resigned myself to that. Yet I take this moment to remember my father and bid him rest.

MATTER OF GLORY

INTRODUCTION

THIS BOOK ON *Paradise Lost* began with curiosity about two apparently discrete problems: first, the meaning of glory; second, the proper identification of chaos. I would not now deny that often for devoted Milton scholars the shortest distance between any two points is all of *Paradise Lost*. Nevertheless, I will record my then unexpected discovery that these ostensibly distinct interests between them encompassed the whole pile and structure of the epic. Such a claim may sound like fairly typical, if tactlessly grandiose, introductory rhetoric, but it readily appears that the statement is at least schematically accurate. As I will argue in this book, chaos is the material basis of God's power — his infinite potency — which, though prior to creation, nevertheless exists as an essential attribute of the deity. Glory, on the other hand, most commonly signifies the very end or final cause of creation. In Milton's philosophy, such glory — apocalyptic or eschatological glory we may call it — consists of the preexistent matter of chaos after it has been shaped and spiritualized into its most fully realized condition.[1] The latent power of chaos and its perfect manifestation in final glory both are for Milton states of being. So obviously, if only in neutral chronological and metaphysical terms, chaos and glory between them include everything. Furthermore, in a notoriously proleptic religion such as Christianity, especially Milton's Christianity, glory also signifies the intervening struggle by which the merely possible of chaos becomes the fully actual of the end time. In Pauline terms (see 2 Cor. 4:17), the faithful in the midst of that struggle find solace in the idea of glory because it implies a conclusion that renders life meaningful. In other words, a believer's sense of glory intimates that coherence and meaning will ultimately resolve the burdensome consciousness of an otherwise relentless succession of petty moments.

Consideration of a believer's convictions about the meaning of life raises issues of psychological import and suggests that a study of glory in *Paradise Lost* should involve more than simply the scheme or framework of Milton's cosmos. We cannot fully understand chaos or glory in Milton's epic apart from the subjectivity of creatures, or apart from consideration of God's motive for establishing creatures distinct from himself. As many Christians traditionally have, Milton believed that glory actually completes the deity or affords him a pleasure that logically he cannot possess on his own. "It consummates the deity," says Luther in characteristically expressive language.[2] In plainer terms, Milton's God wants glory and uses his power to get it. In this book, I describe the transactions of power and glory between creature and creator in terms of the Greek and Hebrew traditions that Milton drew on in composing his epic. I note in passing, however, that from a psychoanalytic perspective, the usual emphasis of Milton scholars on Oedipal issues of law, obedience, and punishment has resulted in the corresponding neglect of the epic's primary, pervasive concern with negotiations between narcissistic longing for perfect recognition and the recalcitrance of an unresponsive reality.

Philologically and etymologically, I have been curious about glory since my first reading of *Paradise Lost*, indeed, since I first read Book I, where in a short space it is used in strikingly different contexts:[3]

> That *Glory* never shall his wrath or might
> Extort from me.   (110–11)

>   the mind and spirit remains
> Invincible, and vigour soon returns,
> Though all our *Glory* extinct.   (139–41)

>   th' invisible
> *Glory* of him that made them   (369–70)

> his heart
> Distends with pride, and hard'ning in his strength
> *Glories.*   (571–73)

> Thir *Glory* wither'd. (612; italics mine in each citation)

C. S. Lewis in one of his evangelical writings once admitted that although the idea of glory "is very prominent in the New Testament and in early Christian writings . . . , it makes no immediate appeal to me at all, and in that respect I fancy I am a typical modern."[4] Even among the less-than-typical moderns who apply themselves to the study of Renaissance literature, the far-flung semantic territories belonging to glory, particularly as traveled by Milton, have gone largely unexplored.[5] Perhaps because the word *glory* is even now a common one, we simply have neglected to ask the obvious questions.

In the passages cited above, for example, does glory mean "unconditional surrender by one's foe," "splendid appearance," "God's invisible essence," "a physical feature that can either flourish or wither," or, as Milton's various usages suggest, all of these? If all, then how do such widely divergent meanings relate to one another? Unfortunately, the remainder of the poem offers no obvious solution. Milton continues to use *glory* and its cognates throughout *Paradise Lost*—more frequently, for example, than he does *fruit.* And he uses *glory* in ways that suggest not only fine discriminations of sense, but apparently opposite meanings. Consequently, part of my purpose in what follows is simply to define and relate the various meanings of glory available to Milton. I do so primarily in chapters 1 and 2, which investigate the Hebrew and Greek roots of glory, and in chapter 3, which discusses the remarkable civil and religious synthesis of these disparate traditions, particularly as it appears in Renaissance literature and in the life and works of John Milton.

The mention above of C. S. Lewis calls to mind what those familiar with Milton studies will no doubt have already recognized, the allusion of this book's subtitle to *A Preface to Paradise Lost.* I wish here to disown any implication that I consider myself Lewis' equal in style, lucidity, or general literary expertise. By this book's subtitle I intend to call attention only to the three following relations to Lewis' work. First, like Lewis, I address the meaning of the whole poem as well as its cultural basis. Second, I consequently follow roughly the same course as Lewis, moving from Milton's classical and biblical models, through his Christian philosophy, and ultimately to particular interpretive issues in the poem. Third, I offer an alternative understanding to *Paradise Lost* in two respects: (1) the epic's relations to its precursors, and (2) the theology of the poem and its relation to Milton's intended meaning.

As Lewis with characteristic common sense and clarity explains, "The first qualification for judging any piece of workmanship from a corkscrew to a cathedral is to know *what* it is."[6] By describing Milton's generic intention, Lewis establishes what E. D. Hirsch has called a "general horizon" for its meaning.[7] Lewis' discussion of primary and secondary epic, particularly in terms of the aesthetic techniques appropriate to each, is most fruitful and I do not propose to improve upon it. I would revise the horizon that Lewis constructs for Milton's epic only when it comes to his discussion of the subjects typical of primary (e.g., Homeric) and secondary (e.g., Virgilian) epics. According to Lewis, epic in its primary stage concerns relatively trivial matters, ones involving merely "human and personal tragedy" against a background of "meaningless flux" (p. 31). The subject of secondary epic develops to include the "adult" theme of suprapersonal vocation and posits a meaningful world in which great endeavors possess long-lasting, general significance (pp. 29–39). In my opinion, however, Lewis' distinction fails to account for the persistent concern of all epics with *glory*, whether personal or suprapersonal. Furthermore, although it may be possible to construe the *Aeneid* as being closer to *Paradise Lost* on a developmental ethical scale measuring adolescent versus mature values, I still would contend that the heart of Milton's epic lies closer to the *Iliad* than to the *Aeneid*. In this book I attempt to demonstrate that the generic subject of epic is properly understood as matter of glory and that for Milton such matter must ultimately be conceived in personal, not public terms.

Lewis' version of Milton's general horizon matches, as for the sake of consistency it must, his analysis of what Milton specifically includes and excludes from the meaning of his work. In keeping with "grown-up" secondary epic's public and suprapersonal thrust, an

Aeneas-like Milton, Lewis claimed, "laid aside most of his private theological whimsies" (p. 92). His aim was to produce a particular effect "on the ordinary educated and Christian audience of his time" (p. 91). Significantly, Lewis' own evangelical method was to emphasize the common essence of Christian beliefs — "mere" Christianity as he called it — and he saw Milton as a predecessor on this eminently brotherly path. But as opposed to Lewis', Milton's ecumenism was most strikingly one of dissimilitudes, brotherly or not, and his heresies are neither so arbitrary as the word *whimsies* suggests nor are they expurgated from his epic for reasons of decorum or the anticipated satisfaction of a mainstream audience. In the chapters that follow I hope to reveal how integral, how precisely unwhimsical, Milton's heresies are to the fictional cosmos of *Paradise Lost*.

That Lewis sees Milton as performing much the same role in the epic genre as Lewis played in the genre of Christian apologetics underscores the great danger besetting anyone who attempts to reconstruct Milton's meaning, that of falling into a circular argument. One defines the general horizon of a given work in the way that suits one's sense of the particulars of that work — and then proceeds to find evidence to confirm the horizon so defined. As Hirsch observes, "The procedure is thoroughly circular; the context is derived from the submeanings and the submeanings are specified and rendered coherent with reference to the context."[8] Lewis thus determines that Milton sacrifices his theological eccentricities for the greater good of Christianity and so misconstrues, for example, Milton's heretical materialism as a "fugitive colour on the poem which we detect only by the aid of external evidence" (p. 90).

Consequently, in accordance with the horizon of decorous orthodoxy that he posits, Lewis almost entirely neglects to mention chaos, an omission that signals a widespread problem in Milton studies. Although unlike Lewis many scholars have paid chaos close attention, no interpreter whose work I have read has been willing to accept, or even really to consider, that the Anarch Chaos and his Consort Night represent the material dimension of God's own being.[9] The deity in Milton's epic, who has generally been received by perceptive readers of all biases as unrelenting and tiresome in his paternal masculinity and didactic authoritarianism, actually profits enormously from the secret possession of a distinctly feminine and incorrigibly unruly source of power — an inexhaustible womb. In chapter 4 I shall argue that Chaos and Night represent an *essential* — I use the word with its full theological force — attribute of God himself and so participate in the fullness of divinity as neither the Son nor the Holy Spirit do.

The slowness of Milton studies to apprehend accurately and in detail the interpretive significance of Milton's unique theology stems, I think, from the implicit assumption of the same orthodox horizon for *Paradise Lost* that Lewis explicitly proposes. True, most scholars willingly concede the presence of materialism in *Paradise Lost*, but they often do so abstractly or without awareness of its vital, pervasive influence in the epic. In this as in other cases, the effect has been to perceive Milton's highly original Christianity as more ordinary than the facts will allow and to reduce his heresies — carefully constructed positions integral to a cohesive, consistent religious philosophy — to "fugitive colours" on a poem portrayed as almost unexceptionably orthodox. The surprising consequences of Milton's heretical theology, his material monism in particular, will comprise a main theme of this book, and in order to explain the material workings implicit in Milton's cosmos, I will often turn to the "external evidence" that Lewis would prefer to discount. A basic premise underlying this study is that to avoid minimizing what may be of crucial import to the meaning intended by Milton, we must consult, as Hirsch again maintains, "the author's typical outlook, the typical associations and expectations which form in part the context of his utterance."[10] In this light, Lewis' contention that in *Paradise Lost* Milton suppressed certain firmly held beliefs for reasons of decorum contradicts what any reasonable assessment of his life and works proclaims: that he frequently defied conventional expectations of all sorts and reinvented decorum whenever he thought it necessary for the expression of his highly original ideas and convictions.

The meaning of the epic that I understand Milton to have intended implies the natural as well as the moral workings of a material creation, a creation that takes shape between the absolute potency of chaos and the perfect actualization of final glory. Within this Aristotelian framework, each creature finds itself inexorably bound to change and motion. Not surprisingly, then, this preface also differs from Lewis' by prominently including among Milton's horizon-setting influences Ovid's *Metamorphoses,* a poem that until recently has been largely ignored as an epic precursor of *Paradise Lost.*[11] Furthermore, given the inevitability of material metamorphosis, the traditional doctrine that God's progeny are not only literally themselves but also figures of divine self-expression becomes for Milton unusually critical in constituting what it means to be a creature. *Only the metaphorical dimension of one's being allows for continuity of identity through time.* In order to be knowable as a creature, indeed in order to be as a creature at all, one must bear the burden of significance. And the content of this significance is always and necessarily the glory of God.

Mention of this necessity raises the topic of the theodicy in *Paradise Lost.* While the middle chapters will be concerned to identify and relate the various kinds of creatures in Milton's cosmos — rebel angels, human beings, good angels — and to describe the moral and natural metamorphoses characteristic of them, the final chapters will turn to Milton's justification of God's ways. On this topic Lewis and I agree that Milton manages at least a partial success. But before I explain this book's relation to Lewis' on this final point, I must first digress in order to justify the importance I attach to the theodicy, an issue that has fallen from attention in much recent scholarship.

Lewis' contention that Milton wrote for the ordinary Christian of his time prefigures the position underlying the contemporary scanting of the theodicy. Finding its most influential expression in Stanley Fish's consensus-forming *Surprised by Sin,* Lewis' basic argument has become dominant in Milton scholarship, though with two significant developments. First, Milton's "ordinary, educated and Christian audience" has increasingly been identified with the relatively orthodox, conservative Puritans of mid-seventeenth-century England. Second, Milton's own views have also increasingly been identified with the views of that audience (an identification which despite its inaccuracy has at least the virtue of admitting that Milton generally intended his works to mean what he believed). Consequently, the catechismal version of *Paradise Lost* proposed by Fish resembles more the work of a Presbyterian didact such as the self-righteous Richard Baxter (seven citations in *Surprised by Sin*) than the work of a politico-religious Independent like Milton. In my view, William Empson's much maligned version of a radical Milton's intention is in historical detail and general conception closer to the truth than Fish's more successful though largely rhetorical invention. Despite his tendency to exaggerate, Empson at least recognized the main point — as did Lewis — that Milton is absolutely serious about his theodicy.[12] Fish, on the other hand, considers Milton's ostensible statement of purpose disingenuous: "'that thou may'st believe and be confirm'd' would have been a more honest — literal is the better word — *propositio* than 'justify the ways of God to men.'"[13]

Given an authorial horizon of relatively conservative Puritanism, one may well construe the stated aim of *Paradise Lost* as ironic bait designed to elicit — so as to correct — the hideous presumption of fallen humankind. In fact, if like Fish and much of recent scholarship we construct Milton's epic intention according to the context of typical Reformation attitudes, we must in the interest of coherence reject the sincerity of his stated purpose. This context after all, as represented by, say, the shared beliefs of Luther and Calvin, was deeply inimical to the very notion of theodicy. The more appropriate horizon for *Paradise Lost*, however, at least on the issue of theodicy, is that associated with Christian humanism.[14] The distinction between these opposed attitudes toward theodicy appears sharply in the debate on free will between Luther and Erasmus, a debate that I will briefly recount in order to clarify my position.

My contention is that Milton's deeply rooted affirmation of free will *requires* us to accept his theodicy as a straightforward attempt to accomplish what he says he wants to accomplish. Erasmus, like Milton, believed in the power of free choice, "which can do and does, in relation to God, whatever it pleases, uninhibited by any law or any sovereign authority" (p. 170).[15] Erasmus particularly maintains — and anticipates Milton in so maintaining — that freedom of choice applies to "the things which lead to eternal salvation . . . , the words and works of God which are presented to human will so that it may apply itself to them or turn away from them" (p. 172). Erasmus thinks it probable, and Milton confirms, that only God's prevenient grace can clear human understanding to the point where free choice becomes possible (p. 66; see *PL* 3, 185f.).[16] At that point, however, Man *can* choose between God and Satan, and that freedom makes a sincere theodicy possible.[17]

Luther admits that "it gives the greatest possible offense to common sense or natural reason that God by his own sheer will should abandon, harden, and damn men as if he enjoyed the sins and the vast eternal torments of his wretched creatures" (p. 244). Luther also understands that the denial of free choice leads reason inevitably to this conclusion, which simply testifies to the character of reason as, in Luther's typically subtle phrase, "the devil's whore" (p. 16). Hence Luther concedes that the assertion of free will is actually "sweating and toiling to excuse the goodness of God" (p. 244), a sweating and toiling that Milton consistently engaged in from the time of *Areopagitica* onward. Yet Luther, though he recognizes the theodical rationale behind the assertion of free will, insists that this primary gesture of theodicy displays fallen humanity's arrogance all the more clearly: "here they demand that God should act according to human justice, and do what seems right to them"; "he may damn none but those who in our judgment have deserved it" (p. 258). Insofar as Luther is concerned, the whole idea of a theodicy appears grossly supercilious, an illusion of freedom and dignity inspired by the devil.

For Erasmus and Milton, however, humankind is neither so insignificant nor so impotent as Luther would have it. Erasmus in fact seems stunned by how little Luther allows humanity as he cites the Reformer's claim that "no one has it in his own power to think a good or bad thought" and remarks only, "these are Luther's actual words," as if the claim refuted itself (p. 64). In effect, Luther reduces waking human consciousness to the state described by Adam as appropriate to sleep (5, 100f.). Even then, according to Adam, "Evil into the mind of God or Man / May come or go, so unapprov'd, and leave / No spot or blame behind" (5, 117–19). Adam's "so unapprov'd," nonsense to Luther, is an index to the distinction between Milton and the main body of Reformation thought. For Milton as for Erasmus, human beings enjoy the active freedom to reason and to choose, and this freedom, while it imposes the heavy burden of responsibility, also entitles reason, if not fully to comprehend the ways of God, then at least to construct a case for continued patience and fortitude even when faced with apparently senseless woe. Such a theodicy need not entail the quixotic task of a rational grasp and approval of all things as they are. As Jeffrey Barnouw writes of Leibniz's theodicy, "[It] relies on formal rational argument in order to justify the persistence of moral striving even in the face of apparent futility."[18]

Even if one were to follow the current fashion, and proclaim that we have no access to the "real" Milton and that the idea of a "real" *Paradise Lost* is theoretically naive, one might at least admit that the failure to account for the consequences of the invented Milton's repeated and emphatic assertion of free will renders the currently accepted version of the author of *Paradise Lost* so inconsistent as to be unworthy of our suspension of disbelief. As Luther understood in his dispute with Erasmus, free will is the "real issue" of the Reformation, "on which everything hinges" (p. 333). To perceive in *Paradise Lost* the intention to suppress questions concerning divine justice or to accomplish an ironic theodicy by undermining the attitude behind theodicy is to place Milton in Luther's camp. Although the similarity in ideas between Luther and Milton is often striking, Luther's kindred spirits with respect to the issue of free will and reason were in Milton's time relatively conservative Puritans such as the Presbyterians. And the political and theological Independent, whose prose, beginning in the mid-1640s and consistently thereafter, stressed human dignity and the nobility and freedom of human reason and will, simply does not belong in their company.

Indeed perhaps the saddest consequence of the success of Fish's invention is that a generation of students has been taught to hear the epic narrator as a censorious preacher, one whose characteristic tone is according to Fish tactless, accusatory, taunting, imperious, and humiliating.[19] Milton at his worst, the Milton of the least admirable moments of the prose pamphlets, has become the Milton of choice, the Milton we hear in the greatest nondramatic poem in English. This book attempts to provide an alternative to so gross a misapprehension, and like Lewis and Empson, in fact like almost all readers of *Paradise Lost* during the first three hundred years of its history, I take the theodicy seriously. Unlike Lewis, however, I do not claim that the shortcomings of Milton's justification of God derive from mistaken aesthetic decisions. Lewis argued that Milton made heaven "too like Olympus," and that the "anthropomorphic details make the Divine laughter sound merely spiteful and the Divine rebukes querulous" (p. 131).[20] But I will contend, as others have, that in Milton's view an author representing God *had* to resort to anthropomorphic figures because they were the ones authorized by God in *Scripture*. Hence, as Empson suggests, any discomfort that Milton's God causes us is appropriate also to the biblical God, or at least to the biblical God of Milton's interpretation. According to this analysis, dissatisfaction with Milton's God grows from a single condition, one which I mentioned early in this introduction: he wants glory and uses his power to get it. Until we come to terms with glory and God's desire for it, we will not be able to come to terms with the theodicy in *Paradise Lost*. I thus turn now to the biblical idea of glory.

1

GLORY IN THE
OLD TESTAMENT

MILTON'S IDEA of glory rests on the foundation of the simple Hebrew word *kabod. Kabod* has at least two distinct, immediately identifiable references: 1) great reputation; and 2) the very being of a substantial entity. Like the modern term *identity, kabod* thus suggests the uncertain reflection and potential dissonance between who someone actually is and how this someone appears to the rest of the world. With reference to God, for example, *kabod* can mean sensible manifestations of his majesty through his creatures — as in the verse, "the heavens declare the glory of God," or it can, as Joseph Mead writes, "denote the *Divine Essence* or *Deity* itself" — as in Milton's condemnation of idolatrous nations for deserting "th' invisible / Glory of him that made them" (1, 369–70).[1] Given the absolute, primary insistence of Hebrew law that God not be confused with his creatures, this fundamental division of meaning in the single word *kabod* demands attention. This chapter, however, will first survey the various meanings, images, and values attached to *kabod* and attempt to suggest their influence on Milton's thought and expression.

Milton's renditions of the psalms suggest that he also recognized the perplexity implicit in *kabod*, especially as it applies to the apprehension of God in and by creation.[2] Consider, for example, his relatively literal translation of Psalm 7:

Let the enemy persecute my soul, and take it; yea, let him tread down my life upon the earth, and lay mine honour in the dust.	Let th'enemy pursue my soul And overtake it, let him tread My life down to the earth and roll In the dust my glory dead, In the dust and there outspread Lodge it with dishonor foul.
(AV 7:5)[3]	(13–18)

While the Authorized Version distinguishes between life and honor (which here translates *kabod*), Milton's addition to line 16 allows a certain ambiguity: "glory" in "my glory dead" can be taken either as a metaphorical restatement of "life" from the preceding line, or, with the following lines, as a reference to the dead man's reputation. In his elaborate version of Psalm 114, Milton alters the rhetorical strategy of the original, which testifies purely to the brute impact of God's presence on an awestruck world, to contend explicitly that Jehovah's wondrous deeds make "his praise and glory . . . known" (6).[4] Similarly, Milton shifts the emphasis in his translation of Psalm 136 — originally a detailed list of God's mercies — to focus on the nature of the splendid being revealed by these mercies (especially 89–96). Despite his departures from the originals, Milton's translations nevertheless hold true to the meaning of *kabod* as it occurs in the Old Testament.

The meaning of *kabod* in the Old Testament begins with the idea of weight.[5] Moses uses *kabod* when he complains that the heaviness of his speech will hinder him as God's spokesman (Exod. 4:10). The intensity of a severe plague or famine could also be denoted by *kabod* (see Gen. 12:10; Exod. 9:3). When St. Paul contrasts the early Christians' "light affliction" with their ultimate reward, an "eternal weight of glory," he may have intended a pun on the Hebrew sense of the term (2 Cor. 4:17). Genesis describes the wealthy Abram as heavy (*kabod*) "in cattle, in silver, and in gold" (13:2). As Luther comments, the transition from *kabod* as material wealth to *kabod* as the magnificent being of God seems natural enough "because wealth and an abundance of all things produce glory and magnificence."[6] Hence, whether it refers to an abundance of mass or to the profundity of an intangible state of being, *kabod* denotes the substantiality and magnitude of what it characterizes.

True glory, therefore, concerns something weighty, sober, and grave—intangibles that are almost tangible. As Luther again remarks, "metaphorically [*kabod*] denotes glory; it signifies that the things are present and that it is not a vain and empty matter."[7] Luther therefore considers his ministry a "weighty" matter because it "serves first to the glory of God."[8] The attention that Reformation and Renaissance authors, Sidney and Spenser in particular, pay to bearing, carriage, pace, and personal gravity is closely related to the belief that the weight of the inner man appears in his deportment. One recalls also the parallel in Aristotle's depiction of *megalopsychia*, or highmindedness, and its appearance in the "slow step," "deep voice," and "level utterance" of the great man (*Nicomachean Ethics* 4.3.1125a14–15).[9]

Milton regularly employs imagery of weight or gravity to glorify people and ideas. The man, for example, who possesses knowledge of God—the infallible mark of *kabod*, as we shall see—sustains "a sorer burden of mind, and more pressing then any supportable toil, or waight, which the body can labour under" (*CP* 1, 801).[10] In *The Reason of Church Government* he argues that episcopacy is excluded "from the solid and grave Ethical law" (*CP* 1, 765). Making use of the connection between *kabod* and visible revelation, Milton particularly associates gravity with sensible manifestations of divinity:

> There is not that thing in the world of more grave and urgent importance . . . then is discipline. . . . Discipline is not only the removall of disorder, but if any visible shape can be given to divine things, the very visible shape and image of vertue.
> (*CP* 1, 751)

In paraphrasing Basil's comparison of the Sophists to night-owls, Milton adds his own clarification: "in weighty matters of visible truth and beneficial knowledge [they] are blind" (*CP* 1, 381). Milton opposes gravity as a virtue to the vice of levity in *Christian Doctrine*, and in *Paradise Lost*, he describes as "grave" the "sober Race of Men," who nevertheless for the sake of light women "yield up all thir virtue, all thir fame" (*CP* 6, 768; *PL* 11, 585, 621, 623). Their seducers he depicts as devoid of glory, "empty of all good wherein consists / Woman's domestic honor and chief praise" (*PL* 11, 616–17). The clergy under Laud follow the example of these early sons of God in that they "suffer'd themselvs . . . to countenance with their prostituted Gravities every Politick Fetch that was then on foot" (*CP* 1, 531). Satan typifies the loss of glory in this as in other respects. Despite his "Regal port," and the ability to dilate his appearance as the occasion warrants, God's scales appear to reveal him "how light, how weak" (*PL* 4, 1012). This reversal of Homer's use of the scales, so that the side of the destined loser kicks up instead of sinking, while it may signal Milton's deference to the Book of Daniel (5:27), also modifies Homer's epic device according to Hebrew values.[11] To Milton, weight signifies true glory.[12]

As Rudolph Kirk explains in his notes to *Animadversions*, "the importance of the differentiation between light and heavy objects was immensely significant both in theology and physics and was, therefore, cosmological, if somewhat allegorical, in implication" (*CP* 1, 671). Confusion about heaviness and lightness signals a "mixed scale of values and lack of understanding of God's natural order" (*CP* 1, 671). Such confusion threatens a return to chaos, where one finds things without weight having weight — "*sine pondere habentia pondus*" (*CP* 1, 671). While weightiness indicates the visible revelation of glorious truth, lightness suggests vanity and deceit. Accordingly, in discussing the Son's possession of divine glory, Milton interprets *bodily*, in the assertion of Colossians 2:9 that "in him dwelleth all the fullness of the Godhead bodily," as perhaps meaning "*solidly*, as opposed to the *vain deceit* mentioned in the preceding verse" (*CP* 6, 273). Similarly, in *Paradise Lost*, Milton juxtaposes his vision of heavenly glory with Satan's exploration of the Paradise of Fools, where a "windy Sea of Land" awaits those who would build "thir fond hopes of Glory or lasting fame" on vain pursuits (3, 440, 449). An "inclement sky" ever threatens "storms / Of *Chaos*" to the vaporous inhabitants (3, 425–26), who are as light as the "devious Air" of their kingdom (3, 489). From earth they fly "up . . . like Aereal vapors" to a world filled with "things transitory and vain," where the vainglorious "find / Fit retribution, empty as thir deeds" (3, 445–46, 453–54).

Milton's association of false glory with preexistent chaos reflects Scripture's equation of *kabod* with creativity and new life. Thanks in part to the abundance of their progeny, Sarah and Abraham set the standard for human *kabod*, suggesting that gravity signals the *kabod* of the biblical female just as surely as gravity signals that of the male. If one tends automatically to show respect to certain men simply because of their grave bearing, certainly one also defers automatically to a woman who will bear children. Raphael thus greets Eve according to the unexpressed *kabod* which nonetheless resides within her: "Hail Mother of Mankind, whose fruitful Womb / Shall fill the World more numerous with thy Sons / Than with these various fruits the Trees of God / Have heap'd this Table" (5, 388–91). The perversion or diminishment of *kabod*, conversely, results in monstrosities such as Satan brings forth, or such as inhabit the Paradise of Fools —"unaccomplisht works . . . / Abortive, monstrous, . . . unkindly mixt, / . . . . / Embryos, and Idiots," including those Giants of "ill-join'd Sons and Daughters born / First from the ancient World" (3, 455–74).

In fact, the generations which follow the misalliance of the Sons of God with the daughters of Cain, "prodigious Births of body or mind, / . . . Giants, men of high renown," with "many a vain exploit" actually pervert the very standards by which men recognize glory (11, 687–88; 3, 465). It is as if humankind's sense of glory itself suffers a miscarriage because of these inglorious prodigies:

> To overcome in Battle, and subdue
> Nations, and bring home spoils with infinite
> Man-slaughter, shall be held the highest pitch
> Of human Glory, and for Glory done
> Of triumph, to be styl'd great Conquerors.
> Patrons of Mankind, Gods, and Sons of Gods,
> Destroyers rightlier call'd, and Plagues of men.
> Thus Fame shall be achiev'd, renown on Earth.
> And what most merits fame in silence hid.
>
> (11, 691–99)

Not surprisingly, the rebel angels set the pattern for the pursuit of glory through military strife (6, 377–85). For the peace-loving Milton, however, fertile, life-sustaining wisdom, not ferocious military prowess, best denotes glory (see Sonnets 15 and 16). But in the cruel world envisioned by Michael, men like Enoch "eminent / In wise deport," suffer at the hands of tyrants unless God protects them (11, 665–66; see also *PR* 3, 68–99).

The failure to show respect or to render praise — *kabod* as fame — to a man of *kabod*, or to God as the source of *kabod*, is the mark of a fool and thus an indication of the negligent one's own lack of glory. The secondary meaning of *kabod*, as the fame or respect owed to a substantial person, makes it an effective antithesis for disgrace or shame, even as the wise man of *kabod* is an effective antithesis for the barren fool: "the wise shall inherit glory [*kabod*]: but shame shall be the promotion of fools" (Prov. 3:35). The use of "inherit" tells us that the wise man or woman does not merely enjoy fame or progeny, but that he stands entitled to it — it belongs to him. All modern prudence aside, a woman of wisdom, such as Sarah or the mother of Christ, will bear children. Biblically, fertility and wisdom imply one another, and both express the creative principle of being indicated by *kabod*.

In the Psalms, *kabod* generally concerns the complementary relationship between man and God. The Psalmist glorifies God with his very being (his own glory): "I will sing and give praise, even with my glory [*kabod*]. Awake psaltry and harp: I myself will awake early" (Ps. 108:1–2; cf. 57:8). "I myself" joins the psaltry and harp as an instrument for the praise of God. The Psalmist also says that God blesses him "to the end that my glory [*kabod*] may sing praise. . . . O Lord my God, I will give thanks unto thee for ever" (Ps. 30:12). Here *kabod* directly parallels the "I" in the verse. In recognizing his dependence on God, he recognizes the complementary nature of his own *kabod*. Similarly, when in *Paradise Lost* Adam and Eve sing their evening praises with "adoration pure / Which God likes best," everything that exists, and even that which will exist, reminds them of their maker:

> Thou also mad'st the Night,
> Maker Omnipotent, and thou the Day,
> Which we in our appointed work imploy'd
> Have finisht happy in our mutual help
> And mutual love, the Crown of all our bliss
> Ordain'd by thee, and this delicious place
> For us too large, where thy abundance wants
> Partakers, and uncropt falls to the ground.
> But thou hast promis'd from us two a Race
> To fill the Earth, who shall with us extol
> Thy goodness infinite. (4, 724–34)

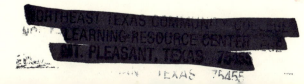

In their psalmic recognition and praise of their creator's glory, Adam and Eve wisely recognize the plentitude of God in creation as the source of their own complementary fertility.

Milton's awareness of the complementary relations that comprise glory also appears in his use of *adore* and *adorn*. In *Paradise Lost*, Milton prefers *adore* to *worship* as a description of creatures' praise of the creator. This preference corresponds to his use of *adorn* with reference to decoration and creation of beauty, including the heavens, idols, buildings, the nuptial bower, and especially Eve: "adorn for thy delight," "with perfect beauty adorn'd," "in naked beauty more adorn'd / . . . than Pandora," "adorn'd / With what all Earth or Heaven could bestow," "adorn'd / With all perfections," "Adorn'd / She was indeed" (8, 576; 4, 634, 713; 8, 482; 9, 1030; 10, 151). According to the *OED*, *adore* and *adorn* derive from similar Middle English roots and in the seventeenth century were used interchangeably. The meanings of *adore* and *adorn* meet in the sense of "to honor" or "to glorify." Eve's "naked beauty," which outstrips Pandora's and symbolizes the beauty of all creation, thus elicits Adam's "adoration pure / Which God likes best" (4, 737–38). In gratefully receiving and recognizing glory as adornment, man adores and moves closer to communion with God. As Luther explains, the "'Glory of God' is . . . something which is given to us by God and because of which we can before Him glory in Him and about Him."[13]

In the Old Testament, the reference of *kabod* to Yahweh himself orders the various meanings and images associated with the term. Milton understood, as did his learned contemporaries and theological predecessors, that the ultimate meaning of *kabod* is simply God: "'glory' in Hebrew denotes the glorious thing itself."[14] Other significations of *kabod*, comprising a symbolism of good as varied and as layered as the symbolism of evil, can always be considered to be manifestations of God, even when they include creatures with reason and free will. Luther explains that "in an active sense the glory of God is the glory that God has in Himself; in a passive sense it is that glory by which we glory in God."[15] Consequently, while glory primarily denotes God himself, it also characterizes revelations of him, so that Milton's concept of glory affects his view of himself as an epic poet-prophet as well as his choice of subject matter and use of figurative language in *Paradise Lost*.

The Old Testament associates the visible manifestations of invisible God with unbearable light, thunder, the sounding of trumpets, lightning, fire, and with moments pregnant with imminent wrath or favor (Exod. 16:7; 33:18–19; Lev. 9:6, 9:23; Num. 20:6; 14:10). Perhaps no passage in *Paradise Lost* better underlines Milton's intimacy with the Hebrew idea of *kabod* than Abdiel's final remarks in Book V:

> Yet not for thy advice or threats I fly
> These wicked Tents devoted, lest the wrath
> Impendent, raging into sudden flame
> Distinguish not; for soon expect to feel
> His Thunder on thy head, devouring fire.
> Then who created thee lamenting learn,
> When who can uncreate thee thou shalt know.
>
> (889–95)

As Hughes notes, Milton here draws upon Moses' warning to the innocent among the blasphemous to escape the impending wrath of God (Num. 16:26). The same glory that as a fiery revelation of wrath devours the disobedient or unlucky can also appear as "propitious Fire" to consume a worthy sacrifice and so to reveal God's approval (see *PL* 11, 441; Lev. 9:24).

In expressing God's glory, Milton relies also on Exodus accounts wherein clouds sheathe the deadly brilliance of Yahweh: "the glory of the Lord abode upon mount Sinai, and the cloud covered it. . . . And the sight of the glory of the Lord was like devouring fire. . . . And Moses went into the midst of the cloud" (Exod. 24:16–18). An unknowable light, surrounded by clouds, thus constitutes Milton's central image of glory: "how oft amidst / Thick clouds and dark doth Heav'n's all-ruling Sire / Choose to reside, his Glory unobscur'd" (*PL* 2, 263–65). In the invocations to Books I and III, Milton even implies that the experience of Moses, who enters the protective and revelatory cloud that covers God's insupportable glory, prefigures his own irradiation by the glory of God within the "cloud . . . and ever-during dark" of his blindness (3, 45).[16]

Although Milton may not have believed that his own face glowed with revelatory brilliance as Moses' did, he certainly knew the rabbinic tradition that before the Fall, Man's face shone with a ray of divine glory, and that after the Fall, Man lost his original brilliance (see 4, 292).[17] Satan and his companions suffer a more drastic darkening, as we learn from the very beginning of the poem's action (1, 84f.). Satan, once "cloth'd with transcendent brightness" has seen his glory depart so that he, as Zephon tells him, "resembl'st now / [His] sin and place of doom obscure and foul" (4, 839–40). Satan suffers not only embarrassment at "his lustre visibly impair'd," but also awe at the virtuous brilliance of unfallen angels and men (4, 850; see also 363–65, 844–49). Just as Satan adopts disguises after his Fall, so postlapsarian Man requires "troublesome disguises" to cover his shame (4, 740).

While creatures' shining faces represent the basic natural symbol of glory, Milton often resorts to clothing imagery — as the citations above testify — to express the paradoxical significances of glory. Clothing thus can represent the glory given by God to creatures, protection from God's own essential glory, or, most familiarly, a covering for shame. It may seem unlikely that Milton would relate clothing to glory (often in association with imagery of clouds), particularly given the fact that unfallen humankind is most glorious in its nudity. Nevertheless, he clearly does so. Consider his 1673 revision of stanza XV of the Nativity ode:

> Yea, Truth and Justice then
> Will down return to men,
>   Th'enamel'd *Arras* of the Rainbow wearing,
> And Mercy set between,
> Thron'd in Celestial sheen,
>   With radiant feet the tissued clouds down steering.
>
>   (141–46; 1645)

> Yea, Truth and Justice then
> Will down return to men,
>   Orb'd in a Rainbow; and like glories wearing
> Mercy will sit between
> Thron'd in Celestial sheen,
>   With radiant feet the tissued clouds down steering.
>
>   (141–46; 1673)

No metrical shortcomings in the earlier version warrant the changes in lines 143–44. But the later version does clarify Milton's meaning. The passage deals with the apocalyptic promise of the Incarnation and the reign of glory in which God's reconciliation of Mercy and Justice, signaled by the Nativity, will finally reinstitute a perfect order on Earth. The semicolon inserted in line 143, along with the assertion that Mercy wears "like glories," attests to the essential unity of Mercy, Truth, and Justice as aspects of God. Consequently, their divine origin is revealed to the world by their "like glories" of light and their "radiant" appearance in the "tissued clouds."

Adam and Eve's loss of their "first naked Glory," according to Milton's gloss, equals the first degree of death and signals "the loss of divine protection and favor, which results in the lessening of the majesty of the human countenance" (*PL* 9, 1115; *CP* 6, 394). The phrase "naked Glory" paradoxically asserts that Man enjoyed ideal, natural protection before the Fall. Shame marks the loss and may be defined as the diminution of glory or alienation from God. "In our Faces evident," as Adam says, shame leaves Man vulnerable before unfallen creatures, who will dazzle mortals "with thir blaze / Insufferably bright" (*PL* 9, 1077, 1083–84). Just as glory is lustrous and brilliant, shame, as we see during Satan's disfiguration on Niphates' top, is "pale" — a word which can translate the Hebrew for "shame" (4, 115). As I hope to demonstrate in chapters 5 and 6, this loss of color has a physiological basis related to the gradual deterioration of being brought about by death.

The fallen Adam's trepidation at the prospect of heaven's shining faces associates him with the cringing Israelites, who shy away from Moses' glowing countenance. Just as fallen Man needs artificial clothing to protect his body and cover his shame, so also does he require more thoroughgoing accommodation, a more opaque veil, in order to accept revelation. Michael's appearance, as observed by Adam, sets the new standard for revelation:

> I descry
> From yonder blazing Cloud that veils the Hill
> One of the heav'nly Host, and by his Gait
> None of the meanest, some great Potentate
> Or of the Thrones above, such Majesty
> Invests him coming.   (11, 228–33)

A shining cloud veiling a hill sends forth a glorious teacher, invested with majesty, "as Man / Clad to meet Man" (11, 239-40). The natural symbols accompanying revelation, as well as its accommodating anthropomorphic vehicle, are thus established by the end of Milton's epic.

In *Paradise Lost* any garment, phenomenon, or material — whether blindness, angels' wings, clouds, hair, darkness, innocence, or even a "Cloud of Fragrance," can act as a veil (9, 425). Milton speaks of his lost vision as being with "dim suffusion veil'd" and of the seraphim, who with their wings "veil their eyes" (3, 26, 382). Before the Fall, man's innocence veils him from the knowledge of evil just as "love unlibidinous" protects husband and wife from sexual infidelity and jealousy (5, 449). Eve needs "no veil," "Virtue-proof" (5, 384-85). Her awesome desirability is alloyed with the perfect singleness of her affection. While Eve's "wanton ringlets" have perplexed some readers familiar with Milton's description, in *Of Reformation*, of the "chaste and modest vaile" of the Church "overlai'd with wanton *tresses*," students of the morally charged language in *Paradise Lost* will recognize that Milton considers "the gaudy allurements of a Whore" as a caricature of Eve's seductive beauty, just as "Grooms besmear'd with Gold" literally travesty Adam's natural majesty (*CP* 1, 557; *PL* 5, 356).

After the Fall, veils function either to hide shame or to protect the fallen from the brunt of true glory. Milton thought of the episcopacy, for example, as encouraging a return to the times before the clear revelation of glory in Christ: "a meere childe of ceremony, or likelier some misbegotten thing, that having pluckt the gay feathers of her obsolete bravery to hide her own deformed barenesse, now vaunts and glories in her stolne plumes" (*CP* 1, 765). These upstart crows slavishly imitate the fashion of the temple "as if they had meant to sow up that Jewish vail which Christ by his death on the Crosse rent in sunder" (*CP* 1, 839). Still, the distinction between pre- and post-Fall veils, or between pre- and post-Christ veils, is more a matter of degree than of kind. All creatures require mediation of God's unbearable glory. The danger lies in mistaking the medium for the source. The Mosaic Law, for example, becomes death for the Pharisees because they grew more enchanted by the veil than by what it hid. In Michael's revelation of the future, whores and tyrants are symptomatic of the fallen attempt to repair the ruins of the Fall through disguise. In order truly to recapture that first glorious adornment, however, one would first have to reestablish something like the original relationship with God enjoyed by Adam and Eve.

The various uses of *kabod* analyzed in this chapter underlie everything that Milton meant by glory. The primary meaning and ontological wellspring of *kabod* is God himself, the infinitely weighty source and governor of all existence. The secondary meaning — that of praise — implies the duty of creatures to respond to their Creator by expressing their gratitude. *Kabod* also accounts for the imagery and language by which Milton portrays glory, that of clouds, thunder, light, fire, fecundity, and clothing. The revelation of God in creation through these and other natural symbols warrants reference to them as glories. Clothing belongs on this list of natural symbols because, in fact, creatures' natural appearances clothe their invisible beings, even as visible creation cloaks invisible God. Only after the Fall does clothing become something extra, something put on as a cover. In the same way, after the Fall, the revelation of God to humankind is perforce less direct, less naked — according to Man's vitiated capacity. The duty of Christians, in Milton's view, is to strip off as many as possible of the unnecessary garments obscuring true glory and, unlike the Israelites overawed by Moses' radiant countenance, to face up to the weight of glory. The trouble with artificial clothing is that fallen creatures tend to forget that God offers it only as a makeshift arrangement, an allowance or dispensation for creatures suffering desperate shame and weakness and badly in need of pretense. And when pretense gives way to pretension, in a travesty of unfallen perfection, clothing becomes rather a wanton obstacle to, than a restrained conveyance of, glory.

2

HOMERIC GLORY

THIS CHAPTER develops Greek ideas of potency and glory and in so doing stresses the inescapable presence and pressure of death shaping and driving Milton's own pursuit of glory. Like the last chapter, however, this one mainly offers background, and it is left to later chapters to justify these historical excursions. Fortunately, neither the Old Testament nor Homeric epic is without interest in its own right.

While the various, occasionally paradoxical meanings that compose the Old Testment idea of glory derive from the single word *kabod*, the Greek version of glory — though simpler and less mysterious than the Hebrew — cannot be summed up in a single word. Nevertheless, certain fundamentals do unfailingly describe the Greek pursuit of glory. First, glory demands sacrifice. The Homeric hero sacrifices himself not primarily on behalf of friends, family, city, or country, but on behalf of a self that he wishes to achieve, a golden self, in Sidney's terms, that lives outside mortal flesh in the thoughts and songs of innumerable generations.[1] At no time in his carefully shaped and sacrifice-filled career does Milton desert the quest for his own version of that self of glory, even if his notion of what makes one glorious differs from the Greeks'. The legendary self of the Greek hero lives in the *klea andron*, "songs of men." *Klea* is the plural of *kleos*, the Homeric word for glory conceived of as reputation or report. In the *Iliad*, when knowledgeable Odysseus, strong Aias, and paternal Phoinix approach Akhilleus to persuade him to return to battle, they find him playing the harp and singing *klea andron* (9, 189).[2]

We should not construe the genitive in the phrase "the songs of men" to mean songs that men sing so much as songs that sing — define or express — men. Some of the old stories tell of great men of the past who, like Akhilleus, have suffered "towering wrath" but who, as Phoinix reminds his beloved pupil, allowed themselves to be appeased (9, 524). In terms of the heroic tradition as critics of Milton have usually described it, Akhilleus should have returned to battle at this point: the Greeks have admitted that without him they cannot win, and Agamemnon has offered to pay huge recompense for his rash appropriation of Briseis, thus adding even more to Akhilleus' already exalted honor. In sum, by returning now to battle, Akhilleus can reap the maximum return of glory. But the story of Akhilleus does not follow the pattern that the heroic tradition allegedly recommends. The hero who spends his time singing *klea andron* rejects whatever tactical lessons about glory are contained in them. Like Milton, he insists on establishing his own glory in his own way.[3]

Timé, Kudos, Areté

In order to grasp the significance of Akhilleus' rejection of glory, however, or rightly to understand Milton's response to Homeric heroism, we must first inspect the terms related to *kleos* as an expression for glory. *Timé* and *kudos* can be translated as "honor" or "status" and "luster" or "charisma," respectively. Like the Anglo-Saxon *wergeld*, or "manprice," *timé* recalls an evaluative system wherein one's worth, defined as one's place in the social network, equals a specific monetary value.[4] In the *Iliad*, however, the lone Akhilleus inverts the usual situation — and this measures his glory — by penalizing the entire Greek army for their leader's detraction from his *timé*. Shakespeare represents a similar situation in *Coriolanus* when Martius calls all of Rome to account for its abuse of his honor. Milton, too, strikes something of an Akhillean figure when he refuses to participate in his countrymen's restoration of tyranny and instead, a sect of one, writes an epic confronting the questionable justice of existence.

Epic conflicts often involve a dispute over *timé*, or great changes in the order underlying *timé*. The classic example is the clash between Akhilleus and Agamemnon over Briseis, but the larger action of the *Iliad* also derives from an affair of *timé*. The Atreidi and their supporters have set the steep price of Troy itself for the rape of Helen (1, 159). The Trojans certainly understand the war in these terms and occasionally, anticipating Milton's Raphael, question the value of even the most beautiful woman compared to the potential loss of human life.

Although Milton regards with a skeptical eye honor paid merely to position, he nevertheless recognizes the propriety of social gradations and of payment in esteem for social worth or dignity of place. It is a common theme in *Paradise Lost*. Satan, for example, parodies Akhilleus' anarchic response to Agamemnon's slight as he rebels against God, thinking "himself impair'd" by the exalted honor proclaimed for the Son (*PL* 5, 665). A more realistic Satan defines his own offense against God as a failure to pay honor due (4, 46f.). The network of relative value implied by *timé* also anticipates and underlies the system of retributive justice that Milton takes for granted as a premise of salvation theory: "die hee or Justice must" (3, 210, 234ff.).

Unlike *timé*, *kudos* has little to do with one's place in society. It exudes from a hero like an aura of success or power. *Kudos* derives from Zeus, and whoever occupies the seat next to him glows in splendor (see, e.g., *Iliad* 5, 906). Zeus also allots *kudos* to winners of competitions or to kings whose authority he recognizes (5, 33; 1, 278–79). As James Redfield describes it, *kudos* is "a kind of star quality," a property of being, "like health or strength."[5] As Stella Revard has noticed, in *Paradise Lost* Homeric *kudos* applies chiefly to the Son, whose radiance is preeminent among the progeny of light.[6]

The most important word, however, for understanding the values expressed in the *klea andron*, and for recognizing the structural analogy between Homer's and Milton's epics, is *areté*.[7] An aristocratic concept, indeed a word derived from a common root with *aristoi* or aristocracy, *areté* generally means "excellence" and applies only to the nobility. As the swineherd Eumaios remarks to Odysseus, "Zeus who views the wide world takes away / half the manhood [*areté*] of a man, that day / he goes into captivity and slavery"

(*Odyssey* 17, 322–23). In Homer, *areté* appears almost exclusively to refer to the strength and skill of a warrior. Such a definition furthers the case of those who associate Satan with classical heroism because, as has been widely remarked, his appreciation of *virtus*, like the early Romans', appears to extend only to its manifestation as raw power. Yet, although *areté* can be distinguished by its emphasis on battle strength, it comes closest, of all the Greek words expressing glory, to the primary meaning of *kabod* simply as internal, invisible, personal weight or impact. In an aristocratic society, *areté* is what *timé* should, ideally, reflect.

Although *areté* does not depend on public recognition, just as *kabod* does not, it nevertheless can only be revealed in action.[8] The inchoate sense of duty that motivates the Homeric aristocrat concerns his responsibility, if not to realize the magnificent potency unavailable to those of low birth, then at least not to subject his family to public shame (*aidos*). As Werner Jaeger remarks, "nowadays we must find it difficult to imagine how entirely *public* was the conscience of a Greek."[9] Hence, when the Greeks seem to lack fortitude in battle, Nestor recommends that Agamemnon "marshall the troops by nations / and then again by clans" so that "each will fight before his clansmen's eyes" (*Iliad* 2, 362–63, 366). Those who share a common heritage obviously take special interest in their kinsmen's performance. Consider then the terrible dilemma of Hektor standing between the crowds of family watching from the walls of Troy and the manslaughtering hands of Akhilleus.

Just as Milton questions the payment of honor simply to social position, he surely does not accept the conservative, aristocratic stand on the matter of inherited excellence. See, for example, his approving citations of John Guillim on honor and merit (*CP* 1, 473) or his condemnations of aristocratic arrogance (*CP* 6, 786). Yet, the conventions of Ciceronian panegyric do not force him to praise Cromwell's "illustrious stock" or Sidney's "glorious name" (*CP* 4, i, 666, 677). Similarly, in praising Parliament, Milton cites their noble ancestry as a "great advantage towards vertue" and "the strength of an inbred goodnesse" as enabling these noblemen to overcome the temptations of privilege, "imitating the worthiest of their progenitors" (*CP* 1, 923). A certain bourgeois complacence even accompanies the invocation of his own "honorable family" (*CP* 4, i, 612).[10] As far as Milton is concerned, differences in created excellence (*areté*) should result in appropriate hierarchical distinctions and dignities (*timé*).

A clearer resemblance between Homer and Milton regarding *areté* lies in their mutual recognition that inborn potency is the first matter underlying human events. Given the *areté* of each participant, a situation will unfold within certain limits. *Kleos* reports what actually happens. In fact, the primary meaning of *kleos* is simply "news." The newlywed and memorably dutiful Thracian youth Iphidamas, for example, "when the word [*kleos*] came" of war at Troy, immediately departed for the battlefield, even before bedding his bride (*Iliad*, 11, 226). (He dies there, incidentally.) As someone has said, literature is news that never gets old, like the news about Troy. For Homer and Milton, then, glory conceived of as *kleos* is a function of history, and history is engendered by the father of the gods.

The distinction between *areté* and *kleos*, or for that matter, between creation and sacred history, focuses attention on the expectations defined by nativity versus the achievements or failures recorded by history. *Areté* is to *kleos* as the rape of Leda is to the Fall of Troy, or as Book IV of *Paradise Lost* is to Book IX. The poignance of the all-important distinction between *areté* and *kleos* appears in the paternal deity's observation of freely willing creatures, possessing a certain, finite potency, who choose to enact an outcome that he immutably foresees. This guaranteed outcome necessarily redounds to his glory. One might object that Homer never recognized, much less believed in, free will, and that Zeus, unlike Milton's God, actively influences events, so that Akhilleus, for example, will return to battle. Yet Milton at least defends Homer and the Gentiles from the charge that they sponsor determinism (*CP* 2, 293–95). And Akhilleus himself speaks of his choice to fight or not and of the ramifications of his choice. Adam and Eve also confront a choice, with its own ramifications. In either epic, the audience already knows the outcome, of course, and neither epic ever pretends otherwise. The fascination of epic lies in witnessing how the exercise of free choice coincides with events as they inevitably must occur. Homer probably would not define his interest in these terms. Yet Milton recognizes the similarity of his task to Homer's and borrows Homer's crucial narrative device when he has Adam consent to a separation from his

other self, just as Akhilleus had consented to separation from Patroklos. In this way, the freedom of choice of Akhilleus and of Adam
is preserved even as the foregone conclusions of the Fall of Troy and
the Fall of Man move the final step toward realization. Eve and Patroklos die; their partners resolve to join them.

Areté, Kleos, and Death

The transition from the splendor of preeminent *areté* to a *kleos*
whose poignance proceeds from an immutably foreseen encounter
with death is the common frame of *Paradise Lost* and the *Iliad.*[11]
Roughly speaking, *areté* — like chaos with respect to God — stands
for potency, or the power of the individual warrior to become a hero
in actual fact. *Kleos* represents or mediates that accomplished fact
after it has occurred. Between these two — nativity and history, we
may call them — lies the existential problem of becoming oneself, coming into being as a consciousness distinct from everything else that
surrounds, defines, reflects, and even infiltrates one's being. Hegel,
whose philosophy reviews the phenomenology of self-consciousness,
described this struggle for selfhood as an attempt to master or to
annihilate the other that is also oneself. And as W. Thomas Mac-
Cary has remarked, Hegel chose to describe this struggle as an all-
or-nothing Homeric duel to the death.[12] In psychological terms, this
battle must be understood as being pre-Oedipal and narcissistic. Mac-
Cary even suggests that while tragedy is the predominantly Oedipal
genre, the conflict in heroic epics is, generically speaking, narcissistic.[13] This distinction readily applies to *Paradise Lost* where critical
attention to the issue of obedience to law (the definitive Oedipal concern) has obscured the essentially narcissistic motive behind both
creation and sin — to propagate or impose one's own image on the
world. In the *Iliad* and in *Paradise Lost,* the epic struggle for self-
consciousness emerges out of the tension between the primary desire for the complete or perfect self of infancy — an illusory self that
never can be realized but is the primal source of all desire — and the
piercing awareness of oblivion, of nothingness and death. The poles
of glory and death represent the psychological limits of desire in the
epic, and the self-consciousness that arises between them is marked
by an intense awareness that one does not either achieve glory *or*

suffer death, but that glory and death mutually define each other. Akhilleus has to come to terms with this condition; Adam and Eve originate it.

Glory and death are cleaving opposites, such that the Greek's singleminded pursuit of *kleos* signifies his horror at the prospect of his own mortality. William Kerrigan has established Milton's own pervasive concern with mortality and particularly with the cruel phenomenology of death. Kerrigan gives voice to Milton's anxiety:

> A good soul labors to temper the body through many hard sacrifices, cleansing the appetites and disciplining the passions; yet at death the refined body must bear all the corruptions shunned in life, invaded at last by the gross earth itself.[14]

For the Greeks as for Milton, the subjection to decay of a carefully trained and disciplined body — an object of religious as well as aesthetic devotion — is a death beyond death. By making what was once beautiful and active loathsome and inert, death strikes at the narcissistic heart of the hero. Although the following argument concentrates on Homer's *Iliad* almost to the exclusion of *Paradise Lost*, it does so to establish an interpretation of Homeric glory somewhat at odds with the version generally accepted by Miltonists. The next chapter will consider the relevance of this revised version of Homeric glory to Milton's life and work.

In the *Iliad*, the possibility of one's strength and beauty becoming carrion for dogs and birds, or of suffering mutilation at the hands of the enemy, represents absolute death, death unmediated by funeral ceremony. Beheading, dismembering, impaling, emasculating, feeding corpses to assorted beasts — all describe the routine treatment of dead enemies by the ancient Assyrians, whose widely reputed ferocity probably influenced Homer's presentation of the horrors of war.[15] Even we moderns must consider the Assyrians remarkable: rather than equivocate or lie outright, they actually boasted of their savagery, nor did they expect to profit financially from their attention to detail.

We see evidence of the Homeric hero's horror of postmortem bodily degradation in Akhilleus' ferocious speech to the mortally wounded Hektor. Akhilleus wishes that the extremity of his passion would drive him, as he cries in the face of the expiring supplicant, "to slaughter you and eat you raw" (*Iliad*, 22, 347). In lieu of that grisly feast, Akhilleus promises Hektor that he will feed him to "dogs and birds . . . every scrap" (22, 354). It appears that behind the desire to feed one's enemies to the dogs lies the fascination with eating the enemy oneself. The hero wishes to become for his enemy what he himself fears most — death, conceived of as a scavenging beast of insatiable appetite.[16]

One does not require a very intimate knowledge of history to see that Akhilleus' frenzied urge to rend and consume his enemy would not have struck seventeenth-century Englishmen as altogether alien or primitive. Consider only the disinterment of Cromwell's carcass, its mutilation and decapitation, the head left to rot atop Westminster. As early as age seventeen, Milton saw vermiculate death even in the blush of beauty. The "lovely die" of the fair infant, "that did [her] cheek *envermeil*," is a Latinate foreshadowing of the "wormy bed" that has taken possession of her beauties ("On the Death of a Fair Infant," 6, 31; italics mine). Certainly Eve's "glowing cheek" bodes no better than the vermilion of the infant (*PL* 5, 10; 9, 887). Perhaps the culmination of Milton's poetic preoccupation with the fate of the body after death, as Kerrigan argues, appears in *Lycidas* when the speaker "imagines . . . an outrage for the body precisely opposite to the rites of civilized burial."[17] Lycidas' body becomes the sport of the waves and fish, just as in Homer the dead warrior's corpse becomes a treat for dogs and kites.

Appropriately, *kleos* is particularly associated with tombstones or burial mounds.[18] Death without a memorial undermines the only mitigation of death these heroes knew — life in the *klea andron*: "the man so remembered was the true man, the essential self, who by his exertions had found his full range and passed outside the changing pattern of his development and into his ultimate reality."[19] Even this limited transcendence is denied to heroes who die without the benefit of witness or ceremony. Telemakhos' lament in Book I of the *Odyssey*, wishing that his father had died at Troy rather than been lost at sea, illustrates the point: "They would have made a tomb for him, the Akhains, / and I would have all honor [*kleos*] as his son. / Instead the whirlwind got him, and no glory [*akleios*]" (1, 240). As the heir of a famous, dead hero, and not of a man missing and presumed dead, Telemakhos could wield legitimate authority over the riotous suitors and restore order to his family's realm.

Death is so important to *kleos* because it allows for a final comparison. *Kleos* depends in part on the givens of the past, including *areté*, but events, and Zeus as their master, modify the ultimate calculation of glory for a given generation. When Odysseus triumphs over Aias in the competition for the armor of Akhilleus, it does not matter that Aias may have done more to deserve it. The simple fact is that Odysseus won it and thus enjoys the greater *kleos*. Aias accepts this conclusion even in death when he refuses to speak to the haunted Odysseus, manifesting the Greek obsession with the end result (*Odyssey* 11, 545ff.).[20] It should come as no surprise that Virgil models the infernal encounter between Aeneas and Dido on that between Odysseus and Aias. Love, like war, often thrives on cutthroat competition, and, for lovers as for warriors, the final outcome generally reshapes in its image whatever provisional character had seemed appropriate to an affair prior to its conclusion. Dido does not care that Aeneas loved and loves her, just as Aias does not care that Odysseus recognizes his merit. What matters to Dido and Aias, to lovers and warriors, is the outcome. In the terminology of modern diplomacy, these are, after all, "vital interests," and such interests, it seems, give men and nations license to kill. Thucydides establishes the corollary to this principle as Pericles in effect proclaims in his funeral oration that one should hope to go out on top: "the unfortunate who has no hope of a change for the better has less reason to throw away his life than the prosperous who, if he survives, is always liable to change for the worse, and to whom any accidental fall makes the most serious difference."[21] As Othello cries at his moment of greatest felicity,

> If it were now to die,
> 'Twere now to be most happy; for I fear
> My soul hath her content so absolute
> That not another comfort like to this
> Succeeds in unknown fate.   (2, 1, 289-93).

Othello can only say this because, like a Greek hero, he possesses a narrative sense of himself as warrior and lover — a "round, unvarnished" *kleos*, but *kleos* nevertheless.

As I noted earlier, Akhilleus' reverence for mere life apparently contradicts his desire for preeminent *kleos*. The famous choice of Akhilleus, to which Milton autobiographically alludes in *The Second Defense* (*CP* 4, i, 588), reveals two versions of death. He can fight brilliantly as a warrior at Troy and win everlasting glory, or he can go peacefully home to a long, quiet life and be buried along with his name (*Iliad* 9, 392ff.). Thetis' lament for her son, however, applies to either choice: "alas, my child, why did I rear you, doomed / The day I bore you" (1, 414). Agamemnon's insult may trigger the wrath of Akhilleus, but their conflict is as settled as it will ever be by Book IX. The dispute with Agamemnon is tangential to Akhilleus' dilemma, even as "the proud man's contumely" is to Hamlet's. Like Hamlet, Akhilleus considers only an apparent choice, which in fact serves to underline the relation between death and the *kleos* that records how one goes to one's death. The world of the *Iliad* is not, contrary to what C. S. Lewis has argued, meaningless or without value. Indeed, its story deals with the inescapable condition of all meaning and value — one's relationship to one's death.[22]

This is not to deny that death is essentially frightful and senseless — even Akhilleus' immortal horses weep at the death of Patroklos (17, 426ff.) — yet in the *Iliad* common mortality allows men to understand one another as nothing else does. The "Fair Patrimony" that Adam ironically laments leaving his sons nonetheless lets men recognize each other as brothers in their suffering (*PL* 10, 818). Phoinix observes that "war / levels men to the same testing" (*Iliad* 9, 441). When Akhilleus knowingly guarantees his own demise by returning to battle, he waxes lyrical in dealing death to others. To a son of Priam, Lykaon, who stands defenseless before him, he says:

> Come, friend, face your death, you too.
> And why are you so piteous about it?
> Patroklos died, and he was a finer man
> by far than you. You see, don't you, how large
> I am, and how well-made? My father is noble,

a goddess bore me. Yet death waits for me,
for me as well, in all the power of fate. (21, 106–10)

As Lykaon sinks to his knees and spreads his arms to accept his death,
he achieves the freedom that Akhilleus himself is exercising, the freedom to accept the inevitable. Here, where it would appear that no
two roles in war could differ more, these two sons of kings are fundamentally alike.[23]

The phenomenon of war presents the extreme spectacle of man
embodying the violation of life with regard to other men. Killing
the one who would kill you focuses the heroic ethos and all its ramifications in a single action. Homer's usage of *areté* substantiates
Griffen's assertion that Homer concentrates "as exclusively as possible on the position of the hero, face to face with destiny at the hands
of another hero."[24] Hektor, for example, defines Homer's characteristic concern when he notes that the battle by the ships will provide
an opportunity for observation and comparison:

> I'll see if Diomedes has the power
> to force me from the ships, back on the rampart,
> or if I kill him and take home his gear,
> wet with blood. He will show bravery [*areté*]
> tomorrow if he face my spear advancing.   (8, 532–36)

Similarly, Akhilleus, having chased Hektor around Troy, tells him,
"summon up what skills [*areté*] / you have," a line which could also
be translated, "recollect all your valor [*areté*]" (22, 268). Hektor follows Akhilleus' advice, thinking to himself, "I would not / die without delivering a stroke, / or die ingloriously, but in some action /
memorable to men in days to come" and then, "collecting all his might
the way an eagle / narrows himself to dive through shady cloud,"
rushes Akhilleus' spear (22, 304–05; 308–09).

In the last books of the epic, in part because of the superfluity
of prophecies and warnings by gods, men, and even his horses, Akhilleus attains his ultimate *kleos* – as if he were already dead – while
he still lives, a phenomenon precisely the reverse of what Keats meant
by his "posthumous existence." Odysseus later reminds Akhilleus'
shade that "we ranked you with immortals in your lifetime" (*Odys-*

sey 11, 484). Walking wide-eyed into the arms of his fate, and, what is more, finally recognizing himself in the dead Hektor, and his own father in Priam, Akhilleus sees through the war even as he participates in it: "it is part of the greatness of Akhilleus," writes Griffen, "that he is able to contemplate and accept his own death more fully and passionately than any other hero."[25]

The ancient Greek, in sum, is characteristically and emphatically preoccupied with death. Rather than accept it and go on from there, the noble hero confronts it as an enemy. As compared to the ancient Greek, the Hebrew of the Old Testament more easily accepted death as a practical necessity, and although the typical Israelite hoped to gain a measure of immortality through his children, it does not appear that he thought obsessively about the final evil. Yahweh is the God of the living and has no sibling in the underworld. The ancient Hebrew concentrated on achieving a long, prosperous life in his family, tribe, and nation. If we can detect any aristocracy in Israel, it is an aristocracy of the righteous — those who obey the Law. As we saw in the last chapter, the exodus from Egypt establishes the paradigm for Israel: the glory of God either shines benevolently, if imposingly, and propitiously consumes sacrificial offerings, or it breaks forth among the faithless and slaughters them indiscriminately. In less spectacular, everyday terms, God rewards the righteous with the weighty glory [*kabod*] of wealth, offspring, long life, and other substantial blessings of human life, while punishing those who displease him with the shame of poverty, disease, and early death. The ancient Hebrew tended to pursue well-being by following God's laws for conduct in everyday situations.[26]

Akhilleus, on the other hand, represents the distinctiveness of the Greeks' sense of glory. Even in the myths that surround his Homeric character, the preeminence of his glory and his death are inextricable. When, for example, it is foretold that Thetis' child will surpass the glory of his father, Zeus and Poseidon cease their competition for her and marry her off to the mortal hero Peleus. Because Akhilleus will by nature achieve preeminent glory, the undying would never willingly accept his presence in their company. His glory, by its very definition excelling others', determines his death. And it is in these circumstances that his epic self-consciousness is born.

In the following chapters, I will maintain that the Hebrew idea of glory most influences the conceptual structure and figurative expression of glory in Milton's epic. The Greek version of glory will aid in analysis of the aristocratic assumptions of heaven and in understanding the range of relations between a potential hero and his society. But, given its focus on death, the Greek's pursuit of glory has more relevance to Milton's choice of genre and subject in *Paradise Lost,* and to the conduct of his own life, than to the particulars of his epic presentation. The next chapter pays further attention to the tradition behind Milton's idea of glory as well as to the emotional urgency and Homeric mold of his desire to excel.

3

GLORY REVISED

THE PRECEDING CHAPTERS — stressing weight, wealth, and wisdom on the one hand and the encounter between aristocratic warriors and death on the other — may seem wildly incoherent. What does Solomon in all his glory have to do with Akhilleus sulking by his ships? And in truth, Milton's idea of glory, faithful in its way to both the Greek and Hebrew traditions, possesses only a troubled coherence. Yet this troubled coherence is just that implied, though never revealed, by the authoritative language of Holy Scripture. Perhaps, to paraphrase Emerson, a preoccupation with coherence is the hobgoblin of little minds and the virtue of minor artists. In any case, though I will not attempt to survey the history of glory from classical through medieval and Renaissance times, I will briefly consider the Roman rehabilitation of Greek glory. More significant for my argument, however, will be the attempt to relate Greek and Hebrew perspectives on glory to Milton's sense of himself as poet and prophet. Biographically sketching Milton in terms of glory, this chapter particularly relies on certain analogies between Milton and Akhilleus to say what cause moved the mighty Englishman to test the strength of his Christian cosmos. But first, to assess the union of Hebrew and Greek versions of glory, we need to consider the strange fate of *kabod* in the New Testament.

Doxa

Perhaps the Greek translator of the Hebrew bible used *doxa* to render *kabod* simply because it stressed the side of *kabod* that he recognized as primary — the opinion of others and not some intangible dimension of the internal man.[1] In any case, Milton from his reading of Plato certainly would have remembered *doxa* as originally meaning "opinion." For Plato, the faculty of opinion acts as an epistemological daemon which has as its object the world "between that which purely and absolutely is and that which wholly is not," in other words, the world of becoming in which man leads his daily life.[2] Gerhard Kittel explains the problem in having a word for *opinion* translate *glory*:

> When the translator of the Old Testament first thought of using *doxa* for *kabod*, he initiated a linguistic change of far-reaching significance, giving to the Greek term a distinctiveness of sense which could hardly be surpassed. Taking a word for opinion, which implies all the subjectivity and therefore all the vacillation of human views and conjectures, he made it express something absolutely objective, i.e., the reality of God.[3]

The use of *doxa* to translate *kabod* thus underlines the possibility of a semantic split in the idea of glory — a split between the objective fact of glory, or the very being of God, and subjective recognition of it.

Milton understood early that right opinion and therefore human glory rests on the humble recognition of one's own genesis. In *Ad Patrem*, for example, he explains, "no requital equal to your desert and no deeds equal to your gifts are within my power; let it suffice that with a grateful mind I remember and tell over your constant kindnesses, and lay them up in a loyal heart" (111–15). Satan similarly recalls the debt he owed, but in his case failed to acknowledge:

> I sdein'd subjection, and thought one step higher
> Would set me highest, and in a moment quit
> The debt immense of endless gratitude,
> So burdensome, still paying, still to owe;
> Forgetful what from him I still receiv'd,
> And understood not that a grateful mind
> By owing owes not, but still pays, at once
> Indebted and discharg'd; what burden then?
>
> (*PL* 4, 50–57)

As noted in chapter 1, the ancient Hebrew would not view the failure to recognize *kabod* as a simple misapprehension; he would consider it robbery. Raphael's narration of the War in Heaven clearly implies that the rebels' loss of right opinion and subsequent failure to glorify God as their creator trigger the rebellion: "We know no time when we were not as now," says the erring Satan, "know none before us, self-begot, self-raised" (5, 859–60). Philo, whom Milton admired as a scriptural commentator, wrote that God instituted circumcision among the Hebrews to eradicate "the impious conceit [*doxa*] under which the mind supposed that it was capable of begetting by its own power."[4] In these terms, Satan impiously asserts what he knows to be a false opinion concerning his own origin. His crime is at once epistemological and voluntary, as befits the close association between reason and will in Milton's ethics.

In rejecting his creator, Satan steals glory due God and earns the title of criminal, fraud, pretender, counterfeiter. And, having refused to acknowledge his own debt, Satan proceeds, "as a thief bent to unhoard the cash / Of some rich Burgher," to steal the right opinion of others (4, 188–89). According to Plato, right opinion can be lost only through theft, enchantment, or force.[5] Satan accomplishes his goal as something of a cross between a thief and an enchanter, defrauding "the greatest part / Of mankind . . . to forsake / God thir Creator, and th' invisible / Glory of him that made them" (1, 367–70). The union of *kabod* and *doxa* in the expression of glory occurs throughout *Paradise Lost.*

For Milton, Man's definitive task in a world of growth and change, and the only way innocently to pursue one's own glory, is to approach the objective glory of God through subjective recognition of it. Socrates hypothesizes that "*doxa* is either derived from *diōxis* (pursuit) and expresses the march of the soul in the pursuit of knowledge, or from the shooting of a bow (*toxov*)" (*Cratylus* 420b). Given the literal meaning of *hamartia* as an arrow missing its mark, the already strong likelihood increases that an etymologically aware Milton consciously tied false *doxa* to sin and right *doxa* to glory. The philosophical connotations of *doxa* concerning the pursuit of knowledge and the nature of the good life elaborate and revise *kabod* in its secondary sense of reverent, awe-filled praise elicited by the source of creation. Just as the pre-Socratic Greek philosophers strove to substantiate the apparent impermanence of physical reality with a single material principle, Plato, following Parmenides and the Eleatic school, posited a rational principle that allowed for evaluation and discrimination in a world of shifting opinion — Truth.

The relation between Truth and Opinion corresponds to that between being and becoming, such that the epistemological struggle to find a ground for meaning corresponds to the metaphysical search for the basis of reality. Although for Parmenides the relation between Truth and Opinion is one of simple opposition, as between reality and illusion, the challenge taken up by Plato and Aristotle was to reconcile the two. The difficulty of accomplishing such a reconciliation underlines the key problem in giving glory to God. If Man expects to glorify God, he must come to understand the world of growth and change — and even his own developing, subjective apprehension of it — as a dimension of the eternal absolute. As Ernst Cassirer contended, preoccupation with problems of knowing, and therefore with defining a fluctuating subject and object, characterizes Renaissance thought.[6] One type of Renaissance heroism is the heroism of the knower, who pursues truth in the face of all hardship. This brand of heroism particularly appealed to Milton.

Classically, the analogy between the Homeric warrior-hero and the hero of the intellect appears in Plato, whose philosopher-king comes from the ranks of a soldier class that depends on the dictates of reason to guide physical force. This new-model warrior, based on the example of Socrates as Alcibiades depicts him in the *Symposium*, takes courage from the ability of reason to analyze the dangers of a given situation and rightly to judge what course best satisfies the demands of justice. Jaeger finds the motives of warriors, statesmen, and poets explicitly identified in Diotima's discourse on *eros:*

> The speech of Diotima in Plato's *Symposium* draws a parallel between the struggles of a law-giver and poet to build their spiritual monuments, and the willingness of the great heroes of antiquity to sacrifice their all and to bear hardship, struggle, and death, in order to win the prize of imperishable fame. Both these efforts are explained in the speech as examples of the powerful instinct which drives mortal man to wish for self-perpetuation. That instinct is described as the metaphysical ground of the paradoxes of human ambition.[7]

Despite the analogy between them, the emphasis on physical prowess in Homer gives way to the celebration of the intellect in Plato. The dictum "virtue is knowledge" preached by Socrates allows the eventual equation of manliness with ethical insight and fortitude. Milton's notion of virtue is essentially the same — a struggle in a world of flux, ruled by shifting opinion, to ascertain the truth and to live by it at any cost.

The picture of Milton daily toiling in the discipline of sword fighting, thinking himself "equal to anyone" and "fearless of any injury that one man could inflict on another," not only is emblematic of the self-control and effort he expended to adopt the personae of orator and poet, but also testifies to the resemblance he saw between the efforts of a warrior and those of a man of letters (*CP* 4, i, 583). As the most famous passages in *Areopagitica* assert, glory awaits all those who exercise their virtue on behalf of truth. Indeed, Milton ventures to suggest in *The Reason of Church Government* that "sects and errors . . . God suffers to be for the glory of good men, that the world may know and reverence their true fortitude and undaunted constancy in the truth" (*CP* 1, 795). The "true warfaring Christian" fights the real battle, regardless of how he fights it.

While Milton certainly drove himself to study and learn for the sake of his own glory, he claimed that the pursuit of right opinion also glorified God. As has been often observed, whenever we find mention of the pursuit of knowledge in *Paradise Lost*, we also find mention of the glorification of God as the end of that pursuit (e.g., 3, 694–97; 7, 115–17). In Prolusion 7, where Milton begins by stating his desire truly to deserve glory and not to "snatch at a false reputation," he goes on to proclaim that the glorification of God should be the end of all learning and inquiry:

> The great Artificer of this mighty fabric established it for His own glory. The more deeply we delve into the wondrous wisdom, the marvellous skill, and the astounding variety of its creation (which we cannot do without the aid of learning), the greater grows the wonder and awe we feel for its Creator and the louder the praises we offer Him, which we believe and are fully persuaded that He delights to accept. Can we indeed believe, my hearers, that the vast spaces of boundless air are il-

luminated and adorned with everlasting lights, that these are
endowed with such rapidity of motion and pass through such
intricate revolutions, merely to serve as a lantern for base and
slothful men, and to light the path of the idle and the sluggard
here below? . . . By our unresponsiveness and grudging spirit
He is deprived of much of the glory which is His due, and of
the reverence which His mighty power exacts. If then Learning is our guide and leader in the search after happiness, if it
is ordained and approved by almighty God, and most con-
formable to His glory, surely it cannot but bring the greatest
blessings upon those who follow after it.   (*CP* 1, 291–92)

The attitude here toward the lazy man, uninspired to live laborious
days or to seek knowledge, resembles the aristocratic Greek's attitude toward the man without *areté*, the low man for whom comfort
and mere survival represent the end of all striving. Similarly, Uriel
implicitly denigrates the angels who content themselves with reports about the new creation rather than venture forth to inspect
it themselves.

As a warrior in the field of opinion and as a poet, Milton invites
comparison with Akhilleus himself. When the opportunity arose to
champion England, the Akhillean controversialist insists that he was
confronted with two lots "set before [him] by a certain command
of fate." But Milton claims that, unlike Akhilleus', his choice did not
involve glory and honor conceived of strictly in the context of fame,
but rather it concerned duty, which is "of itself more substantial than
glory" (*CP* 4, i, 588):

> I do not covet the arms of Achilles. I do not seek to bear be-
> fore me heaven painted on a shield, for others, not myself to
> see in battle, while I carry on my shoulders a burden, not
> painted, but real, for myself, and not for others to perceive.
> (*CP* 4, i, 595–96)

In this excerpt, we can see how the various strands of Hebrew and
Greek glory meet in *doxa*. Akhilleus' shield was generally understood
to symbolize universal knowledge. Akhilleus' heroism appears both
in the strength that enables him to carry the shield and in the intel-

ligence that enables him to understand it. The dispute between Odysseus and Aias for Akhilleus' armor was traditionally understood to represent a division of the qualities possessed by the ideal hero. As George Sandys commented, the shield was "too heavy for Odysseus" and "not to be understood by Ajax."[8] Milton disavows Akhillean glory insofar as it is considered merely to indicate renown. Nevertheless, he sees himself strong enough to carry the burden of duty, a conviction expressed in terms that associate duty with weighty *kabod.* Milton's revision of glory, it appears, synthesizes *kabod* and Homeric glory. The burden that Milton carries on his shoulders is an epistemological prerequisite for Christian glorification — the consciousness of oneself as a creature, something made, circumscribed, finite. This is the burden that Satan refuses to accept, the burden of acknowledging the source of one's being.

Milton's description of himself may thus remind one of Aeneas carrying Anchises out of Troy. And indeed, one of the concerns of the next section will be to decide whether Milton operates more on the model of the burdened, pious Aeneas or on that of the grandiose Akhilleus. In any case, unlike Aeneas', the patrimony that Milton acknowledges is not so much that of his own father, nor even that of the fatherland. The burden that Milton carries on his shoulders, and fights to sustain in his epic, is the constant duty to achieve or maintain the right opinion of God. Only in the fullness of being and time can true glory be realized or perfect knowledge attained. Until then, it is war.

Milton and the Meaning of Glory

One premise of recent Milton scholarship is that *Paradise Lost* uses "traditional" or "classical" heroism to characterize evil. In so doing, the argument goes, Milton instructs his audience as to the shortcomings of such heroism and recommends seeing heathen epics as "demonic parodies" of Christian revelation.[9] More straightforward resemblances between Milton and the heathens are generally reducible merely to form.[10] This critical premise has much to recommend it. Unlike the Christian hero, after all, the classical hero pursues glory in part because of a narcissistic insecurity that arouses desperate competition and lurid vengeance. And it is justifiable to associate such pernicious egomania predominantly with the culture of ancient Greece and Rome. "Life in fifth-century Athens," remarks Phillip Slater, "seems to have been an unremitting struggle for personal aggrandizement — for fame and honor, or for such goals as could lead to these."[11] Not only must the hero succeed, but, ideally, everyone else should fail: "nothing seemed to have meaning to the Greek unless it included the defeat of another."[12] To win glory, one must inflict death — and herein lies the best grounds for a comparison between Satan and the classical hero.

The passionate slaughter of Hektor and abuse of his corpse identifies Akhilleus with death itself, a savage carnivore littering the field with victims. Akhilleus' wrath, pride, and malice toward Agamemnon, based on what he takes as an insult to his honor, anticipate Satan's response to God's elevation of the Son. Like Akhilleus, Satan sees the failure of the king as identical to his own success. Satan, too, comes to see himself in Death. Yet the resemblance between Satan and Akhilleus is not so straightforward as it might seem. Agamemnon *does* slight Akhilleus, after all, and the insult triggers a conflict in him that transcends the squabble over Briseis. The wrath of Akhilleus arises from his contention and atonement with his own death and destiny, a contention and atonement of significance not only for aristocratic warriors.

"Battle strength," as Stella Revard calls it, thus constitutes only part of what Homer means by *areté*.[13] How tiresome the *Iliad* would be if Akhilleus, like Diomedes, for example, were remarkable simply because he runs swiftly and wields a spear and sword better than anyone else. Homer does claim such preeminence for Akhilleus and absolutely refuses to mitigate the brutality of war. But Homer finds battle an endlessly fascinating spectacle primarily because it levels men to the same testing. Perhaps simpleminded imitations of Homer in part account for the "tedious havoc" of the epics that Milton disdains (*PL*, 9, 30). Milton, however, clearly distinguishes the jousts and feasts of the tradition from the works of Homer, and so should we. In the *Iliad* Homer focuses on warriors facing their own death and on the transition between life and death. Milton's argument surpasses Homer's in part because it concerns the origin of the condition against which Akhilleus rages.

Although no one would deny the influence of Homer on Milton,

Virgil's *Aeneid* is often perceived as mediating between the sharply contrasting heroic ideals of the *Iliad* and *Paradise Lost*. Medieval and Renaissance authors moralized the secular death and rebirth of Venus' son as a triumph of virtue over temptation, a mode of heroism with which Milton certainly sympathized. The *Aeneid* preserves an apparently doomed Homeric hero, who is mustering himself to find death in the fateful night, and transforms his *kleos* and the *kleos* of Troy into a new ideal of glory—the immortality of the virtuous state. C. S. Lewis' view of the transition between Troy and Rome implies a maturation of the meaning of glory. "With Virgil," says Lewis, "European poetry grows up"; compared to Aeneas, Akhilleus is "little more than a passionate boy."[14] While Akhilleus is absorbed with himself, Lewis argues, Aeneas sacrifices his heart's desires in order to perform the will of Jupiter.

Among the Greeks, glory was mainly an individual concern. In Rome, however, the state conferred glory according to community values, values reducible—*dulce et decorum est*—to an inevitable few. Augustine analyzed the Roman consensus regarding glory as a case in which the desire for national preeminence promoted individual sacrifice on behalf of the state: "The zealous desire of this one thing suppressed all other inordinate affects: and hence they desired to keep their country in freedom and then in sovereignty, because they saw how baseness went with servitude, and glory with dominion."[15] The analysis of the desire for glory as a cupidinous passion able to restrain other inordinate desires influenced attitudes toward glory throughout the Middle Ages and Renaissance. In Italy the idea of national fame inherited from Roman authors "stood as a permanent ideal before the minds of Italians," says Jacob Burckhardt, and constituted "a moral postulate" that governed "all the aspirations and achievements of the people."[16] Shakespeare took it for granted that the pursuit and maintenance of reputation buttressed the state, and when one of his characters—say, Duke Vincentio—neglects reputation, it generally signals a corresponding negligence of social duty. In *Othello*, for example, Cassio's response to being cashiered explicitly links the two.

A strong argument can be made that in his service to Cromwell, Milton consciously follows the Roman model of glory, in which individuals achieve preeminence only inasmuch as they exemplify or reveal the excellence of a virtue-loving community. Milton thus justifies his praise of particular public figures by claiming that he actually praises their virtues. Nor would Milton have had to resort to Roman authors for a theoretical or theological justification of such praise. The revered Sidney understood that Puritan moral philosophers, "with books in their hands against glory," would prefer authors to ignore individual exemplars and concentrate on the idea of virtue itself.[17] "Rudely clothed for to witness outwardly their contempt for outward things," the moral philosophers condemn individual glory as a false motive for the pursuit of virtue because it appeals to the passions and not reason.[18] But Sidney nevertheless contended that a mere "wordish description" of virtue "doth neither strike, pierce, nor possess the sight of the soul."[19] Sidney believed in the propriety of what Milton's lady calls the "flame of sacred vehemence," which can move "dumb things . . . to sympathize" and the "brute Earth" to "lend her nerves" on virtue's behalf (*Comus* 795–97).

Though Milton is not, practically speaking, indulging in poetic fiction when he praises Cromwell and Fairfax, the principle remains the same: "public testimony is indeed a great ornament to virtue" (*CP* 4, ii, 791). The man being praised merely exemplifies and particularizes the real subject, which is virtue itself. For this reason "there are those times and occasions when appropriate praises are not indecorous, even to the most saintly and modest men" (*CP* 4, ii, 735). Milton of course believed that the good man should be content with virtue alone and repeatedly maintained that "to the extent that any man is virtuous, so stands he less in need of extrinsic testimony" (*CP* 4, ii, 791). But, as Milton's contemporary and fellow Puritan John Robinson claimed, "words are like cloathes, used first for necessitie, after for convenient ornament, and lastly for wantoness."[20] Milton's condemnation of the praises recorded on behalf of Alexander More indicates that he agreed with Robinson's analogy:

> He has provided for himself not virtue, but mere opinion as a cover for his vices, so that when he is uncovered, when he is detected, he is no longer able to hide his villainy.
>
> (*CP* 4, ii, 791)

The eulogies of his friends upon himself, rendered null by his own villainy, have been used as wrappers, not for covering the vilest wares, the usual fate by which bad writings perish, but for covering the foulest filth of his own villainies.

(*CP* 4, ii, 794)

Like the preceding citations of Sidney's *Defense*, these excerpts recall the clothing imagery associated with *kabod*. Recognizing that reputation often arises from a false rhetorical covering, Milton understood that filling the roles of poet and orator exposes the artist who "knows the charms / that call Fame" to a kind of corruption more appropriate to a procurer. Spenser, who illustrates Sidney's prescription for poetry, establishes the thematic and metaphorical precedent that Milton follows. Una is dressed with the beauty and modesty appropriate to Truth and Wisdom. Because she stands for true revelation of God, she is decorously outfitted and covered by a veil. Spenser characterizes the false artist Archimago by having him dress Duessa in a "glorious show" that hides her deformities.

Milton's willingness to lavish praise on virtuous men like Cromwell and Fairfax may therefore suggest that, like Sidney before him, he wishes to negotiate a compromise between the extreme iconoclasm advocated by some Puritans and the Papists' alleged love of images for their own sake. In any case, he recognized the power of poetic language to transform men's opinions, for good or ill, and felt the role of poet or orator to be one of terrible responsibility, a task of glory indeed, but glory with accent on the primitive meaning of mere weight. Opinion (*doxa*), Milton understood, is crucial to mankind's pursuit of glory, making the battle for opinion the battle for the soul. Hence the poet or orator must himself be as worthy as his subject and ought not presume "to sing high praises of heroick men or famous Cities, unless he have in himselfe the experience and the practice of all that which is praise-worthy" (*CP* 1, 890).

Hence, it would seem that Milton bears the strong influence of the Roman ideal of national glory. How might I then explain my initial impression that the proper literary model for Miltonic glory is more Homeric than Virgilian? Tillyard's brilliant and persuasive argument concerning Milton's epic ambitions offers one possibility.

According to Tillyard, Milton's disappointment over the Restoration would not allow him to write the Virgilian, national epic that he had originally conceived.[21] In terms of this argument, one might claim that political events transformed Milton from a dutiful neo-Roman, shaping the opinions of a nation on behalf of virtue, to a figure of Akhillean alienation, expressing a cosmic sense of disappointment at a world that has denied him the fruits of his labor and sacrifice. The Milton of the revolution is the Roman; the Milton of the Restoration is the Greek. Indeed, I believe there is much truth in this: Milton undoubtedly admired the Roman ideal; even in *Paradise Lost* the ideal community of heaven bears a resemblance to the Roman state. And yet, I do not think that such an argument accounts for all the facts. One does not suffer the alienation and disappointment of an Akhilleus unless one has all along entertained the narcissistic expectations of an Akhilleus.

Perhaps I can make this point clearer by returning to the character of Aeneas, who displays serious inner divisions. For all his piety, he lacks the integrity of Akhilleus, who, despite his terrifying violence, is undoubtedly fully present, fully Akhilleus, regardless of whether he is slitting the throats of human sacrifices or weeping with and embracing Priam. The ambivalence of Aeneas, however, reverberates through an epic corridor that stretches from Troy to Rome. He seems incapable of wholeheartedness, taken with "the tears of things" and perhaps wishing that he had died at Troy or stayed with Dido. He achieves epic glory with such reluctance that his individuality dissolves into the general character of the Roman state. In founding Rome, he effectively leaves himself behind.

Milton, on the other hand, exults in his unique role as state spokesman and sees his youthful dreams of glory fulfilled on this stage for his individual excellence. He refers to his controversy with Salmasius as a "single combat" against "the contentious satellite of tyrants, hitherto deemed unconquerable, both in the view of most men and in his own opinion" (*CP* 4, i, 556):

> When one man above all, swollen and complacent with his empty grammarian's conceit and the esteem of his confederates, had in a book of unparalleled baseness attacked us and wickedly assumed the defence of all tyrants, it was I and no

other who was deemed equal to a foe of such great repute and to the task of speaking on so great a theme. . . . I did not disappoint the hope or the judgment of my countrymen about me, nor fail to satisfy a host of foreigners, men of learning and experience, for by God's grace I so routed my audacious foe that he fled, broken in spirit and reputation. (*CP* 4, i, 549)

Though he knew that his decision meant blindness, Milton entered the lists against Salmasius, showing that "it is not in warfare and arms alone that courage shines forth, but she pours out her dauntless strength against all terrors alike" (*CP* 4, i, 550). "Any stout trooper" could match Milton's contribution in the physical battle, but he alone of all Englishmen could make certain "that truth defended by arms be also defended by reason — the only defence truly appropriate to man" (*CP* 4, i, 553).

C. M. Bowra says of the heroic Greek that where "common sense . . . deplores dangerous ventures . . . the vaulting ambition of the heroic mentality . . . appeals to instincts and desires beyond morality and regards happiness as an unworthy or irrelevant aim."[22] No doubt morality figured into Milton's dispute with Salmasius, but certainly his "vaulting ambition" and "heroic mentality" led him to pursue the controversy despite the mortal threat to his eyesight. What is more, his palpable love of fame, of being exalted among men, throbs in the passages where he describes his victory over Salmasius. He pictures himself looking "from on high" upon an adoring throng of "all the most influential men, cities, and nations everywhere":

> Wherever liberal sentiment, wherever freedom, or wherever magnanimity either prudently conceals or openly proclaims itself, there some in silence approve, others openly cast their votes, some make haste to applaud, others, conquered at last by the truth, acknowledge themselves my captives.
>
> (*CP* 4, i, 555)

As he had said of Shakespeare, a Horatian Milton now says of himself, "I have erected a monument that will not soon pass away" (*CP* 4, i, 685).

Judging from the language that Milton uses to describe his aspirations and his heroic exploits, I conclude that Akhilleus, not Aeneas, is the better literary model for Milton's own heroism. He consistently exhibits a competitive desire to defeat utterly any disputant, a narcissistic tenderness toward his own image, and an almost limitless fury at anyone who would assault that image. His pamphlets are the literary equivalent of Homeric combat, where you kill the one who would kill you and achieve glory in victory. If one takes into account Milton's opinion of the "pretious life-blood of a master spirit" present within one's writing, such battle sounds neither so metaphysical, nor so risk free, as one might otherwise suppose (*CP* 2, 493). Although one might argue that during the interregnum Milton sponsored a Christian, English version of Roman national glory, he by no means played the part of a reluctant, Aeneas-like hero. In Milton's view, England followed his lead in the arena where it counted most — the arena of opinion. The individual glory and exaltation he had always desired for himself he found in fulfilling the role of national prophet.

Imagine then his dismay when England is taken away from him. The country of the faithful — once actively re-forming in the image of truth that he represented — actually deserted him, slandered him, persecuted him. To suggest that, because his countrymen disappointed him, Milton no longer felt they deserved to have an epic written in their praise is to put the matter so weakly as to obscure the real issue. A direct assault had been made on Milton's glory. The grand, reassuring image of himself basking in the adulation of all the virtuous men in Europe — seeing himself in their reflection of him — had been shattered. The God of history, whose justice had been so often invoked as the power behind the Commonwealth, had allowed the wrong side to win.[23] The image of Milton now offered by his nation was that of a monster: a contemptible, criminal object of ridicule, struck down for his slanderous lies. Milton in *Paradise Lost* examines the workings of a cosmos that could allow such a bitterly disappointing situation to occur. More to the point, he considers how such an order could come to be if God is indeed just in his ways to men. The following chapters thus detail the workings of Milton's fictional world, and man's place in it, before finally addressing the problem of theodicy.

4

DIVINE POTENCY

THE PREVIOUS CHAPTERS suggest that the subjective, emotional basis of Milton's pursuit of heroic excellence may best be understood in terms of Greek glory, particularly in terms of the Greek hero's horror at the prospect of death and his corresponding desire for immortal fame. The Hebrew *kabod*, on the other hand, which establishes glory rather as an immanent principle of existence than as a transcendent end to be sought after, contributes more to Milton's metaphysics and cosmogony than to his zeal for everlasting life. We can see this clearly in Milton's idea of divine substance. Although he elaborates this idea in language appropriate to Aristotelian philosophy, the heart of the matter — that God's weight (*kabod*) anchors existence — is biblical.

The prime question in any philosophy concerns the nature of being and its occurrence in reality — *what* is and *how* it is. This question, at once ontological and metaphysical, arises under the rubric of substance because the definition of substance has for millennia focused on the relationship between the stuff of existence (ontology) and its disposition (metaphysics). Inasmuch as it originates in the material principle of God's essential being, "the stuff of existence" roughly defines the primary meaning of *kabod* — the "invisible / Glory" of the divine essence (*PL* 1, 369-70). Chapter 1 argued for the importance of weight in Milton's scheme of values. In creating, God in effect assigns a certain "weight" or *kabod* to a portion of his previously undetermined matter. Although the metaphysical signifi-

[53]

cance of weight was apparently a commonplace of Renaissance theology and physics, the philosophical implications of heaviness and lightness can be traced to Aristotle.[1] The following chapter, by elaborating *kabod* (weight) in Aristotelian terms, will not only outline a characteristically Miltonic synthesis of Hebraic and Hellenic traditions, but also define the conceptual configuration of glory as a principle at once ethical and cosmological. Moreover, in detailing the relevance of substance to glory, this chapter also provides an accurate definition of Milton's concept of substance, a concept that scholarship has yet to explain satisfactorily, though its crucial place in his theology has been duly noted.[2]

I thus propose to explain Milton's ideas about substance – his philosophical elaboration of *kabod* – according to Aristotle's treatment of the subject. Centuries of commentary presented Renaissance readers with a variety of Artistotles from which to choose, and even though the Aristotle Milton met at Cambridge was most certainly a Scholastic one, it is equally certain that his perception of the ancient Greek was also colored by a variety of other influences. These might include, among others, the humanist Erasmus; the Jesuit schoolman Suarez; the neo-Aristotelian Julius Caesar Scaliger; or the rabbinical Aristotelian Ibn Gabirol.[3] To distinguish the various influences on Milton's own version of Aristotle would be a large task and one outside the scope of my argument. Still, it is useful to remember that when we speak of the impact of Aristotle on a Renaissance writer, we refer not simply to the effect of a single man, but to an enormously varied tradition of great historical and intellectual complexity. This argument, however, employs Aristotle only as a relatively accessible point of reference. The aim here, in fact, is to indicate a crucial Miltonic deviation from Aristotle's concept of substance.

Consider first some of the similarities between Milton's ideas about substance and those of Aristotle. Milton's opposition to creation ex nihilo depends on ideas which also appear in Book VII of the *Metaphysics*, a book from which Milton quotes in Prolusion 4:[4]

Everything that comes to be comes to be by the agency of something and from something and comes to be something.
(*Metaphysics* VII.7.1032a12)

It is impossible that anything should be produced if there were nothing existing before. Obviously then some part of the result will pre-exist of necessity; for the matter is a part; . . . and it is this that becomes something.

(*Metaphysics* VII.7.1032b30)

Compare the preceding remarks from Aristotle with the following from Milton's *Christian Doctrine:*

It is clear, then, that the world was made out of some sort of matter. For since "action" and "passivity" are relative terms, and since no agent can act externally unless there is something, and something material, which can be acted upon, it is apparent that God could not have created this world out of nothing. . . . It was necessary that something should have existed previously, so that it could be acted upon.   (*CP* 6, 307)

The usual explanation of Milton's opposition to creation ex nihilo rightfully points to his citation of the Hebrew, Greek, and Latin verbs for "to create." Milton understood these words to indicate in Genesis, as in other contexts, creation as a shaping or production out of some preexistent material (*CP* 6, 305–6). One need not, however, deny the relevance of Milton's philological observation in order to see that he relies on Aristotelian reasoning for his doctrine of creation.

Creation is an active God's work, the "Six days' acts" that bring forth an ordered realm from the passive, if stormy deep (*PL* 7, 601):

> Thus God the Heav'n created, thus the Earth,
> Matter unform'd and void: Darkness profound
> Cover'd th' Abyss: but on the wat'ry calm
> His brooding wings the Spirit of God outspread,
> And vital virtue infus'd, and vital warmth
> Throughout the fluid Mass.   (7, 232–37)

This Aristotelian interaction between active and passive principles appears on every level of Milton's universe.[5] As Raphael says, only "in the fruitful Earth . . . receiv'd" do the beams of the sun "unactive else, thir vigor find" (8, 96–97). The "solid good"of passive matter is no recalcitrant clay to be pounded into shape; it participates in a fertile union which produces everything that exists in Milton's epic. The solidity and fertility of God's matter associate with the Aristotelian passive principle biblical imagery belonging to *kabod*.

Milton deviates from Aristotle's framework in his unique identification of the passive, material cause of creation, but this deviation even more closely links *kabod* and substance. In Aristotle's view, matter exists independently, an eternally restless, passive counterpart to the unmoved mover. Aristotle will not allow his absolutely serene and eternally actualized God any part in the pure potency of the first matter. In contrast, Milton maintains "that matter should have always existed independently of God is inconceivable" (*CP* 6, 307). Matter could not have existed apart from God simply because "it is only a passive principle, dependent upon God and subservient to him; . . . there is no inherent force or efficacy in time or eternity" (*CP* 6, 307). For Milton, God comprehends both the active and the passive principles of creation.

Thus far we have been considering substance as the undifferentiated matrix — matter — out of which creation, including individual beings, is produced. William B. Hunter, Jr., has maintained that Milton borrows this notion of substance as the ultimate substratum from the Stoics and that he uses it to allow for the underlying unity of the Father and the Son.[6] A later chapter will address the evidence of Milton's Arianism. For now, it should be noted that the idea of substance as the ultimate substratum did not originate with the Stoics, at least not insofar as Milton employs it. As I have just demonstrated, the concept appears already in Aristotle — but not as a distinct category apart from substance as individuality.[7] Indeed, in Aristotle and in Milton substance refers both to the undifferentiated first matter and to the individuality of particular creatures, just as *kabod* refers both to the very being of God and to the individual manifestations of that being in creation.

One way of looking at substance is as that which makes a thing what it is by its very nature, what we might call its essence. Milton writes that "nature or *natura* implies by its very name that it was *natam*, born. Strictly speaking it means nothing except the specific character of a thing" (*CP* 6, 131).[8] When defining something — setting it apart from all else — one should express this specific character or essence. Milton explains in his *Art of Logic* that "*a perfect definition is one which consists solely of causes constituting essence*" (*CP* 8, 310). God transcends definition if only because no causes precede him (*CP* 6, 137). His essence is "increate" (*PL* 3, 6).

What we try to get at by way of definition, therefore, is the *essence, nature, specific character*, or *substance* of a thing. These terms are synonymous for Milton insofar as they indicate the quiddity of an object or, in Aristotle's words, "what it is said to be *propter se*" (*Metaphysics* VII.4.1029b13). Nor are these the only terms Milton uses. When writing about God's proper identity, Milton invokes the term *hypostasis*, "which is variously translated *substance, subsistence*, or *person*," and "is nothing but the most perfect essence by which God exists from himself, in himself, and through himself" (*CP* 6, 140–41).[9] Aristotle also regards these concepts as equivalent: "each primary and self-subsistent thing is one and the same as its essence" (*Metaphysics* VII.6.1032a5); "essence will belong just as 'what a thing is' does, primarily and in the simple sense to substance" (*Metaphysics* VII.4.1030a29).

The reason we cannot define God's essence, to use Aristotle more precisely, rests in our inability to comprehend his form. Of Aristotle's four causes, says Milton in his *Art of Logic*, the formal cause constitutes the essence of a thing: "a thing can indeed be said to *be* through other causes, but only through form to *be that which it is. Therefore by its form a thing is distinguished from all other things*, that is, by a distinction which they call essential" (*CP* 8, 234). We must grasp the form of an object if we would define it because a definition explains "*what a thing is*"; "it defines the essence of a given thing and circumscribes it as if by its limits" (*CP* 8, 310). But the form of "uncircumscribed" God is to be without form, to be infinite.

Before creation — and creation is first and foremost a circumscription (*PL* 8, 225–31) — the matter which comprises the passive dimension of God rests "in a confused and disordered state" (*CP* 6, 308). An essential attribute of the creator, however, this matter is unlimited, without form. Undoubtedly attracted by the latent parallel to the Hebrew view of creation as the glory of God, Milton emphatically endorses the Greek understanding of creation as an arrangement or ordering, the adornment of chaos.[10] God adorns matter by bringing forth finite substances out of his own infinite substance.[11]

The finite *kabod* of creatures complements and testifies to the infinite *kabod* of God. Man cannot know matter apart from such ostentation, the defining mask or veil by which God suggests his own limitlessness.[12] Hence Adam's perusal of himself and the earth around him leads him to the conclusion that "some great Maker . . . / In goodness and in power pre-eminent" authored all (*PL* 8, 278–79). Milton knew early that just as language clothes thoughts, making them known even as it obscures them, so specific qualities, or accidents, clothe substance and make it knowable (*Vacation Exercise* 18–26, 80–82). Similarly, in broader, theological, terms we know God only through his word and works, which veil his infinite essence. Like *kabod*, substance refers both to that which underlies being as we know it and to the finite phenomena that we in fact know.

Aristotle points out that before any parcel of matter comes to be a substance, we cannot know it because it "is neither a particular thing nor of a certain quantity nor assigned to any other of the categories by which being is determined" (*Metaphysics* VII.3.1029a20). Likewise, in *Paradise Lost*, before God endows matter with the beautiful forms of creation, it constitutes a profound chasm of "unessential Night" whose "abortive gulf" threatens "utter loss of being" (2, 439–41):

> Illimitable Ocean without bound,
> Without dimension, where length, breadth, and highth,
> And time and place are lost;
>
> . . . .
>
> For hot, cold, moist, and dry, four Champions fierce
> Strive here for Maistry, and to Battle bring
> Thir embryon Atoms . . .
>
> . . . .
>
> Light-arm'd or heavy, sharp, smooth, swift or slow,
> Swarm populous, unnumber'd.   (2, 892–903)

Milton's chaos bears some likeness to Aristotle's first matter, which, as one scholar puts it, "has no fixed shape, . . . and . . . cannot therefore be distinguished by the position or arrangement of its parts; nor does it have a definite size, since it may exist in a more contracted or a less contracted form."[13]

Although he admits that Milton's chaos resembles Aristotle's first matter in some ways, A. B. Chambers argues that it "resembles Plato's more closely than any other of the cosmological antecedents."[14] No one will deny the influence of Platonism, and especially of Neoplatonism, in Milton's work. But Chambers goes on to claim that the Platonic aspect of chaos in *Paradise Lost* explains "the alienation of Milton's chaos from Milton's God" and in doing so asserts a false premise, namely, that "Chaos and Night are the enemies of God," "opposed to him only less than hell itself."[15] The fault in this argument will appear as we further develop the crucial point of agreement between Milton and Aristotle.

The significant similarity between Milton's chaos and Aristotle's first matter appears in the fact that Milton, in accordance with Aristotle, deletes weight, "the 'objective correlate' of our sensations," from chaos.[16] Milton describes chaos as a "vast vacuity," a "hollow dark" (*PL* 2, 932, 953). For Milton as for Aristotle, "weight must . . . attach only to the visible elements that are formed from the primal unity."[17] Aristotle's deletion of weight from the first matter — allowing it to seem like anything or nothing — shifted emphasis from "the opposition between appearance and reality as the conceptual cradle of change" to "a new opposition between potency and act."[18] Milton accepts this stunningly original aspect of Aristotle's philosophy; it forms the basis of all conflict and growth in the universe of *Paradise Lost*. Milton does not write of a Platonic universe where the variance between appearance and reality gives rise to the evils of change and impermanence. For Milton, change, motion, is a condition essential to the definition of good and evil. Good creatures grow to completion in their God-given forms; Milton refers to such creatures as "accomplisht," as "perfection" (*PL* 4, 660; 5, 29). Evil creatures, on the other hand, refuse to become what God wants them to be and are "perverse, . . . monstrous, . . . prodigious," "unaccomplisht," and "abortive" (2, 625–26; 3, 455, 456). Regardless of whether one prefers to describe creatures as substantial, finite manifestations of an infinite essence or simply as revelations of God's glory, the fact is that Milton's idea of substance or *kabod* incorporates the dynamic, Aristotelian accent on potency and act and on change or motion as the ordained mode of God's glory in creation.

Martin Luther's theology offers an analogue to Milton's thoughts about substance. As Charles Trinkaus has observed, the great Reformers wrestled with the problem of "what kind of possible connection could be established between the remote and sensually ungraspable reality of God and the world order he has established."[19] Luther likens the world order to a mask or veil of God: "the whole creation is a face or mask of God," wrote Luther, "behind which He wants to remain concealed and do all things"; anything good that happens, God himself performs under the cover of such masks.[20] Neither Milton nor Luther adopted the inferential approach to creation associated with the Deism of the Enlightenment. They did not think it possible or desirable to dis-cover anything about God. As Philip Watson says in describing the "mediated immediacy" of Luther's God in creation, "we do not reach God by inferring his existence, nature, and attributes from His masks and veils, but God Himself comes to meet us in them."[21] Milton's concept of substance is consistent with this notion of mediation; indeed, it all but requires it. In *Paradise Lost* the message is, in some sense, the medium: the smell of bacon cooking differs fundamentally from a ringing alarm clock as a signal for breakfast time.

When, for example, God announces his intention to save Man, the surrounding angels apprehend the purposed good before they are explicitly informed of it:

> ambrosial fragrance fill'd
> All Heav'n, and in the blessed Spirits elect
> Sense of new joy ineffable diffus'd:
> Beyond compare the Son of God was seen
> Most glorious, in him all his Father shone
> Substantially express'd, and in his face
> Divine compassion visibly appear'd,
> Love without end, and without measure Grace.
>
> (3, 135–42)

Here as elsewhere, the Son's countenance best articulates his Father's *kabod*, but God also reveals his merciful intention through an unspeakable sense of joy that suddenly permeates heaven, an ambrosial fragrance that evokes the angels' awareness and knowledge of God. As W.B.C. Watkins observed, "Beatitude itself Milton makes essentially pleasure in seeing, hearing, feeling, smelling, tasting God."[22] The angels characteristically respond to their heightened apprehension of God with songs that express their awareness and dances that represent apocalyptic harmony (3, 345–415; 5, 620–25). The perfection of such knowing praise, along with willing participation in heavenly harmony, comprise the glory of God, and it is in this divinely orchestrated reflexivity that he takes delight (5, 626–27).

God and Chaos

One consequence of Milton's philosophy of *kabod* lies in the fact that before God makes part of chaos into the prepared matter out of which he will form individual creatures, it logically must constitute a dimension of his own essence.[23] It belongs to him *propter se* — "uncreated," "illimitable," "boundless" (*PL* 2, 150, 892; 7, 168). Existing in God "substantially," it is pure potency, containing the "seeds of all subsequent good" (*CP* 6, 308). Isabel MacCaffrey agrees that while Milton "shows a troubled distrust of the unformed potentiality of nature," he still "admits its necessity."[24] She compares what Satan discovers beneath the surface of heaven, "materials dark and crude / . . . / . . . in thir dark Nativity," "Th' originals of Nature in thir crude / Conception," with chaos, "the Womb of nature," where the elements of creation appear "in thir pregnant causes mixt" (6, 478–82, 510–11; 2, 911, 913).[25] "A little chaos," as MacCaffrey says, "is thus allowed to make part even of the brilliant actuality of heaven."[26]

But MacCaffrey, like Chambers, will allow God no share in the potentiality of his creation; "God," says MacCaffrey, "is pure actuality."[27] In absenting God from chaos, MacCaffrey agrees not only with Chambers, but also with Walter Curry. Curry argues that the matter of chaos cannot be "a 'part' or diversification of God's essence," because that would make Milton "a rank materialist and a pantheist."[28] But Milton is a materialist, rank or not, and he is a pantheist as well, if pantheism means a belief that all matter originates in God and will finally return to participate in apocalyptic harmony with him. Only in the interval measured by space and time do we find creatures who move according to their own wills toward or away from God. Curry claims that God contains chaos as water contains an air bubble; it is not "substantially" a part of God.[29] But the poet calls chaos "infinite" and "boundless," and because only God manifests these attributes, Curry must assert Miltonic hyperbole in order to maintain the distinction between God and chaos: "the poet while postulating a void or vacuum, attributes to it merely a hyperbolic infinitude; for him only God is infinite."[30] God, however, does not say that he *surrounds* the boundless deep; he says that he *fills* it without exerting his will over it:

> Boundless the Deep, because I am who fill
> Infinitude, nor vacuous the space.
> Though I uncircumscrib'd myself retire,
> And put not forth my goodness, which is free
> To act or not.   (7, 168–72)

When Milton refers to the state of chaos as "void" or "vacuum," he is indicating, as I have already suggested, that unformed matter is without weight; it does not yet fulfill any role in creation according to God's will. God has yet to assign actuality to its potency. Chaos has weight only in the sense that its formlessness is essential to God. Conceptually, it equals his invisible *kabod* because it bears the possibility of all things. "Sable-vested *Night*" and the material state of chaos thus represent the dark, silent, female dimension of God – the infinite power to bring forth. Chaos does the talking for the pair, as befits decorum, but also because by his presence he allegorically represents the absence of God's formative will. That which is absent from Chaos' anarchy is the volitional power that speaks from the clouds in Book III or through the Son in Book VII. But it is Chaos and Night who lend substance to those words.

One might object that we cannot accept material chaos as part of God because Milton personifies the metaphysical status of this material condition in the guise of the Anarch Chaos, and Chaos cooperates with Satan. But Chaos merely acts according to the material nature of his realm. Being prior to the will of God – prior to the beginning (a possible translation of *anarch*) – he tends to favor any action which furthers chaos: "*Chaos* Umpire sits, / And by decision more imbroils the fray / By which he Reigns" (2, 907–9). While

Satan works to thwart the will of God, Chaos by definition is inclined to remain free of it because the imposition of God's will on matter is his negation. In other words, Chaos does not cooperate with Satan out of an evil inclination to deviate from God's will. Rather, he cooperates because he represents a state of being which is not subject to God's will. His visage is not *dis*composed but "*in*-compos'd" (2, 989; italics mine). Hence, Chaos objects equally to the creation of hell and to the creation of this world; all creation threatens his kingdom (2, 998ff.).[31]

Chaos thus speaks for that part of God which has not been determined, his potential if you will. Milton's unorthodox belief that potential is essential to God follows necessarily from his unstinting emphasis on the absolutely free will of God as the ultimate agent. In the famous passage from Book VII, which I quoted above, God's potency and freedom to act imply one another. If God did not include potentiality, he would not enjoy freedom of action: "God cannot rightly be called Actus Purus, or pure actuality, as is customary in Aristotle, for thus he could do nothing except what he does do, and he would do that of necessity, although in fact he is omnipotent and utterly free in his actions" (*CP* 6, 145–46). God can form countless creatures, worlds, and so forth out of his infinite matter and yet remain the same as when he started. God always possesses infinite matter without form, pure potential, as an essential and therefore as a "formal" attribute. Not until he separates it from himself does it become the substratum proper. Thus when the Son turns the golden compasses "round through the vast profundity obscure," part of infinite God becomes finite and therefore no longer a part of God *propter se* (*PL* 7, 229).[32] It stands at a curious in-between state, no longer of God's essence and yet not belonging to any other essential being. That is why I call it the substratum proper; it does not bear a substantial relationship to God, nor does it bear any other form. It is "matter unform'd and void" but not infinite — creation ready to take shape (*PL* 7, 233). This matter, when God endows it with form, becomes "the property of another" (*CP* 6, 309). And this articulation of the substratum into individual substances occurs according to God's will. What creatures are in and of themselves is a divine inheritance.

Identity and Relation

Thus far, this exploration of Milton's concept of substance has clari-
fied the puzzling duality in the meaning of *kabod*, and therefore in
the meaning of glory. Like *kabod*, substance at once denotes God's
essential being and also the creatures that derive from that being.
Furthermore, the infinite nature of God's own *kabod* insures that
we can only know him through his finite productions. As Luther
would claim, if Man desires knowledge of God, he must forsake the
category of mere being and content himself instead with apprehension of God "in the category of relation."[33] Although Luther, unlike
Milton, never argues that God contains matter, they nevertheless
agree that reality presents in various forms versions of God himself —
samples, to one degree or another, of what God is like. For any
given creature, God resides in one's relations to the rest of creation,
and these relations consist in form and matter.

Aristotle maintains that "in everything which is generated matter
is present, and one part of the thing is matter and the other form"
(*Metaphysics* VII.8.1033b19). Matter and form, Milton likewise says,
are "internal causes . . . the things which go to make up the object
itself" (*CP* 6, 308). But for Aristotle, the form, though it never occurs apart from matter, is nevertheless distinguishable from any particular parcel of matter. The actual piece of matter that happens to
constitute an object at any given time is the "this" and the form the
"such" of an individual entity:

Is there . . . a sphere apart from the individual spheres or a
house apart from the bricks? Rather we may say that no "this"
would ever have been coming to be, if this had been so, but
that the "form" means the "such," and is not a "this" — a definite
thing; but the artist makes, or the father begets, a "such" out
of a "this"; and when it has been begotten, it is a "this such."
(*Metaphysics* VII.8.1033b19–24)

Hence Aristotle says that "the begetter is of the same kind as the
begotten (not, however, the *same* nor one number, but in form)"
(*Metaphysics* VII.8.1033b30). For Aristotle, particular members of
a given genus, even particular instances of the same individual taken

through time, differ on account of *matter* but are recognizably the same because they share a common *form:* "They are different in virtue of their matter (for that is different), but the same in form" (VII.8.1034a7).

Milton, however, reverses Aristotle; for him, "matter constitutes the common essence, and form the proper" (*CP* 8, 234).[34] I cannot overemphasize the importance of this innovation for an understanding of *Paradise Lost.* If he were to rephrase Aristotle, Milton would say that the begetter is of the same kind as the begotten *not* because they partake of the same *form,* but *because they share the same matter.* Thus God begets the Son out of his own substance even as parents bring forth children (who are essentially different from them) out of their own matter. The difference between the human and the divine parent-child relationship lies in the fact that, unlike a human parent, God the father is infinite, beyond any limiting form, and thus absolutely free. While God's unlimited matter, his *kabod,* is the indispensable prerequisite of his absolute freedom to act, his omnipotent will actually constitutes reality out of the infinite possibilities of chaos. His will determines the form of glory in creation by assigning a particular portion of *kabod,* in a particular condition, to each creature. God's own Son represents or sums up the forms that God has chosen to create out of himself and thus is finite, the actual revelation of God's absolute freedom. We might well call the Son God's living choice.

God is "the source of all substance" (*CP* 6, 308) and so unites the various perspectives that can be taken on substance. God "substantially," or *propter se,* contains undifferentiated matter, the "substratum." What we think of as the formless substratum is an essential attribute of God. When he creates, God "admits various degrees" to this matter (*CP* 6, 308). Accordingly, we find generic distinctions between rocks, men, and angels based on their respective distances from God on a graded continuum, "more refin'd, more spirituous, and pure, / As nearer to him plac't or nearer tending" (*PL* 5, 475–76). Despite the convenience they provide our understandings, we should remember that, for Milton, genera do not exist in what we know of reality, neither as forms nor as degrees of substance.[35] What really exists are proper forms. Form, the first principle of Milton's metaphysics, constitutes reality as finite beings in space and time know it. Matter, the first principle of Milton's ontology, serves as the ground out of which reality is produced even though it never occurs in reality by itself.[36] The actual participants in reality, particular rocks, men, or angels, are differentiated according to their proper forms, which distinguish them from all other entities. For Milton, God's matter can be summed up in the phrase "a heterogeneous and substantial virtue" (*CP* 6, 308): substantial because it partakes of God's own essence or substance, and heterogeneous because out of it he can generate or make a variety of essences or substances apart from himself, inferior to him according to degree and distinct from him and one another according to form. In a larger sense, everything is of the same genus — God-kind.[37]

As Raphael explains to Adam, therefore, "one first matter all" is "indu'd" by God "with various forms, various degrees / Of substance" (*PL* 5, 472-74).[38] Milton uses *endue* when he wants to refer to God's creation of beings formally distinct from himself. Hence Beelzebub recommends that the rebels study man to learn "of what mould, / Or substance, how endu'd" — in other words, out of *what* degree of matter were they made and *how* that matter is disposed (2, 355-56). Satan eventually supposes that Adam and Eve are "earth-born perhaps, / Not Spirits," but made in the divine image and therefore worthy of love, "such grace / The hand that form'd them on thir shape hath pour'd" (4, 360-61, 364-65). We learn later that man is "endu'd / With Sanctity of Reason" (7, 507-8). *Endue*, in the sixteenth and seventeenth centuries, had a variety of meanings, according to the *OED*. It could mean "to assume" (a form), "to put on" (clothes), "to cover," "to invest," "to endow," "to bestow," or — and here the *OED* uses Milton as an example — "to be inherent in" (Sonnet 7, 8). Here again, Milton's diction suggests imagery intimately associated with the Hebrew *kabod*. Man is endued with a form, therefore, which should be considered God's natural gift to man, as freely bestowed as it can be freely misused, just as can any inheritance.

Whereas distinctions between creatures reside in form, in matter rests the unity of creation, the possibility for apocalyptic communion, the avenue and vehicle for communicable good:

> one Almighty is, from whom
> All things proceed, and up to him return,

If not deprav'd from good, created all
Such to perfection, one first matter all
Indu'd with various forms, various degrees
Of substance, and in things that live, of life;
But more refin'd, more spiritous, and pure,
As nearer to him plac't or nearer tending
Each in thir several active Spheres assign'd,
Till body up to spirit work, in bounds
Proportion'd to each kind.   (*PL* 5, 469–79)

Angelic and human intellect differ "but in degree, of kind the same" because they are made of the same matter (5, 490). Even the beasts, though certainly inferior to man in degree, "reason not contemptibly" (8, 374). Raphael thus can eat human food and convert what is good for man "to proper substance" for an angel — that is, to the degree of matter appropriate to angels in general and to the particular matter which at the moment comprises Raphael (5, 493). Men, on the other hand, could not survive on angels' food since grosser human nature needs grosser food. The higher can function on a lower level, but the lower cannot function on the higher. Only the highest can function on all levels because through his matter he contains "virtually . . . and eminently . . . what is clearly the inferior substance (*CP* 6, 309).

As an analogy, one which Milton himself suggests (*PL* 8, 626), we might say that a gas contains both its liquid and solid states, but virtually or eminently. Degrees of temperature separate the liquid and solid states from the gaseous state. A molecule of a gas is the same as a molecule of a solid except that it moves faster. If we wanted to press the analogy even further, we could say that the faster a molecule moves, the closer it comes to being everywhere at once. In something like the same fashion, Milton pictures his angels as possessing spiritual speed and, like two units of a gas, being capable of occupying what appears to be the same place at the same time. Raphael blushingly boasts that where Adam and Eve become one flesh, angels can interpenetrate. The closer one gets to God, therefore, the more distinctions between individuals become purely formal. In heaven, God's *kabod* flows through spiritual forms without hindrance. This state of being is analogous, thanks to the mutual will for communion, to the involuntary communion of chaos. But in heaven, the apparent "chaos" follows recognition of separation and desire to overcome it.

Although men cannot yet enjoy the angelic life,

> time may come when men
> With Angels may participate, and find
> No inconvenient Diet, nor too light Fare:
> And from these corporal nutriments perhaps
> Your bodies may at last turn all to spirit,
> Improv'd by tract of time,
>
> .   .   .   .
>
> If ye be found obedient, and retain
> Unalterably firm his love entire
> Whose progeny you are.   (5, 493–503)

Empson mentions that Eve may have thought of this speech while she was being tempted.[39] After all, it does imply that the efficient cause for moving up in the created order is found in food. But if she does remember this speech when she decides to eat the apple, she must ignore the efficient cause upon which all agency is predicated— the will of God as expressed in the prohibition against eating the apple. Eating happens to be a material path through which God's will is accomplished, but there can be no doubt that his will is the formal cause. In *Paradise Regain'd*, Christ eats angelic food only after his obedience to his Father's will has been thoroughly sifted. The original plan for human beings saw them on earth "till by degrees of merit rais'd / They open to themselves at length the way / Up hither, under long obedience tri'd" (*PL* 7, 157–59). Like all matter, the stuff out of which Man takes his being is "susceptible to augmentation and remission, according to [God's] will" (*CP* 6, 308).

Substance for Milton is thus not a static condition of being even though it is the principle that underlies it. Instead, it implies a process, the working out of God's will in the stuff of existence. Unlike Neoplatonic philosophers and theologians before him, Milton did not see the source of evil in matter's reluctance to submit to God's will. For rational beings, the prerequisite of evil or of good rests in form, in a creature's separateness from other creatures. Once God, according to his will, makes a parcel of matter "the property of another," that is, gives it form, it can choose to work according to God's intention for his matter or attempt to thwart it. This is how the physics and metaphysics of substance can give rise to an ethical conflict of epic proportions. Thus a Lucretian epic on the nature of things coincides with the mysterious Christian drama of God's intent and its realization, a union that can best be understood in terms of glory, Milton's principle of coherence in *Paradise Lost*.

5

THE METAMORPHIC EPIC

THE LAST CHAPTER presented Milton's idea of matter as a unique, philosophical synthesis of Greek and Hebrew traditions. Whether or not Milton thought specifically of biblical glory in philosophizing about divine substance, the split in the meaning of substance parallels the split in the meaning of *kabod:* in either case, the reference can be to the very being of God, as well as to its manifestations in creatures. Furthermore, in neither case should one see these meanings as distinct; they imply one another and proceed from two perspectives on the same topic. By the end of the last chapter, it also became apparent that Milton's philosophy of glory might elucidate the reconciliation of science and ethics — of the natural and moral realms — in *Paradise Lost.* And it is this reconciliation that subsequent chapters consider in assessing the destinies of creatures in Milton's epic.

It bears repeating that Milton's version of substance owes much to Aristotelian thought. Where Platonists tended to see reality as perfectly constant, and change as belonging to the shadowy world of appearance, Milton, like Aristotle, saw change as the mode of reality's progress from chaos to perfection. Milton stressed potency and act, not appearance and reality. The nature of creation is such that creatures *must* change in order to become what God wants. Consequently, in order to attain the final glory of apocalyptic communion, creatures must recognize God and his will; they must desire what he desires, as fully as possible.

Apocalyptic glory, as a physical state of being, differs from the anarchy of chaos primarily through the recognition and desire shared by those who participate in beatitude. Milton's insistence on matter as the common principle uniting creatures and creator renders the formal separation from God as finally inconsequential. Through a moral and natural process of refinement, creatures can voluntarily reunite with God. Recognition and desire — proceeding from reason and will — are the dynamic agents of creaturely glory in *Paradise Lost*. They bring about the substantial metamorphoses that are at once morally just and naturally fitting.

This chapter places Milton's vision of metamorphosis toward glory in the intellectual context of the seventeenth century. It examines nutrition as a metamorphic process and comments on the relevance of alchemy to the metaphorical equation of knowledge and food. Finally, returning to death as the negation of glory, it characterizes Satan's son as a kind of antinutritional force, a famine that renders recognition impossible.

Natural Metamorphosis

Milton was familiar with a wide range of literature that may be termed metamorphic, including, but not limited to, Ovid's veritable encyclopedia of classical mythology. Ovid's *Metamorphoses* had long since been moralized, but even in this more palatable format, mythology was on the decline during the seventeenth century. Rationalists, Metaphysical poets, and Puritans alike tended no longer to trust or use myth, a tendency in which we see evidence of the growing faith in reason and experimental science.[1] Moreover, Davis Harding has contended that by 1630 the Ovidian influence on Milton had waned because a would-be Christian epic poet could not allow himself to be associated with the poet of love.[2] Yet, in my opinion, Milton remains very much an Ovidian poet of Spenserian extraction in *Paradise Lost*. Of Milton's early poetry John Reesing wisely asserts that "two opposite kinds of transformation are open to human beings and determined for each person by the moral choices he makes: metamorphosis into a beast or into a God."[3] *Paradise Lost*, if anything, is the culmination of Milton's poetry of metamorphosis and clearly ties the potential for transformation to the power of love. Nevertheless, Milton cannot be considered, as Harding rightly claims, merely Ovid's apprentice.[4] Although Milton scarcely abandons myths of transformation, *Paradise Lost* does testify to its native intellectual climate by its attempt to naturalize metamorphosis. Milton grounds metamorphosis in science as well as sapience, transfiguring the moralized fictions of Ovid into verities.

For Milton, all knowledge bears moral significance. In this respect, he is more medieval than modern in his viewpoint. Yet his picture of the natural world was far less consistent, more scientifically accurate, and therefore more problematic, than a medieval man's. However psychologically complex the motivation behind his heresies, the unique cast of Milton's Christianity may be described in terms of a reversal of accommodation theory, with Milton bringing the baby talk of traditional doctrine into line with the grown-up truths of an increasingly empirical and insistently logical attitude toward the world. As Edward Tayler remarks, "Milton stands at one of the critical junctures of Western history, marked broadly and a little inaccurately by the shift from forms of medieval realism to the kinds of nominalism present in Hobbes."[5] Inchoate science mixed unpredictably with traditional beliefs and supernatural speculation. The pulmonary circulation and oxygenation of blood, for example, was discovered by Michael Servetus (a physician burnt at the stake in Calvin's Geneva) as he attempted to demonstrate that the infusion of Spirit into the blood through the nostrils made conception by a virgin physiologically plausible.[6] Milton, too, is a Janus figure in intellectual history, an advocate of the new science and a political independent, one who disdained mere tradition and looked to the future for vindication, but who nevertheless "wrote the last great epic, the last all-embracing synthesis of all knowledge, . . . the last integration of a world-view that had already disintegrated."[7]

In terms of intellectual history, Milton has thus been seen to occupy a position almost precisely at the point of cleavage between cultures devoted, respectively, to religious and scientific pursuits.[8] The application of an increasingly scientific habit of mind to scholastic and mythological preoccupations does not seem incongruous in the generation preceding Milton's. Joseph Mead (d. 1638), a tutor in Milton's own college, aside from being the most influential intellectual leader of the surge in millennial speculation during the early seventeenth century, excelled also as a linguist, botanist, and mathematician.[9] While we do not question the lack of consistency in Mead's interests, we do feel surprised to learn of the deep involvement of men like Newton, Whiston, and Priestly in the intricacies of millennarian computations.[10] In assessing the career of the brilliant Victorian natural historian Phillip Gosse, surprise turns to ridicule and finally to pity as a strangely detached Edmund Gosse portrays the conflict between his father's scientific studies and biblical obsessions.[11]

Like most great works of the English Renaissance, therefore, *Paradise Lost* may be seen as transitional in character, written during a period of shifting epistemological assumptions. In *Hamlet*, by way of illustration, the tenets of medieval and Renaissance Christianity are expressed in the context of a ghost story, with faith in the afterlife expressed by the threats and superstitions that parents use to enforce their children's obedience. Although Hamlet is obsessed with the appearance of the ghost and with identifying him as his father, the real recognition scene in *Hamlet* occurs in the graveyard, when the clowns toss up the skull of Yorick. Whereas the appearance of his father's stern ghost prompted only irresolution and instability, the tender memory of Yorick accompanies Hamlet's growing resolution and independence. Hamlet remarks that singers, courtiers, lords, ladies, lawyers, politicians — even Alexander, Caesar, or Yorick — are ultimately recognizable in any death's head. What lies beyond that witness of common mortality is silence. No extravagant ghost meanders through the final moments of *Hamlet*; the rest is merely natural skulls and corpses.

Nor does Hamlet stand alone. The unremittingly natural end of *Lear* proceeds from a notoriously implausible beginning.[12] *Macbeth* and *Othello* begin with the overtly supernatural and with accusations of enchantment, respectively: *Macbeth* drives to the perfectly natural fulfillment of predictions of seemingly supernatural events; *Othello* records Iago's almost scientific experiments on his general's psyche and makes an issue of his decidely uncloven feet.[13] Even in the *Faerie Queene*, where Spenser begins with True Religion, Holiness, and the Archmagician Hypocrisy, the final cantos offer a vision of the Goddess Nature and her judgment of Mutability. *Paradise Lost* makes no exception. It opens with an awesome depiction of ruined virtue, evil on a cosmic scale, and ends with a small, flawed, but hopeful human pair walking into our world and its checkered future: a man, a woman, and a world that we recognize as our own.

Inasmuch as he does not depict metamorphosis as merely mythical or moral, Milton reflects the increasingly scientific bias of his times. Metamorphosis in *Paradise Lost* thus draws upon Renaissance science and, in typical humanistic fashion, upon the authority of classical natural philosophy. Milton, as we have seen, accepted the commonplaces of Greek physics — as did Ovid before him — and founds his cosmos on premises that Lucretius gave most elegant expression: 1) "nullam rem e nilo gigni divitus umquam" ("divine power produces nothing whatsoever out of nothing"); and 2) "natura neque ad nilum intermat res " ("nor does nature reduce things to nothing").[14] The earliest and most influential exponents of regulated transformation as the mode of being in time were the pre-Socratics. Milton would not have considered these philosophers irrelevant to his religious studies; as Werner Jaeger has argued, they considered questions appropriate also to theology.[15] They simply conceived of these questions in the context of physics, a context for theology that comes as less and less of a surprise to moderns. Of all the pre-Socratics, Anaxagoras — whose thought filtered down to the seventeenth century through Aristotle, Lucretius, and Simplicius — seems most congenial to Milton because of his interest in nutrition as it relates to medicine and natural philosophy.[16]

Other reasons than the metaphorical congeniality of their systems recommend comparison between Anaxagoras and Milton. Plutarch records that Anaxagoras "was the first to enthrone in the universe, not Chance, nor yet Necessity, as the source of orderly arrangement, but Mind (Nous) pure and simple."[17] The first principle of creation in *Paradise Lost*, voiced by the eminently rational Creator himself, is that "Necessity and Chance / Approach not mee, and what I will is Fate" (7, 172–73). Milton would also certainly have admired Anaxagoras for his influence on Pericles: "the man who most consorted with Pericles, and did most to clothe him with a majestic demeanour . . . who lifted on high and exalted the dignity of his character, was Anaxagoras."[18] He exalted Pericles, says Plutarch, by lifting him "above superstition, that feeling which is produced by amazement at what happens in regions above us."[19] Plato also refers to the wisdom of Anaxagoras regarding matters commonly subject to superstition.[20] Socrates is represented as particularly acknowledging his debt to Anaxagoras in the *Phaedo*, a dialogue notable for its profound influence on Milton, especially the account (in *Comus*) of the metamorphoses appropriate to the truly chaste and the lewd, respectively.[21] Anaxagoras disappointed Socrates only because the natural philosopher stressed rather the mechanics of existence than its rational perfection, its goodness. In *Paradise Lost*, as I have suggested, Milton wishes to fuse the mechanical interest of Anaxagoras — how phenomena occur — with the ethical one of Socrates — why things should be as they are.

The resemblance between Milton and Anaxagoras primarily resides in the importance each attaches to the process of nutrition. Given a creation that represents the intellect and will of God in a material format, eating effectively promotes, as Raphael teaches, a natural communion between God and an almost infinite variety of creatures (*PL* 5, 404–26). Throughout his earlier works Milton identified one's choice of food with the development of one's moral character: the temptation of the lady in *Comus;* the diets of different poets described in Elegy 6; the "charming cup" sipped by the virtuous, versus the "thick intoxicating potion" swallowed by the impure, in the *Apology for Smectymnuus* (*CP* 1, 891–92). Similarly, Milton's invective against the prelates and royalists often indulges in graphic descriptions of digestive disorders. But in *Paradise Lost* the equation of diet and moral knowledge is by no means merely figurative. Aspiration comes naturally as well as morally to Man, and a diet of the Great Nourisher's special provisions can actually refine one's material being. To object that Man's moral status alone ultimately determines the nature of his being is to misunderstand the point. Life in the Garden is inseparably moral and natural. "Planted with the Trees of God," the Garden boasts fruit designed to effect unfallen Man's immortal destiny (*PL* 7, 538). In part because of the special food found only in the Garden, God must expel Adam and Eve from their Paradise so that they will eat "mortal food, as may dispose him best / For dissolution wrought by Sin" (11, 54–55). Unfallen Man enhances his stature as a creature and actualizes the glory of his resemblance to God by physically, not just intellectually, assimilating the *kabod* of his creator. Things change drastically after the Fall, when only by "Faith and faithful works" can Man be "refin'd" (11, 63–64).

When Raphael describes the give-and-take of cosmic harmony in terms of nutrition, he chooses the process first employed by Anaxagoras to clarify the problem of becoming:

> But how is it possible, that one substance preponderates and fills a thing in greater mass than the others present? . . . This preponderance is gradually produced only through Motion, . . . the result of a process, which we commonly call Becoming. . . . Continually the like is added to the like . . . through nourishment. . . . The homogeneous is always segregated from the heterogeneous and transmitted (e.g., during nourishment, the particles of flesh out of the bread &c.).[22]

From the time of Paracelsus through the middle of the seventeenth century and the experiments of van Helmont, the phenomenon of digestion justified the work of the alchemists.[23] Furthermore, Anaxagoras was cited early as an authority in alchemy, a moral-natural discipline to which Milton repeatedly alludes in the depiction of his cosmos.[24] Like Anaxagoras, the alchemists saw in nutrition an everyday miracle of metamorphosis.[25] Yet, neither the alchemists nor Anaxagoras were interested in digestion as modern biology understands it. For Anaxagoras, nutrition conveniently illustrated the nature of becoming. He saw the world of change as an organizing process, like digestion, that sorts out an original confusion. For the alchemists, this process took on the moral dimension of spiritual advancement, and digestion thus provided a model for what has been well described as psycho-chemistry.[26] Any reader of Ben Jonson will recall the moral and spiritual claims of alchemy. Its goal is purification, and it involves a *gnosis* wherein the stages of the alchemical process symbolize progress toward glorious redemption.[27]

Anaxagoras, like Milton, posits the confusion of chaos as matter's original condition — "All originated from All" — but offers no vision of apocalyptic realization when God will be "All in All."[28] In Milton's system, however, once God distinguishes creatures from his primal whirligig, they can through their own knowledge and volition move either to a chaos-like condition of loving excitation and interpenetration, or to the solitary confinement of alienate individuality. As I noted earlier, though chaos contains no essences — no distinct creatures—approximately the same condition of material confusion, though a very refined confusion, is the apocalyptic product of rational love: "regular / Then most, when most irregular they seem" (*PL* 5, 623–24). As we have seen, however, the apocalyptic chaos stems from the will to yield to another and ultimately to God: "Easier than Air with Air, if Spirits embrace, / Total they mix, Union of Pure with Pure / Desiring" (8, 626–28).

Facelessness: Metamorphosis and Death

If love and proper nutrition combine materially to purify creatures and propel them toward the glory of apocalyptic harmony, logically one would expect that hate and malnutrition account for the reverse motion, toward shame and death instead of glory.

Nutrition makes creatures more themselves and more like God, and the heart of glory is God-like distinction. But death renders a creature indistinguishable from the rest of nature. Yorick finally cannot be distinguished from Gertrude: "let her paint an inch thick, to this favor she must come" (*Hamlet* 5, 1, 193–94). Macbeth observes that the day of his wife's death differs not in the least from any other day. Cordelia enjoys no privilege over dogs, horses, even rats. As countless logic texts have insisted, "All men are mortal; Socrates is a man; Socrates is mortal." Where in these propositions is the man who was beloved of Alcibiades, his maddening irony and investigation of virtue, or his insistence that the unexamined life is not worth living? What happens to Socrates in the course of these propositions?

In discussing the *Iliad*, I argued that the brute fact of death, portrayed as a fierce predator, was essential to Homer's vision of Akhilleus' glory. Homer saw heroism in the warrior's capacity to look death in the face, to be always on the precipice of his mortality and to know it. Milton, too, depicts Death as a monster of measureless appetite, one who appears first as something like an epic warrior. By the time he infects our world, however, he enters as if he were all nose for scenting, and all mouth for consuming, his prey (*PL* 10, 265–81). If, as has been often noted, Sin resembles Scylla, then surely Death resembles Charybdis, a vortex that sucks the very being—the *kabod*—out of creatures.

Milton's poetic expression of death incorporates natural philosophy in part by developing Ovid's portrait of Erisichthon in the *Metamorphoses*. Although Ovid's natural philosophy is really no more than a premise for his fiction, he nevertheless uses the same scientific basis as Milton for the universe of change that he depicts. Both claim that all forms arise ultimately from an original chaos that contains in a swirling mixture the embryonic materials of nature.[29] The tale of Erisichthon follows the story of Baucis and Philemon, a pious couple transformed at the hour of their death into trees sacred to the gods (*Met.* 8, 620–724).[30] Baucis and Philemon, like Adam and Eve, exemplify pious respect, hospitality, and a laudatory attitude toward the divine. Erisichthon, however, spurns worship of the gods and perversely persists in cutting down a magnificent oak, sacred to Ceres, even after it gives signs of its holiness (8, 738–76). Ceres, the goddess of fruitfulness, bids Famine reside within Erisichthon: "hot famine raves through all his veines: / And in his guts, and greedy pallat raignes" (8, 828–29). Famine obeys Ceres, as Death does God, "Though their endeavours still opposed stand" (8, 814–15). Like Death, Erisichthon would happily devour everything, but the more he eats, the more he hungers (*Met.* 8, 834; see *PL* 11, 600–1). In a sequence parallel to the one in Ovid, therefore, the ravenousness of Death enters the world of *Paradise Lost* as punishment for the defilement of a tree sacred to a God of fruitfulness.

Milton chooses as a model for Death an Ovidian figure remarkable chiefly for his limitless hunger because dying reverses the nutritional process designed to bring creatures to their perfectly realized identities as participants in God and heaven. Other than hunger, Death's chief characteristics are deformity and insubstantiality (*PL* 2, 706; 11, 494, 513). Satan's first reponse to Death, labeling him "miscreated," accurately indicates the nature of Death as an entity (2, 683). Unlike other creatures, he lacks the shaped *kabod* that marks God's progeny. Instead, he is an ontological sink, a black hole of glory. An anti-Proteus, Death invades rational creatures and makes them all the same, incapable of recognition or desire: "many shapes / Of Death, and many are the ways that lead / To his grim cave" (11, 467–69). One by one he grabs creatures by the throat and forces them to become like him — insubstantial and deformed.

The first stage in the process of death, as Milton defines it in *Chris-*

tian Doctrine, includes the "lessening of the majesty of the human countenance" (*CP* 6, 394). Death attacks the face first because for Milton the face especially proclaims a creature's glorious resemblance to God, and thus its identity. As I noted in the first chapter, the bodily locus for the transmission and revelation of God's *kabod* is the face. Uriel's brightness may announce his stature even when his back is turned, but not until his "radiant visage" appears do we learn his identity as "interpreter" of God's "great authentic will" (3, 646, 656–57). "The image of thir glorious Maker" shines in the faces of Adam and Eve (4, 292). Milton in his blindness most laments the lost sight of "human face divine" as a source of wisdom (3, 44). In Sonnet 23 the vision's face is "veil'd," making it remarkable that "love, sweetness, goodness, in her person shin'd / So clear, as in no face with more delight" (10–12). Lucifer's "count'nance, as the Morning Star that guides / The starry flock" first allures the rebel angels, and the turbulence that penetrates his "borrow'd visage" first betrays the stranger in Paradise (*PL* 5, 708–9; 4, 116).

When Milton asks the celestial light to shine inward, he gets to see the face of the Son as it substantially reflects the being of the Father. After the vagaries of hell and chaos, Book III in effect lets the reader look Truth in the face. Unfortunately for fallen men, the face of Truth, as Spenser contended, is veiled, while Error, though in itself faceless — without glory or identity — is countenanced by custom. Milton offers a Spenserian allegory of this dangerous epistemological condition in the *Doctrine and Discipline of Divorce:*

> Whether it be the secret of divine will, or the originall blindness we are born in, so it happ'ns for the most part, that Custome still is silently receiv'd for the best instructer. Except it be, because her method is so glib and easie, in some manner like to that vision of *Ezekiel,* rowling up her sudden book of implicit knowledge, for him that will, to take and swallow down at pleasure; which proving but of bad nourishment in the concoction, as it was heedlesse in the devouring, puffs up unhealthily, a certaine big face of pretended learning, . . . that swoln visage of counterfeit knowledge. . . . To persue the Allegory, Custome being but a meer face, as Eccho is a meere voice, rests not in her unaccomplishment, until . . . shee ac-

corporat her selfe with error. . . . Hence it is, that Error sup-
ports Custome, Custome count'nances Error.

(*CP* 2, 222–23)

Milton traces the deceptive appearance of false opinion to the rash
ingestion of custom's dictates. By expressing the effects of false opinion in nutritional terms, Milton characteristically links knowledge
and food as agents of substantial metamorphosis, and this linkage
again recalls the translation of Hebrew glory (*kabod*) by a Greek
word for opinion (*doxa*). Error, conceived of as false revelation,
might remain faceless, and thus never be mistaken for truth, if men
were more selective about what they swallowed. Milton's use of the
simple device of the brightness or dimness of creatures' faces as the
poetic conveyance of their identities in relation to God is itself countenanced by the belief that the eternal reward of heaven consists in
a face-to-face communion with the Lord. As Merritt Hughes claimed,
"to most of the theologians of the Renaissance the immortality of
man . . . was so intimately bound up with the beatific vision that
they quite subordinated the idea of eternal life to that of the vision
of God as part of human experience in the life to come and, frag-
mentarily, in the life that we now know."[31]

The Old Testament petition that God make his countenance shine
upon us underlies Milton's reliance on the face as an index of being,
or of a creature's standing in relation to God. Simply put, a creature's
glory, particularly as it appears in its face, enables others, including
God, to recognize it. The essential scriptural authority, however,
for Milton's poetic connection of countenance, glory, recognition,
and metamorphosis is found in Paul's Second Epistle to the Corin-
thians. Paul adapted the pagan mythology of metamorphosis to his
evangelical purposes among the gentiles. For Paul, the divine glory
reflected on the face of Christ underwrites the process of gradual
metamorphosis from unredeemed mortality to blessedness: "we all,
with open face beholding as in a glass the glory of the Lord, are
changed into the same image from glory to glory" (3:18). Unques-
tionably, the passage from glory to glory implies the possibility of
error, as must any process that involves an attempt "to become other
than ourselves . . . and remain ourselves at the same time."[32] In
Christian terms, the problem may be expressed in Luther's admoni-

tion: "You must always pass from glory to glory, yet into the same form; not from the glory of Christ into the glory of the angel of Satan, who simulates glory."[33]

Appropriately, as the redemption of Man is discussed in Book III, Milton focuses on the transmission of God's intent through the face of the Son. He does so, I think, because he recalls Paul's contention that by faith in Christ man can gradually be "transformed" (*metamorphoumetha*). Joseph A. Fitzmyer, S.J., relates Paul's doctrine to the prevalence and popularity of metamorphosis in Greco-Roman literature.[34] According to Fitzmyer's analysis of Paul's theory of Christian metamorphosis, "the Creator is the source of the *doxa* that shines on the face of Christ as on a mirror; Christ is thus the *eikon*, the likeness of the creator, and in turn reflects the same *doxa* on the faces of those who turn to him with unveiled faces."[35] Paul's explanation of Christ as *eikon* exactly fits Milton's rendition of him in *Paradise Lost* (3, 138-41, 383-89; 5, 719-20; 6, 680-82, 719-21; 10, 63-67). The same glory that appears in the revelation of light out of darkness in creation shines in the face of Christ, and versions of that glory shine in the faces of all unfallen and redeemed creatures.

From the time of his earliest poetry, Milton consistently relies on the possibility of metamorphosis as an answer to nature's humiliating death sentence and abrogation of glory. Death, through his frosty rape, transforms the Fair Infant from a rosy cheek'd beauty to food for worms, but death in her also is transformed as Milton's consolation represents her as a heavenly mediator. The possibility of such a metamorphosis for the dead culminates in the consolation of Lycidas as the drowned man rises to become the "genius of the shore." Lycidas' resurrection is naturally represented by the daystar, which sinks into the ocean, "yet anon repairs his drooping head, / And tricks his beams, and with new-spangled Ore, / Flames in the forehead of the morning sky" (*Lycidas* 169-71). The primary, natural symbol of renovation is thus expressed as the restitution of the world's face, and Lycidas' assumption of his large recompense follows the same pattern: "with *Nectar* pure his oozy Locks he laves" while the saints above "wipe the tears for ever from his eyes" (175, 181).

The following chapters elaborate Milton's depiction of beatitude or damnation as the end result of a metamorphic process leading toward face-to-face knowledge or estranged ignorance. As I argued earlier, the epistemological nature of the progress toward glory would have been implied by the New Testament use of *doxa* for *kabod*. But the fact that the approach to glory involves understanding and will does not make salvation the prize for solving an intellectual puzzle. As I mentioned in chapter 4, Milton agreed with Luther that God himself comes to Man under the mask of creatures. For fallen beings in particular, the problem is really one of internal adjustment — of accepting, or admitting, the sense that surrounds them. In Milton's material cosmos, the flux of Man's world constantly reflects the glory of God, if only Man can recognize it, as Michael says, "compassing thee round / With goodness and paternal Love, his Face / Express" (*PL* 11, 352–54).

Chapter

6

WITHERED GLORY

M ILTON'S ARISTOTELIAN DICHOTOMY between potency and act, as detailed in the last two chapters, presumes that change and motion are necessary to a creature's substantial development toward the final perfection of its being. As Northrop Frye has described this metamorphosis, "the creature moves upward toward its creator by obeying the inner law of its own being, its *telos* or chief end which is always and on all levels the glorifying of God."[1] "The glorifying of God," conceived of as an engine of metamorphosis, requires an intellectual and voluntary appreciation of the creator and his will, or what I have called recognition and desire of the divine. Furthermore, Milton's unorthodox vision of the material community of creation and creator allows this moral, epistemological progress to be accompanied and symbolized by a natural process of aspiration, a nutritional, alchemical process accomplished through the ingestion and assimilation of God's bounty. The perfect communion of the apocalypse represents the final stage of this metamorphic process, in which recognition and desire are finally fulfilled as fully realized creatures unite with the source and object of glory.

The risk in such a cosmos, where mutability is the inescapable condition of being, is that creatures will turn their backs on God, refusing to recognize the creator or to desire communion with him. In this case, creatures undergo a reverse metamorphosis, involving diminished recognition, failed desire, and natural degradation. Evil creatures thus suffer increasing alienation instead of communion, shame instead of glory, and self-consumption instead of divine nourishment.

The perverse metamorphosis of evil creatures is measured, as is all metamorphosis, by the glory of God as reflected in the face of the Son. The Father suffers the War in Heaven only so that the Son may win the glory of victory, and the Son triumphs by displaying his Father's essential being: "He . . . on his Son with Rays direct / Shone full; hee all his Father full exprest / Ineffably into his face receiv'd" (*PL* 6, 719–21). The Son's chief weapon is thus his super-charged countenance, "into terror chang'd / . . . too severe to be beheld" (6, 824–25). Even the chariot that carries the Son to victory is memorable particularly because of the "fourfold-visag'd Four" that reflect the wrath of God against the rebels (6, 845). As the battle-ready Son reminds us, the transformation of evil creatures propels them toward a negative end, an apocalypse of estrangement and horror:

> in the end
> Thou shalt be All in All, and I in thee
> For ever, and in mee all whom thou lov'st;
> But whom thou hat'st, I hate, and can put on
> Thy terrors, as I put thy mildness on,
> Image of thee in all things. (6, 731–36; see 3, 319–41)

At the center of the poem we thus witness both sides of the promised end: the revitalized, good angels, united under their head, observe as the hopelessly fallen leap into exile.[2] "Hard'n'd more by what might most reclaim, / Grieving to see his Glory," the rebels find that the glory reflected in the Son's countenance effects an entirely different metamorphosis for evil creatures (6, 791–92). Instead of communion and pleasure, evil creatures can expect grief and a physical as well as spiritual hardening that makes heavenly harmony impossible.

Burned Beyond Recognition

If, as I have suggested, unfallen creatures glorify God by acknowledging his bounty in the food that sustains and improves them, fallen angels, "insatiate" for their own glory, get eaten away at the same time that they refuse to eat. The fire of hell, according to Sandys, "ever feeds on the bodies of the damned; which suffer no diminution; but afford unconsumable nourishment" (p. 211). The corresponding effects of gnawing remorse appear in Satan's face, which, as he ponders his fate, changes "with pale, ire, envy and despair" (*PL* 4, 115). Unlike the face of Christ, transfigured with splendor on a mountaintop, or the face of Moses at Sinai, glowing behind its veil, Satan's face during his disfiguration is "dimm'd" (4, 114). Satan's "borrow'd visage" thus "marr'd" and "disfigur'd," reveals him to be one of the fierce spirits of hell, spirits whose chief physical characteristic is their dim obscurity (6, 116, 127). Such dimness is a symptom of self-consumption, a physical condition that, as in the myth of Erisichthon, matches a spiritual and moral self-obsession.

Scholars have commented on the correspondence between the landscape of hell and its occupants, a correspondence that Milton has Satan acknowledge in the declaration, "myself am Hell" (4, 75).[3] In Burton's words, Satan is "an epitome of hell," so that Milton's description, "the hot Hell that always in him burns," may well be taken literally (9, 467).[4] Sandys expresses a common opinion among Renaissance authors when he explains that "palenesse, the going and comming of the colour," is a physiological symptom of anger, caused "by the burning of the spirits about the heart" (p. 341).[5] I believe that Milton depicts a Satan whose insides have in fact caught fire because of this congregation of inflammatory spirits. Furthermore, it appears from the construction of Pandemonium that "all the demons" suffer much the same torment. The "fiery Deluge" of Hell, "fed / With ever-burning Sulphur unconsum'd," produces the "metallic Ore, / The work of Sulphur" mined by Mammon and his brigade (*PL* 1, 68–69, 673–74).[6] In light of the Paracelsian theory of matter as based on sulphur, and the association of sulphur with mining and metals, one may see the erection of Pandemonium as an objective correlative for the transformation of the demons into hardened sinners.[7]

In alchemy, sulphur is the agent that works toward the perfection of form in matter. So long as there is sulphur present, the matter has not yet reached its final form. According to Joseph Duchesne, who zealously defends Paracelsus and the new chemistry in a tract on "the original and causes of Mettales," any creature may be considered imperfect insofar as it has not reached its final form.[8] Though Duchesne refers specifically to the production of metals from "breathes and vapoures," he, in principle, includes all creatures as subjects of his transformational chemistry — "for the perfection of anything is but by putting on of forme."[9] Even angels, being imperfect, contain sulphur, "a matter apt to be set on fire," so that in fallen angels a process analogous to metal making occurs, their airy substance being "sublim'd with Mineral fury" into a coarser, harder substance (1, 235).[10] The heat of Satan's angry passion may be supposed to have ignited the unconsumable sulphur within him, whereby he is "killed, made blacke, calcined and burned."[11] Milton thus suggests a scientific rationale for the traditional association of sulphur with evil and hell as he presents the fallen angels, like the matter of hell, being metamorphosed by burning sulphur into darker, more solid, almost metallic, substances.[12] As the result of a process that Duchesne describes in terms of digestion, Satan's remains eventually will consist of a hard, charred lump, "Adverse to life" (7, 239).[13]

The nutritional reversal that the demons undergo has its intellectual counterpart. The sad state of the fallen angels' ability to know is made immediately apparent to us in Book I: "If thou beest hee; But O how fall'n! how chang'd / From him, who in the happy Realms of Light / Cloth'd with transcendent brightness didst outshine / Myriads though bright" (1, 84–87). The first speech in *Paradise Lost* depends on the conditional subject — "if he" — and that fundamental doubt never gets resolved. Prior to this expression of remediless ambiguity, the narrator describes hell with the exclamation "O how unlike the place from whence they fell!" which emphatically conveys not only the difference between heaven and hell, but also the impossibility of measuring that difference (1, 75). Hell is like nothing else, not even itself. The "how unlike" of the narrator and the "how fall'n! how chang'd" of Satan's address, even though they do not begin questions, retain their full interrogative force. Questions imply the possibility of answers. The questions of the fallen angels get transformed into exclamations simply because hell holds no answers. Part of the hope abandoned at the entrance of hell is hope of knowledge, a hope based on the faith that the law of identity stands. From the first moments of his epic, Milton consistently de-

picts the confusion of lost identity through the diminution and dis-
figurement of a creature's original glory.

Milton allegorizes Satan's confusion when he has the Prince of
Hell fail to recognize himself in his own daughter-beloved and son-
grandchild, a failure attributed to the "dire change / Befall'n . . .
unforeseen" (2, 820–21). Satan soon learns that — like Beelzebub, Sin,
and Death — he, too, is hardly recognizable:

> Think not, revolted Spirit, thy shape the same,
> Or undiminished brightness, to be known
> As when thou stood'st in Heav'n upright and pure;
> That Glory then, when thou no more wast good,
> Departed from thee, and thou resembl'st now
> Thy sin and place of doom obscure and foul.
>
> (4, 835–40)

Intentionally and unintentionally, Satan continually goes unrecognized. Even God, as he judges fallen Man, ostensibly fails to detect
Satan in the serpent. Moreover, Satan consistently expresses surprise at what he himself has become morally and physically, surprise at his loss of glory:

> abasht the Devil stood,
> And felt how awful goodness is, and saw
> Virtue in her shape how lovely, saw, and pin'd
> His loss; but chiefly to find here observ'd
> His lustre visibly impair'd.   (4, 846–50)

The last moment of Satan's consciousness that we witness presents
a creature wonder-struck by what he has finally become:

> a while he stood, expecting
> Thir universal shout and high applause
> To fill his ear, when contrary he hears
> On all sides, from innumerable tongues
> A dismal universal hiss, the sound
> Of public scorn; he wonder'd but not long
> Had leisure, wond'ring at himself now more.
>
> (10, 504–10)

Satan loses not only the public glory be sought, but also any sem-
blance of his former self; he has gone well beyond recognition, beyond glory, beyond identity.

Throughout the first two books, Milton insists on the irreducible
uncertainty underlying even the simplest matters of opinion in hell.
Satan rhetorically adapts to this ambient imbecility by shifting to
others the burden of a universe of ignorance. To the alleged Beelzebub he remarks, "into what Pit thou seest / From what highth fall'n"
(1, 91–92). Beelzebub knows no more than his chief about their location or its position relative to heaven, but Satan manages to give
the impression that *he* does, relying on Beelzebub's pride to prevent
anxious queries. The interrogative pronouns and subjunctive mood
that Satan uses throughout his first speeches indicate that he despairs
of really knowing anything. Nevertheless, he and Beelzebub reas-
semble the rebel forces in order to resolve several issues: "how we
may henceforth most offend / Our Enemy, our own loss how repair, / How overcome this dire Calamity, / What reinforcement we
may gain from Hope, / If not what resolution from despair" (1,
187–91). The council of Book II must be considered a charade not
because Satan and Beelzebub rig the outcome, but because none of
the questions on the agenda has an answer.

We expect that, once off the lake, Satan will have cleared his head,
but instead, as he plants his feet on land, "if it were Land," "the lost
Arch-Angel" asks,

> Is this the Region, this the Soil, the Clime,
>   . . . this the seat
> That we must change for Heav'n, this mournful gloom
> For that celestial light?   (1, 228, 242–45)

"Lost" not simply in the romantic sense of a homeless, restless, rebel,
Satan plainly does not know where he is, and his partners in crime
share his confusion: "Abject and lost lay these, covering the Flood, /
Under amazement of thir hideous change" (1, 312–13). In Book I,
therefore, Milton carefully establishes the fallen angels as nonenti-
ties, strictly from nowhere, and beyond recognition because of "thir
hideous change." As I mentioned previously, the risk entailed by
metamorphosis is that, in trying to become other than oneself, one

might lose all continuity and become something entirely different. This certainly is what occurs in Book X. But even in Book I, the amazing metamorphosis of the fallen angels signals their loss of identity in God's eyes. They no longer possess names, nor will they until false men entitle them gods (1, 361–65).

Despite the fact that they have suffered an abrupt loss of their created identities, Satan insists that the rebellion "was not inglorious" (1, 624). He nevertheless admits that "th' event was dire," particularly "this dire change / Hateful to utter" (1, 624–26). Satan, in other words, claims that though they have changed and lost so much of their original glory that they can scarcely recognize one another "(far other once beheld in bliss)," the actions that caused this change were not in themselves inglorious (1, 607). Satan affects to understand hell simply as a consequence of losing the war and ignores its reflection of his withered glory. His diminished understanding and loss of right opinion (*doxa*) thus prevent him from perceiving the full significance of his perverted, shrivelled potency (*kabod*). Having created the possibility of a hermeneutic circle by dividing the rebellion from its existential consequences, Satan leaps to a misinterpretation that denies the coherence of significant relations between part and whole. Satan's final speech of Book I, belying the appearance of improvement in the rebels' condition, echoes the sophistry and ignorance of his first:

> what power of mind
> Forseeing or presaging, from the Depth
> Of knowledge past or present, could have fear'd
> How such united force of Gods, how such
> As stood like these, could ever know repulse?
> For who can yet believe, though after loss,
> That all these puissant Legions, whose exile
> Hath emptied Heav'n, shall fail to re-ascend
> Self-rais'd, and repossess thir native seat?   (1, 626–34)

What? How? Who? Essentially the same multitudinous uncertainties and unintended ironies underlie all of Satan's speeches to his companions dear, speeches that consistently reveal the physical and intellectual consequences of lost glory.

Of all the demons, only Belial seems to have some understanding of the nature of hell. He argues that by banking the fires of their own hatred, the rebels can expect God much to "remit / His anger" so that "these raging fires / Will slack'n" (2, 210–11, 213–14). Belial at least implies the principle of correspondence between a creature and its situation that Satan, in Books I and II, attempts to ignore but, ironically, affirms: "what matter where, if I be still the same" (1, 256). The council in Book II is ostensibly called to consult on how best to regain their "just inheritance of old," as if their former state of glory were still appropriate to them (2, 38). But the rebels are not "the same" and the radical uncertainty regarding who they are is signified by their visible loss of glory. Belial at least acknowledges a certain fitness, a justice, in having beings who hate God occupy a place whose torments vary according to the intensity of their hatred. He thus comes close to admitting the principle of pain that Milton had formulated by the early 1640s:

> Though it were granted us by divine indulgence to be exempt from all that can be harmfull to us from without, yet the perversnesse of our folly is so bent, that we should never lin hammering out of our owne hearts, as it were out of flint, the seeds and sparkles of new misery to our selves, till all were in a blaze againe. And no marvell if out of our own hearts, for they are evill; but ev'n out of those things which God meant us, either for a principall good, or a pure contentment, we are still hatching and contriving upon our selves matter of continuall sorrow and perplexitie. (*CP* 2, 234–35)

All of reality, not just hell, reflects creatures' attitudes toward God and, simultaneously, his attitude toward them. Satan's experiences during his travels, as we have already seen, testify to the accuracy of Belial's understanding of hell. Wherever he goes, Satan is tormented by the internal, portable hellfire produced by his hatred of God. Creation, even one's personal portion of it, inasmuch as it derives substantially from God, is like a one-way mirror in which creatures can perceive themselves as they appear to God. If, in Luther's terms, we may describe creation as a mask of God, it is a mask that materially expresses, in the creature's own image, divine wrath or pleasure. The peace or unrest within creatures permeates their worlds.

Belial's proposal, however, does indulge in a single pervasive inconsistency, one later adopted by Mammon. He maintains that the demons may grow accustomed to the anguish that inevitably accompanies their constitutional dissatisfaction with their situation: "chang'd at length, and to the place conform'd / In temper and in nature" (2, 217–18). Mammon includes Belial's hope for such an impossible metamorphosis in his own plan for a separate empire: "Our torments also may in length of time / Become our Elements, these piercing Fires / As soft as now severe, our temper chang'd / Into their temper" (2, 274–77). Mammon further contends that the elements of hell, a place fundamentally inhospitable to created life, can be refined so that products beneficial to life can be manufactured:

> Our greatness will appear
> Then most conspicuous, when great things of small,
> Useful of hurtful, prosperous of adverse
> We can create, and in what place soe'er
> Thrive under evil, and work ease out of pain
> Through labor and endurance.   (2, 257–62)

The conservationist's parody of a developer, Mammon is hell's industrialist, out to reshape the world in a plastic, utilitarian image of himself while at the same time accomplishing a metamorphosis of himself into plastic. How can hell's "corrosive Fires" become wholesome or even unharmful (2, 401)? How can creatures whose original natures lack all harmony with their current environment ever adjust to it?

They cannot. And the impossibility of their position defines hell. The identity of a thing with itself is the basis of all reason, all assurance, all happiness, but the only hope the devils have is the complete loss of their created identities and the establishment of new ones. The real matter before the council is what to become: to be as they were is no longer possible; to be as they are means oblivion and pain. To lose all consciousness of their original selves and start over seems the only path open to them. But God either cannot or will not allow them to take that path. They are forever tormented by the world as it represents God's will and by themselves as inhabitants of that world. Milton thus unites the myth of Tantalus, eternally thirsty in sight of water, with the myth of the Lethe, a drop of whose waters erases all trace of who one was (2, 604–14). The fact that "*Medusa* with *Gorgonian* terror" prevents the waters of oblivion from touching their lips suggests that the rebels have become fixed like stone, artifacts of their own discontent. The irony of Satan's many metamorphoses is that fundamentally he refuses to change. He will take any shape he feels he must take in order to remain opposed to God's goodness. His only identity now is one of essential dissatisfaction and discomfort with the disposition of existence. The hell imagined by Milton thus relies on Ovidian figures of isolation, expressions of what Harold Skulsky has described as "deformity and alienation driven to the limit of the imaginable — solitary confinement in one's own body."[14]

The "study of transformation," says Skulsky of certain of Ovid's myths, "is the story of the self as it endures a catastrophic physical change."[15] Ovid sometimes offers such changes simply as poetically just deaths, but occasionally the poignance of the change resides in "the persistence of a mind alienated from all selves including the self it belongs to."[16] Calisto, for example, becomes a bear, but "her minde shee still possest; / And with continuall grones her griefe exprest; / With pawes strecht up to heaven, accus'd her fate" (*Met.* 2, 485–87). The innocent Actaeon, whose fate, like the innocent Scylla's, associates him with Satan's daughter-mate, undergoes an even more pitiful transformation, into a deer torn to pieces by his own dogs (3, 176–290). Dante first accommodated the horrors of Ovid's cruelest, and often entirely unjust, changes to the just God of Christianity, locating only in hell such vicious transformations and radical instability of self.

For both Dante and Milton, the last resort of the damned, starved for recognition and the identity it partly confers, is to build fame among undiscriminating men.[17] Yet they also affirmed, as Ovid did before them, that the primal confusion attendant on a state of lost identity is hardly assuaged by the dubious remedy of fame. Like Milton's Paradise of Fools, Ovid's house of fame owes its character to the uncertainties and equivocations that pervade human opinion, a realm not as unreliable nor as confused in perception as hell, but

one that Milton nevertheless saw as fraught with uncertainties born
of hell:

> Hither the idle Vulgar come and goe:
> Millions of Rumors wander too and fro;
> Lyes mixt with truths, in words that vary still.
> Of these, with newes unknowing eares Some fill;
> Some carry tales: all in the telling growes;
> And every author addes to what he knowes.
> Here dwels rash Error, light Credulity,
> Dejected Feare, and vainly grounded Joy;
> New rais'd Sedition; secret Whisperings
> Of unknowne Authors, and of doubtfull things.
>
> (12, 52–61)

The equivocations of fame in the world of opinion reflect the vulnerability of identity in the world of becoming. At the extreme, a
loss of glory (not just fame) such as Satan suffers makes doubt a
metaphysical condition, not only an epistemological one. Suddenly,
creatures can become other than themselves. Their shiftiness, hypocrisy, and unreliability correspond to a state of being about as de-
pendable as a hallucination. Ovid's house of fame appropriately
stands "Amid the world, betweene Aire, Earth and Seas," its ambiguous locale reminiscent of the Paradise of Fools' position on a "windy
Sea of Land" (*Met.* 12, 40; *PL* 3, 440). And just as the falsely religious in the Paradise of Fools will actually become their clothes, so
Satan and his followers as easily and as involuntarily become ser-
pents (*PL* 3, 478–91; 10, 504–45).

Desire in Hell

Given that Milton's characterization of hell recalls Ovid's most ironic
and implicitly cynical depictions of the human condition, one still
searches for some explanation of the fallen angels' desire to inflict
their evil on others. Like the victims of Ovid's most bitter transformations, the rebels are "excluded by their past from understanding . . . anything but their own forlorn uniqueness."[18] What makes
these alienated and isolated creatures into agents of evil? One may

suppose generally that love, the search for identity, and metamorphosis are connected topics, and that a loss of identity — a loss of glory — is often accompanied by the attempt to inflict similar anguish on others. But I wish to examine the problem of evil in *Paradise Lost* specifically by considering the psychology of love and its relation to metamorphosis in the Ovidian tradition. Others have ably cited instances of verbal indebtedness to Ovid and of *retractio* and *contaminatio* in the construction of the action.[19] What interests me here is the concentration on love and hate as the emotional bases of metamorphosis and how Milton's use of Ovid illuminates this theme.

In some ways, Satan and his crew resemble forsaken lovers, though we should remember that they themselves, by their excessive self-love, initiate the divorce from God. As George Sandys comments on the fable of Narcissus, "a fearfull example we have of the danger of selfe-love in the fall of the Angells; who intermitting the beatificall vision, by reflecting upon themselves, and admiration of their owne excellency, forgot their dependance upon their creator" (p. 160). The narcissism of the rebel angels, which contrasts with and yet prefigures the innocent self-love of the newborn Eve, associates them with Ovidian figures who are driven by self-love and ambition either to deny or to contend with the gods. In either case, the guilty party attempts to steal the glory that properly belongs to the divine. Thamyris, for example, is blinded for contending with the Muses, and Sandys comments that he suffered "a fate deservedly inflicted on those, who dote on their owne gifts, and value them more than the giver" (p. 528).[20]

Milton allegorizes Satan's narcissism in describing the birth of Sin according to the birth of Minerva. Sin represents the wisdom of Satan even as Minerva does the wisdom of Jove. Satan's daughter or feminine side, the part of his psyche that once submitted to God, has now become distinct from and devoted to Satan himself. Satan fails to recognize this feminine, submissive creature in part because he himself has hardened into a perverse masculinity. Without that part of him that owes allegiance and submission to someone outside himself, Satan finds it as impossible to repent as he does to make love. Emotionally and physically obdurate, "gross by sinning grown," Satan suffers a hardness of heart and of substance (*PL* 6, 661). Only disdain and testicularity are left him. The wisdom of Satan, it seems, equals the inability to submit or yield to God, making him, as in Athena's epithet, *promachos*, "first in battle," or, in the language of hell, "Leader of those Armies bright," "foremost to stand against the Thunderer's aim" (1, 272; 2, 28).

This Hebrew Bellona's bridegroom is thus cast out from heaven not so much because of his rebellion or attempt to usurp God's place, but because he has become incapable of submission, and instead exhibits an irremediable priapism of the spirit. Having lost the ability to yield to another, and particularly to love the God "whom to love is to obey," Satan and his followers both reject and are rejected by their former love (8, 634). The hatred exhibited by the devils has much of the emotional character associated with love gone sour. In commenting on the story of Medea, Sandys explains that "No hatred is so deadly as that which proceeds from alienated love" (pp. 341–42). God's indifference to the fallen angels' vain attempts at revenge, an indifference he expresses by permitting them to do what they please, is in fact the most effective way to inflict pain on them. He is like the once loving husband who responds to his once beloved wife by saying that no matter what she does, he will continue not to acknowledge her existence. It is as if God were to say, "Frankly my dears, I don't give a damn," and in so saying, damned them.

Andrew Marvell defined the structure of love in precisely the way that allows us to recognize in Satan the extremity of desire:[21]

> My Love is of a birth as rare
> As 'tis, for object, strange and high;
> It was begotten by Despair
> Upon Impossibility
>
> Magnanimous Despair alone
> Could show me so divine a thing,
> Where feeble Hope could ne'er have flown
> But vainly flapped its tinsel wing.
>
> And yet I quickly might arrive
> Where my extended soul is fixed
> But Fate does iron wedges drive,
> And always crowds itself betwixt.
>
> (*Definition of Love* 1–12)

Like Milton's Satan before him, Marvell's lover finds himself "from despair / . . . high uplifted beyond hope," in pursuit of an impossible object, an aspiration that will lead him ever further into misery and despair (*PL* 2, 6–7). Admittedly, Marvell's lover presumably desires a woman whereas Satan desires God's dominant position. Both loves nevertheless are foiled by, and at the same time derive their power and poignance from, the opposition of fate, whether considered as an impersonal force or as the will of God. Both loves also fix the poles of a cosmos of love that stretches between them; God is above all and Satan below all. If they were to unite, as Marvell's lover suggests with respect to his beloved, "the world should all / Be cramped into a planisphere" (*Definition* 23–24). The Fall of Satan creates distance, creates space, and Milton wrote of, to use Masson's phrase, "a universe of space."[22]

The devils' enmity to God may therefore be seen as an attempt somehow to continue relations with him. Even angry recognition is better than no recognition at all. Their revenge and their love will be satisfied only if they can harm him or cause him misery, because they believe that his joy derives from causing them pain. They thus wish to bring evil out of his good in order to "grieve him," just as Satan and Beelzebub consider "how we may henceforth most offend / Our Enemy" (*PL* 1, 167, 187). God appears to them as the "angry Victor," the "Torturer," and as the inventor of "Torments," such as "Tartarean Sulphur, and strange fire" (1, 169; 2, 64, 69–70). The policies advanced by Moloch, Belial, and Mammon turn on these attitudes: Moloch wishes to direct God's own torments against Heaven, to cause God the dismay and anguish that the devils currently suffer; Belial ostensibly suggests lying low so that later they might catch God napping and take vengeance when he least expects it; and Mammon promotes a life apart from God, showing him that they can be happy without him. All these are ploys of estranged love. Freud might identify the relations between God and the devils as governed by the vicissitudes of sadism and masochism, an unholy perversion of complementary relations between exponents of a once heavenly love.[23] One never knows, however, how much of God's sadism lies at the door of the devils' fallen attitudes. Suffice it to say that, although the devils talk as if they have entered a power struggle and couch their discussions in military idiom, at the heart of their machinations is a failed love.

In true Ovidian fashion, Satan plans to inflict pain on his former lover by attacking those dear to him. If God no longer cares for the fallen angels, he *does* care about others and can, they hope, be affected through them. Beelzebub describes Man as "like to us, though less / In power and excellence, but favor'd more / Of him who rules above" (2, 349–51). Made not in the image of God, says Beelzebub, but "like to us," Man appears as a rival, "favor'd more" than the rebels. Satan refers to Man as the "Son of despite, / Whom us the more to spite his Maker rais'd / From dust" (9, 176–78). Regardless of the accuracy or inaccuracy of his interpretation of God's actions, Satan's own intention is certainly based on spite (2, 385; 9, 177). His plan brings to mind Medea, who in pursuing vengeance ignores Jason himself and instead attacks innocents: Jason's new wife, Creusa; her father, Creon; and even the children that she herself bore to Jason. Sandys remarks that prior to her vengeance, Medea's face goes red, then pale, even as Satan's borrowed visage betrays his passionate thoughts before he proceeds to attack Man (*Met.* p. 341; *PL* 4, 114–16). Medea poisons Creusa and Creon with naphtha, an infectiously fiery substance that also darkly illuminates Milton's hell (*Met.* p. 342; *PL* 1, 729). Naphtha, it seems, symbolizes the violence that proceeds from love gone bad. Eve's eyes thus dart "contagious Fire," a libidinous naphtha that inflames Adam's senses and leads to the spite and alienation that accompany the Fall of Man (*PL* 9, 1036).

Not surprisingly, Medea's story connects her as closely with Adam and Eve as it does with Satan. Before turning to Adam and Eve and their resemblance to Satan, however, I wish to recapitulate some relevant principles regarding metamorphosis in *Paradise Lost*. Metamorphosis for Milton has physical and spiritual components. Though for the sake of analysis we distinguish between these components, they in fact comprise a whole that, particularly in Paradise, does not admit division. The physiological process that chiefly expresses the metamorphic character of Milton's cosmos is nutrition. The emotional and spiritual process that chiefly expresses its metamorphic character is love. Both processes may be considered epistemological in the sense that they are modes of knowing God that allow for recognition and love of him and by him. Notably, the rebel throng satisfies neither hunger nor sexual desire, "plagued / And worn with Famine" and tormented by "fierce desire / . . . / Still unfulfill'd with pain of longing" (10, 572–73; 4, 509–11). As we are about to see, the situation for humankind differs greatly.

7

MARRIAGE AND METAMORPHOSIS

A S I NOTED in the last chapter, Beelzebub claims that Man is made "like to us" (*PL* 2, 349), and although it may be inaccurate to claim that God creates Man because Satan fell, it does seem as if the Fall of Satan through chaos clears a space for Man in the cosmos.[1] Until Satan plummets through the depths, the sole created reality is heaven, and being in heaven means being with God. But the nature of even unfallen Man presumes distance from God, and the idea of distance from God is inextricably tied to the Fall of Satan. As William Kerrigan has noted, two distinct visions of existence surround the invocation to light: Satan's, which expresses seemingly infinite distance and separation; and God's, which expresses presence and an almost pantheistic unity of space and time.[2] The scale of Man's vision lies somewhere between the fragmentation and alienation of Satan's ever-expanding universe and the perfect immediacy of God's abiding immanence.

God's awareness that his new creation may be considered reparation for the loss of the rebels underscores humanity's unique significance as a medium for divine expression (7, 150–56). Roughly speaking, Adam and Eve are war babies, part of a creative celebration of victory conveying the resilience and versatility of God in the face of evil and loss. The meaning of our existence is, thus, inextricably linked to the origin of evil and distance. Our world dangles from its golden chain off "that side Heav'n from whence [Satan's] Legions fell," and God designs Adam and Eve to "open to themselves at length the way" to heaven (2, 1006; 7, 158). Unlike Satan but according to his model, therefore, Man legitimately strives for glories above his created station. Like Satan, Adam gives birth to a daughter-mate in his own image, according to his own desire, and even for Adam this desire at first appears contrary to God's will. Satan, however, in accepting Sin's devotion, rejects God in favor of himself. Eve's devotion to Adam, on the other hand, is ordained, in Pauline terms, as a reflection of the love that Man owes God. Furthermore, Adam and Eve, like the devils, can be described through the Tantalus myth, but through an inversion of it, in which moderate desires are perfectly satisfied. Book IV pictures Adam and Eve reclining on the soft banks of a fountain, with "compliant boughs" yielding them delicious fruit, the rinds of which serve to scoop "the brimming stream" that flows immediately beside them (330–35). No Gorgonian terror fixes Adam and Eve in this fate; unlike the devils, they enjoy the fluidity of being able to become other than they are, an otherness that does not involve the loss of their created identities. Hence, although the similarities between humankind and the fallen angels prompt us to compare them, the comparison also underlines the differences between them. Other similarities and differences define the relations between Man and God.

Regardless of the categories of analysis one chooses, humanity's relative position in Milton's metamorphic cosmos remains the same — fixed by the tension between opposite poles, a definitive tension and yet dynamic in its susceptibility to time and motion. For humankind to continue as humankind, therefore, it must sustain that tension — and thus maintaining equilibrium, change without changing. The alternatives to this steady negotiation of opposing forces are an unlikely, ontologically expansive leap toward heaven and divine presence, or a suicidal plunge toward hell and Satanic absence. The first alternative is only unlikely, not impossible, because God could empower it, his will being irresistible. The second alternative is what would occur if one went against God's wishes to attempt such a leap. (There is no such thing as gravitational force in Milton's cosmos, only willpower.)

I have made humankind's position sound rather simple, as modern critics of *Paradise Lost* often do in their eagerness to accuse their first parents and declare God justified. But despite the indisputable fact that ultimately one chooses either to eat the apple or not, the increasingly subtle and overwhelming variety of the world in which that ultimate choice incessantly applies puzzles the will. It all begins easily enough, with God guiding an instinctively apt Adam by the hand. But soon the developmental tasks become more complex and God delegates the role of counselor to a sophisticated functionary, whose angelic ethnocentricity undermines his ostensibly didactic purpose. It may be a Satanic moral to the story, but surely one of the generally unrecognized lessons of *Paradise Lost* is that one should beware of smiling seraphim, or pretend that one is not at home when they drop by for lunch. In the next chapter, I shall have occasion to consider in detail the relations between human beings and unfallen angels. The current subject, however, is Man's suspension between God and Satan.

Marriage and Miltonic Metaphor

Phenomenologically, one could describe humankind's developmental task as that of establishing, and maintaining through time, a voluntary, self-conscious position between All (God) and Nothing (Satan), or, in logical terms, between tautology and contradiction. As I suggested earlier, one could make a parallel analysis in language appropriate to almost any category of investigation — epistemological, physical, metaphysical, psychological, and so forth. But I wish to characterize humankind's phenomenological problem from a linguistic perspective, viewing Adam and Eve as metaphorical creatures: we understand them in terms of similarities and differences between them and God or Satan, and in terms of proximity and distance — both spatial and chronological — with respect to heaven and hell. It may seem careless to confuse modes that modern linguistic theorists deem distinct: the axis of synchrony, to which metaphorical similarity and difference belong; and the axis of diachrony, to which metonymic proximity and distance belong.[3] But Milton imagines a cosmos in which these apparent oppositions are not substantial and can be transcended. Man's metaphorical relations to God and Satan are simultaneously metonymic, simply because of the common material basis of being as graded into degrees of proximity or distance. While the universal applicability of metonymy implies the ontological solidarity of Milton's cosmos, metaphors nevertheless presume (by pretending to ignore) the metaphysical distinctions that formally distinguish and relate the parts of a whole. Consequently, in *Paradise Lost* metaphorical assertions of identity between distinct beings or processes enjoy the abiding ontological authority of metonymy. For unfallen creatures, the metonymic force behind metaphor predicts and renders intelligible the metamorphoses that inevitably overcome participants in a universe of potency and act. They guide creatures in their movement toward God.

It bears repeating that Milton's understanding of the nature and function of metaphor is consistent with his material monism, and that "sameness" is a substantial reality, not merely the intellectual product of a synthesizing mind. Chapter 4 used Luther's terms to express the immediacy of God's substantial presence in creation; creation masks or veils a God who is *really* there. Milton's deity, more literally than Luther's, permeates reality and the events, or states of affairs, that constitute reality. Because God authored each being out of his own infinite matter, and because each creature potentially can participate in the apocalyptic apotheosis, each creature may properly be understood as a metaphor for God in a cosmos constituted by a network of such metaphors.

With reference to biblical hermeneutics, it follows that Milton should accept the validity of biblical metaphor with a wholeheartedness unusual among humanist exegetes, who, as good Neoplatonists, generally interpreted figurative language as, in Salutati's phrase, "that falseness of skin."[4] Milton scholars, notably R. M. Frye, have identified Milton's hermeneutics with Calvin's, which holds that God allows anthropomorphic metaphors to express him for the same reason that parents use baby talk with small children — to bring things down to their capacity.[5] Calvin particularly objected, for example, to a literal reading of "repent" in a description of a change in God's attitude.[6] Milton, however, citing the same passage, exhorts his readers to believe that God indeed "did repent" (*CP* 6, 134).[7] Although Milton admits that no figure of speech can convey God's essence, he nevertheless views biblical metaphors as the way to think about God sanctioned by God:

> We may be certain that God's majesty and glory were so dear to him that he could never say anything about himself which was lower or meaner than his real nature.
>
> (*CP* 6, 136)

The key difference between Calvin and Milton is thus as follows. While for Calvin and most other Renaissance exegetes *metaphorical* ultimately meant "false," or at least "potentially misleading," for Milton all knowledge of God is metaphorical until the apocalypse. Although *apocalypse* implies an *uncovering* of truth, it would perhaps be more accurate to describe ultimate revelation as the completion or perfection of "knowledge in the making" (*doxa*). In any event, the fullness of truth resides potentially in divine metaphor, just as God unfolds in temporal creation the potency of his otherwise unknowable essence. Metaphors *are* the "literal" truth, insofar as Man can know it in time. Hence, those who allow the divine will to be expressed in their lives may be said to live a "true poem," as true in its own way as the true poem of Scripture — itself a collection of the lives of those who performed or opposed the will of God. According to Milton, anyone who claims to have separated the "real truth" from the metaphor exalts his own authority over God's word and works, as if to demonstrate that "our concept of God was not too debased, but that his concept of us was" (*CP* 6, 136).

Given that humanity's understanding of its dynamic relations with God and creation is by nature metaphorical, the marriage between Adam and Eve is established as perhaps the most efficacious and portentous of figures.[8] As Paul Ricoeur describes metaphor, in it "'same' and 'different' are not just mixed together, they also remain opposed"; "'the similar' is perceived *despite* difference, in spite of contradiction."[9] Hell is the realm, to use Ricoeur's terms, of mere difference, of opposition and contradiction. Human reality, on the other hand, may be described, in Ricoeur's terms, as "the site of the clash between sameness and difference."[10] Humanity subsists in a progressive, metaphorical version of eternal truth. In Platonic terms, temporal creation offers a moving image of eternity. But we must remember that for Milton, unlike Plato, eternal reality does not yet exist, even if it is immutably foreseen. Unfallen creatures, after all, are originally and ultimately part of God, but for now they reside somewhere in the midst of time, developing their divine heritage.

No part of human reality better accommodates to Man the rewards and risks of divine resemblance than wedlock. Consider, for example, the idea of marriage espoused in the divorce tracts:

Wee know that flesh can neither joyn, nor keep together two
bodies of it self; what is it then must make them one flesh, but
likenes, but fitnes of mind and disposition, which may breed
the Spirit of concord, and union between them? If that be not
in the nature of either, and that there has bin a remediles mis-
take, as vain wee goe about to compell them into one flesh,
as if wee undertook to weav a garment of drie sand. It were
more easy to compell the vegetable and nutritive power of nature to assimilations and mixtures which are not alterable each
by other; or force the concoctive stomach to turn that into flesh
which is so totally unlike that substance, as not to be wrought
on. For as the unity of the minde is neerer and greater than
the union of bodies, so doubtles, is the dissimilitude greater,
and more dividuall, as that which makes between bodies all
difference and distinction.   (*CP* 2, 605-6)

Milton here describes marriage in terms of the nutritional and physiological processes that in *Paradise Lost* constitute the physical mode
of advance toward heaven. Some marriages are naturally impossible,
and to force the antipathetic partners to remain in them is to sentence
them to an earthly version of hell's irreconcilable differences: "can
any law or command be so unreasonable as to make men cleav to
calamity, to ruin, to perdition?" (*CP* 2, 605). The contradiction entailed by life within such a "marriage" has its original in the contradictions of hell, where the inhabitants characteristically attempt
to make, among other impossible metamorphoses, "useful of hurt-
ful" (*PL* 2, 259).

Though the hell of a bad marriage results from the union of a
man and a woman fundamentally unsuited to each other, some difference is nevertheless essential to the pleasure and diversion that
wedded union provides labor-wearied partners:

no worthy enterprise can be don by us without continuall plodding and wearisomnes to our faith and sensitive abilities. We
cannot therefore alwayes be contemplative, or pragmaticall
abroad, but have need of som delightfull intermissions, wherein
the enlarg'd soul may leav off a while her severe schooling;
and like a glad youth in wandring vacancy, may keep her holli-

daies to joy and harmles pastime: which as she cannot well
doe without company, so in no company so well as where the
different sexe in most resembling unlikenes, and most unlike
resemblance cannot but please best and be pleas'd in the apti-
tude of that variety.   (*CP* 2, 597)

Several points worth mentioning, aside from the importance of difference, occur in this passage from *Tetrachordon*. First, the development of Man's rational potency requires labor: for fallen Man, it
takes "continuall plodding"; but for unfallen Man, too, the approach
to God involves diligence and steadfastness. Second, for fallen Man,
"proportionably" to unfallen, marriage offers delight and diversion
from divinely appointed labors (*CP* 2, 597). Third, though marriage
therefore appears to be related to the ascent to God in the same way
that vacation is related to vocation, marriage is, especially for unfallen Man, designed as an aid to, and not as a diversion from, Man's
heavenly aspirations. This last point is crucial to understanding Man's
fate in Milton's epic, and we will return to it later.

The difference that fosters diversion and recreation in marriage
is not only sexual. For Milton as for the rest of Christianity, the union
of husband and wife authoritatively resembles the union of the
Church with Christ (see *CP* 2, 606). The union of same and different
on the human scale of husband and wife prefigures the glory of the
ultimate transcendence of difference, when God shall be "All in All."
The husband fills the role of God and the wife the role of creation:
"man is not to hold her as a servant, but receives her into a part
of that empire which God proclaims him to though not equally, yet
largely, as his own image and glory: for it is no small glory to him,
that a creature so like him, should be made subject to him" (*CP* 2,
589). The union of man and woman in marriage, like the final harmony it models, is a union that consists in reasonable love and obedience, not in loss of identity. In fact, a husband and wife most fully
actualize the glory of their different sexes through marriage — "most
resembling unlikenes, and most unlike resemblance."

Earlier I argued that nutrition and love express complementary
aspects of the quest for knowledge in Milton's thought. In *Areopagitica*, for example, the pursuit of truth often appears in nutritional
terms (see *CP* 2, 512–13). But Milton describes the painstaking pro-

cess by which the disparate parts of truth are united in terms similar
to those that he uses to depict wedded union:

> To be still searching what we know not, by what we know,
> still closing up truth to truth as we find it (for all her body is
> *homogeneal*, and proportionall) this is the golden rule in *The-
> ology* as well as in Arithmetick, and makes up the best har-
> mony in a Church; not the forc't and outward union of cold,
> and neutrall and inwardly divided minds.   (*CP* 2, 551)

> out of many moderat varieties and brotherly dissimilitudes that
> are not vastly disproportionall arises the goodly and gracefull
> symmetry that commends the whole pile and structure.
>
>   (*CP* 2, 555)

The way to unity in marriage or in worship is to build harmony
out of sympathetic diversity. The true genius is the master of metaphor, according to Aristotle, because he discerns the hidden relations and harmonies that bring order to the world.[11] As John Halkett has claimed, "Milton's conception of matrimony as a harmony
of souls and wills is a direct result of his conviction of universal order";
marriage exemplified "the universal law of unity in division."[12]

Perhaps reason and choice threaten to collapse into each other
in Milton's theology in part because one must choose to submit to
metaphorical sameness in order to achieve the harmony of understanding and agreement. And one must do so in full recognition of
the differences that metaphor attempts to transcend. Ricoeur expresses
this facet of metaphor in a paradox that fits also the relations between Adam and Eve – "to yield while protesting."[13] Milton defines
the actively willed passion of obedient love as "subjection, but re-
quir'd with gentle sway, / And by her yielded, by him best receiv'd, /
Yielded with coy submission, modest pride, / And sweet reluctant
amorous delay" (*PL* 4, 308–11). The culmination of the description,
"delay," defines the yearning for, but resistance to, union suggested
by the assonant roll of long vowels over the throaty "luct" of reluctant. "Delay" also makes a remote rhyme with "sway" as it suggests
the muted opposition that that sway must overcome.[14] Difference

as well as resemblance constitute wedded love, just as difference as well as resemblance constitute a metaphor.

The heart and soul of marriage, then, is a vital harmony, and for Milton harmony between man and woman consists both in natural and in voluntary fitness.[15] In a fallen world, natural incompatability frequently occurs, due mostly to errors in judgment that lie undetected until after the ceremony (*CP* 2, 249–50). Despite the pronouncements of Church and state, however, no marriage, defined as harmony, can exist under such conditions, and thus divorce is justified by natural incompatability just as surely as it is by jarring perversity of will. In the Garden, though, the natural suitability of Eve to Adam is a divinely provided advantage to sure union. They need only manage the concord of their wills in order to maintain harmony. Appropriately enough, then, while nutrition provides the dominant natural metaphor in *Paradise Lost* for the intellectual incorporation of variety into a unified whole, marriage offers the best volitional metaphor. For though reason and choice seem to coincide, they nevertheless remain at least formally distinct. Raphael offers advice on both aspects of harmony and seems suited to do so by his traditional expertise in health and, supposedly, in affairs of the heart.[16]

Long-standing precedents justified the division of harmony into intellectual and volitional components. Given the banquetlike setting of Raphael's and Adam's discussion, we first remember Plato's *Symposium*. The speech of the physician, Eryximachus, defines the pursuit of harmony in love as a natural, medical problem, and thus as one amenable to an intellectual solution. Aristophanes, however, narrates an etiological myth of sin and punishment to explain the palpable desire for, and frequent absence of, harmony in human love. Socrates, drawing on both speeches, conclusively defines love as the natural and intellectual desire for beauty — which to the Greeks primarily meant harmony — and the soul's corresponding aspiration for immortality.

In the biblical tradition, intellect and will were even more clearly isolated as the bases of harmony. Beginning with Paul, Christians commonly analyzed the fallenness of the human condition, its lack of harmony, in terms of our vitiated rational nature and infected will. Joseph Mead of Christ's College developed the commonplace Christian dichotomy in terms well suited to an analysis of Raphael's teaching:

> The *Ascent* of the Soul unto God by the contemplation of crea-
> tures is either the *Ascent of the Understanding,* to know him,
> or the *Ascent of our Will,* through obedience to worship him.[17]

The purpose of creation is to reflect the glory of God and finally to join in that glory. By the intellect's inquiry into the natural order, Man can learn how, by nature, he fits into the harmony of creation. But as he understands the natural order, Man also must learn to conform himself to his part in creation's embodiment of divine glory. The metaphor of wedded love suits the expression of this side of glory because continuing harmony in marriage subsists mainly on the choices of conscious agents.

Milton thus found precedent in both the pagan and the Christian traditions to justify the stress he placed on the love of Adam and Eve, a stress interpolated by him into the original story.[18] The metaphor of marriage, like that of nutrition, is also a metonymy; in either case, the metaphor not only indicates the harmony in which God's glory finally consists, but also helps constitute that harmony. As with Raphael's analogy of the flowering plant (*PL* 5, 479–88), metaphors in *Paradise Lost* never simply transmit meaning. They rather participate in the progress toward glory as, simultaneously, they signify the goal of that progress. By loving each other, Adam and Eve can grow in conformity to God's will. In other words, by achieving harmony on a human scale, their right opinion (*doxa*) about God and themselves is strengthened and heightened. They can thus better advance toward the final glory of union with, and participation in, God.

Adam's Metamorphoses

Given the intelligibility that existentially forceful metaphors lend metamorphosis in an unfallen world, it follows that one of the most significant differences between Satan and humankind will lie in their respective states of knowledge. In a sense, the devils' epistemological perversity consists chiefly in a lack of appreciation for divine metaphor. As we have already seen, Satan and his followers awaken in Book I to discover themselves in radical uncertainty as to who, where, or what they are. Adam first awakens under similar conditions, but his progress toward God begins immediately and is accompanied by his heightened awareness concerning his situation. Adam's "instinctive motion" heavenward, "as thitherward endeavoring," prepares us for the first conclusion drawn by his naturally upright reason and will, that the "great Maker" responsible for creating him and the world should be sought out and adored (8, 259–60, 278). Scholars have virtually ignored the significance of the unfallen Adam's brief sojourn outside the Garden, yet it represents one of the least precedented scenes in Milton's version of Genesis and sets the pattern for later developments in Man's status.[19] The movement of Adam from Eden to the Garden proper, and from a second state of unconsciousness, which Adam likens to "my former state / Insensible," to renewed and enhanced consciousness, marks the first step toward heavenly glory (8, 290–91). Every subsequent transformation of Man's condition similarly matches his attempts to know God better, to improve in *doxa*. Sleep punctuates these attempts and provides a special medium for encounters between Man and God. Poetry is the language of metamorphosis, but sleep, as Keats understood, is its proper realm, the realm of creation and transformation, wherein the boundaries of recognition are tested. With the exception of the stupor from which the rebels awaken in Book I, the devils never sleep, just as they do not eat or enjoy sex. (When Satan awakens rebellion, he, like Macbeth, murders sleep. We should assume, though, that the restless rebels nevertheless desire sleep, just as they do food and sex. "God is also in sleep," and that makes it impossible for the devils to rest their cares [12, 611].)[20]

As Adam learns more about his world and the subjects of his kingdom, he draws inferences about God.[21] If Books I and II, for all their similes, declare the impossibility of meaningful relations between hell and anything else, Books V through VIII insist on significant comparisons between the realms of Man and God. The only thing that the devils discover in hell is the unremitting anguish involved in their loss of glory and corresponding estrangement from God; God no longer knows them, and they no longer know God.

Adam, on the other hand, discovers that the quest for knowledge of God is inextricably involved with his partaking of the pleasures of Paradise:

> O by what Name, for thou above all these,
> Above mankind, or aught than mankind higher,
> Surpassest far my naming, how may I
> Adore thee, Author of this Universe,
> And all this good to man, for whose well being
> So amply, and with hands so liberal
> Thou hast provided all things: but with mee
> I see not who partakes. In solitude
> What happiness, who can enjoy alone,
> Or all enjoying, what contentment find?   (8, 357–66)

Adam combines two large questions: the first directed at learning more about God; the second at confirming his opinions about himself as the recipient of God's nurture. Both questions address the same issue, Man's resemblance to and difference from God — or the nature of human glory.

Adam's subsequent request rests on the premise that Man requires a "fit and meet" partner in order to maintain his analogical relationship with God. Like creation with respect to God, Eve depends on Adam for direction and without him lives "to no end" (4, 442).[22] She praises Adam as her "Author and Disposer" (4, 635), and when in Book VIII Adam extolls God's solitary sufficiency — "in thy secrecy although alone, / Best with thyself accompanied" — we may recall Eve's similar words to Adam in Book IV: "thou / Like consort to thyself canst nowhere find" (8, 427–28; 4, 447–48). At the birth of Eve the entire world seems once again to have been metamorphosed, just as it did when Adam moved from Eden to the Garden itself. As he had been previously, Adam is put to sleep and awakens to a fresh creation. Seeing the Garden for the first time, Adam remarked, "what I saw / Of Earth before scarce pleasant seem'd" (8, 305–6). Seeing Eve for the first time, he says, "what seem'd fair in all the World, seem'd now / Mean or in her summ'd up, in her contain'd / And in her looks" (8, 472–74). The analogical nature of their marriage appears emblematically as Adam leads Eve by the hand to the nuptial bower, away from God's direct, parental presence. Before, it had always been God — leading Adam by the hand to the Garden, leading Eve to Adam.

As before, this last step in Man's metamorphic progress is accompanied by physical movement, this time from the Garden to the "Nuptial Bow'r," another, even more sacred place within the rest of creation, "a place / Chos'n by the sovran Planter" (8, 510; 4, 690–91). Like the Garden with respect to Eden, the bower restates and refines the rest of creation, either by confluence of the subtle — "selectest influence," "sign of gratulation," "gentle Airs" — or by exclusion of the gross — "other Creature here / Beast, Bird, Insect, or Worm durst enter none" (8, 513–15; 4, 703–4). In sum, as in Donne's *Holy Sonnet Fourteen*, Adam has been transformed from a creature outside the Garden, where he began life in search of a creator, to an inhabitant of the Garden, where he finds himself elevated to the status of vassal with authority over a Garden kingdom. Finally, he becomes a lover enjoying marriage as symbolized by the bower, a place where Man can recognize himself as a private creature with a will apart from God's, capable of accepting or rejecting his divine lover.[23] "To know no more" than to follow her husband's will, says Eve, "is woman's happiest knowledge and her praise" (4, 637–38). So Man must "know to know no more" than to obey "him whom to love is to obey" (4, 775; 8, 634).

Twice referred to as "mysterious," wedded love holds something of the status of a sacrament for Milton in that it especially represents and leads to the profound intimacy — the most personal kind of knowing — that God desires with his creatures (4, 743, 750). The first knowledge of God that Adam desires would confirm the hypothesis proposed by his natural intellect: I am; therefore, God is. The second kind of knowledge that Adam achieves inspires a bond of obedience, a feudal relationship between lord and subject: Adam accepts the obligation to serve his superior, to rule over his inferiors, and, implicitly, to understand himself in relation to those below and those above him. The movement to the Garden answers Adam's desire for the first kind of knowledge because the Garden is the definitive place of God's direct appearance to Man; meeting God in the Garden confirms what Adam had already concluded to be true. The interdiction of the fruit befits the second kind of knowledge, a knowledge that involves a more profound and accurate admission of dependence. Abstention from the forbidden fruit not only signifies obedience; it also signals the fact that Man eats of the fruit of the rest of God's trees, and thus advances in status, only by God's favor and permission. God's other command, however, to "be fruitful, multiply, and fill the Earth," concerns what is primarily Man's own realm, "the sole propriety / In Paradise of all things common else" (7, 531; 4, 751–52). Married love can teach Man in human terms about the reconciliation of love and obedience in the movement of creation toward God. Clearly, Eve engenders the awareness of love in Adam's world: "from that time infus'd / Sweetness into my heart, unfelt before, / And into all things from her Air inspir'd / The spirit of love and amorous delight" (8, 474–77). Intellectual ardor motivates Man to seek a creator, and deeper awareness of his state motivates loyalty and obedience. But only love can motivate the glorious union that God ultimately desires.

No doubt others have felt, in the dialogue between creature and creator in Book VIII, Adam's brief anxiety about God's plans for him. For a moment it almost seems as if Adam may be entertaining the possibility of immediate union with God, even though he realizes also that such a union would call for an extraordinary exercise of divine power (8, 429–31). Such a desire, though a bit premature, is precisely what Adam should feel, and in this respect, Eve is conceived both as a substitute and as a medium of delay that will lead to that final union. Adam's only parent is about to leave him. Adam will be compensated for this loss ("this turn hath made amends") with a companion whose comings and goings he can control, who will be to Adam as Adam is to God (8, 491). The eventual irony is obvious, and in the next chapter I give detailed consideration to the separation between Adam and Eve. For now, however, I simply wish to claim that Eve is, from the beginning, intimately connected to Man's aspiration for final glory.

The mythological figure by which Milton indicates this intimate connection is Ixion. Commentators generally interpreted the myth of Ixion as a warning against ingratitude toward God, but, in a related sense, it was also understood to express the evils of mistaken opinion, especially with respect to the desire for glory. As La Primaudaye put it, "Ixion . . . had to do with a cloud, supposing it to have been the goddesse *Iuno*, whereupon the Centaures were engendered. Even so worldly men imbracing vaine-glorie only, which is but a false shadow of true vertue, all their doings deserve so small commendation, that if they were well waied, they should rather be found worthy of blame and dishonor, than of honor."[24] Sandys seconds La Primaudaye: "Ixion is said to have begotten [the Centaurs] on a Clowd, formed like, & mistaken for *Juno:* representing the vaine pursute of imaginary glory, attempted by unlawful meanes; and the prodigious conceptions of Ambition" (*Met.* p. 564). Joseph Mead alludes to Ixion in his analysis of the Fall: "When an evil *End* is presented unto us in the counterfeit of a good, . . . we are made to embrace *Nubem pro Junone*, and find our selves deceived in the event."[25]

Milton consistently uses the tale of Ixion to characterize false opinions regarding the source and pursuit of glory, especially with respect to marriage or desire for a mate. Given the Old Testament image of God's glory residing in clouds, an image on which, as we have seen, Milton models his presentation of God in *Paradise Lost,* it should not surprise us that Milton takes full advantage of the Ixion myth. In the unfinished *Passion*, Milton begins with sorrow that, if the poem had been completed, would, I believe, have been demonstrated to have been mistaken and self-indulgent.[26] If so, the allusion to Ixion, describing the speaker's sorrows as an "infection" begetting "a race of mourners on some pregnant cloud," would imply that his sorrow results from false opinion and represents, as the paired allusion to Echo suggests, a narcissistic turning away from the true glory of the cross (*Passion* 55–56).[27] In *Animadversions* Milton argues that the people of England, should they submit to the prelates' mistaken version of the Church — and the Church as Christ's bride is, after all, the legitimate vehicle for Man's aspiration to glory — will have become the "Bastards, or the Centaurs of [the prelates'] spirituall fornications" (*CP* 1, 728). In *Paradise Regain'd*, Christ condemns pagan philosophers, who "in themselves seek virtue, and to themselves / All glory arrogate," in terms that recall the myth of Ixion:

> Who . . . seeks in these
> True wisdom, finds her not, or by delusion
> Far worse, her false resemblance only meets,
> An empty cloud. (*PR* 4, 314–15; 318–21)

The key passage, however, for understanding the relevance of Ixion to Milton's idea of marriage and humanity's aspiration for glory appears in *Tetrachordon:*

> as he ordain'd it, so doubtles proportionably to our fal'n estate he gives it; els were his ordinance at least in vain, and we for all his gift still empty handed. Nay such an unbounteous giver we should make him, as in the fables *Jupiter* was to *Ixion,* giving him *a cloud* instead of *Juno,* giving him a monstrous issue by her, the breed of *Centaures* a neglected and unlov'd race, the fruits of a delusive marriage, and lastly giving him her with a damnation to that wheele in hell, from a life thrown into the midst of temptations and disorders. But God is no deceitfull giver, to bestow on us for a remedy of lonelines, which if it bring not a sociable minde as well as a conjunctive body, leavs us no lesse alone then before.   *(CP* 2, 597–98)

The metamorphic potency of the marriage between Adam and Eve, its influence on humankind's relations with God, is underlined by Milton's often noted allusions to the Ovidian myths of Narcissus and Echo and Apollo and Daphne. Eve's innocent if ominous infatuation with her own image reminds us of Narcissus' self-love, while her flight from Adam recalls Daphne's escape from the importunate Apollo's assault on her chastity. In both cases, Eve innocently reflects Satanic self-love and disdain for submission. The difference between God's rendition of himself to Adam — "Whom thou sough'st, I am" — and Adam's rendition of himself to Eve — "whom thou fli'st, of him thou art" — represents the range of attitudes that one may adopt toward the source of one's being *(PL* 8, 316; 4, 482). When Eve's reluctance is overcome, however, the Ovidian myths of frustration and vain love are themselves metamorphosed into examples of the fulfillment of desire. The lesson appears to be that the satisfaction of humankind's desire for glory requires only delay and willingness to go along with metaphor.

Consequently, the myth of Ixion does not appear in *Paradise Lost* to characterize the marriage of Adam and Eve. But the fact that Satan in Book IX spies Eve "veil'd in a Cloud of Fragrance" and, at least for the benefit of her ears, mistakes her for the "Queen of this Universe" should bring the myth of Ixion to mind (425, 684). The deformed children of their union, the "race of mourners" that Eve will bear, similarly encourage a reading of the events leading to the Fall in terms of "the vaine pursuite of imaginary glory" and tragically mistaken opinion on the part of all involved. It is to these events that I turn in the next chapter. But first, I wish to make some final observations.

The love of Adam and Eve — the harmony of their union and the pleasure that derives from it — depends on their awareness and gradual transcendence of their difference. "Delay," in other words, helps Man better to know how happy he is and will be. The risk that logically must accompany Man's greatest earthly delight also accompanies God's pleasure in the loving obedience of his creatures (3, 107). But the disdain that prevents a rebellious creature's submission to God finds decorous modulation in Eve's "Virgin Modesty, / Her virtue and the conscience of her worth, / That would be woo'd, and not unsought be won" (8, 501–3; cf. 4, 770). Hence, the reasoning behind Milton's theological emphasis on free will, and consequently on his understanding of original sin, can also be found in the divorce tracts. The theodicy in Milton's epic and the ideal of wedded bliss propounded in the pamphlets insist absolutely on a single premise: in order for there to be harmony, there must be the possibility of discord and therefore of divorce. Adam and Eve in love form the metaphorical creature Man, who fills the ethical and logical space between the contradiction of hell and the tautology of heaven.

Chapter

8

A TRIUMPH OF DIFFERENCE

AN ALTERNATIVE TITLE to this chapter might be "The Triumph of Differance," if I wished to allude to Derrida and recent Continental critical theory.[1] Those familiar with post-structuralist criticism will see how such a chapter might proceed. Surely, what occurs with the Fall can be (and probably has been) described as a Satanic deconstruction of divinely ordained metaphors of presence. What was glorious becomes shameful. Our first parents become our murderers. Food and procreative love, instead of acting as media of enhanced life and communion, now become metonymies of absence as they propel humans to nothingness and death (*PL* 11, 471–546, 603–99). Nor would it be difficult to argue that Satan is "always already" there, on Earth as in heaven, an eternal Ixion encountering empty clouds and producing monstrous offspring of antiknowledge and antibeing.

I nevertheless prefer to avoid the Satanic form of rationalism and the brand of criticism that goes with it. It strikes me as being impertinent and, all too often, tedious and self-indulgent. Milton was himself familiar with the Scholastic version of deconstruction, and though he understood and accepted the logical ramifications of what Ockham and his followers had to say, they were mainly irrelevant to his poetry. We admit that the human intellect can discover no sure ground for meaning; where we presumed presence, we can demonstrate only absence. But such observations have little to do with the substance or transformations of human lives; with relations between husbands and wives, parents and children; with work and recreation, desire and disappointment; with the matter of glory. These are the human concerns of the tragic poetry of the Fall, and, following Milton, I choose to encounter them by reference to the Ovidian and Spenserian tradition of metamorphosis. First, however, I wish to complete the assessment begun in the last chapter of humankind's relative position in Milton's cosmos.

Of Men and Angels

As I said earlier, angels are remarkable primarily for their proximity to God. They live in heaven, where God "pours forth his glory and the brightness of his majesty in a particular and extraordinary way" (*CP* 6, 311). Despite the angels' exalted location, scholars customarily stress their striking, unorthodox similarities to human beings in Milton's epic. Yet, humanity's metaphorical nature distinguishes it from angelic nature, and lack of sensitivity to this distinction has, I think, misled readers who compare humankind and angels and find the former lacking.[2] Nevertheless, good reasons persuade us to admit angelic and human similarity: both kinds of creatures are made of matter, experience time, are supposed to serve, obey, and praise God, and, on a homier level, eat, sleep, and enjoy sex as an expression of love:

> food alike those pure
> Intelligential substances require
> As doth your Rational; and both contain
> Within them every lower faculty
> Of sense, whereby they hear, see, smell, touch, taste,
> Tasting concoct, digest, assimilate,
> And corporeal to incorporeal turn.   (5, 407–13)

>   Let it suffice thee that thou know'st
> Us happy, and without Love no happiness.
> Whatever pure thou in the body enjoy'st
> (And pure thou wert created) we enjoy
> In eminence, and obstacle find none
> Of membrane, joint, or limb, exclusive bars:
> Easier than Air with Air, if Spirits embrace,

Total they mix, Union of Pure with Pure
Desiring; nor restrain'd conveyance need
As Flesh to mix with Flesh, or Soul with Soul.
(8, 620–29)

The importance of food and sex as symbols of communion accounts
for their rhetorically emphatic placement at either end of the discussion between Raphael and Adam. As I have already argued, love
and nutrition illustrate the motion of creation toward God and apocalyptic glory. Love and nutrition also allow for distinctions to be
drawn between men and angels.

In heaven, for example, angels find that tables are "set, and on
a sudden pil'd / With Angels' Food" (5, 632–33). "Rubied Nectar
flows" or "vines / Yield Nectar" while "mellifluous Dews" spontane-
ously appear, and the ground is "cover'd with pearly grain" (5, 633,
427–30). When the cups of Adam and Raphael flow, however, it is
because Eve pours so attentively. Just prior to Raphael's description
of the wondrous feasts in heaven, suddenly and effortlessly supplied,
the narrator has described Eve's relatively laborious visits to "each
bough and brake, / Each Plant and juiciest Gourd," and her painstaking preparation of a feast deliberately designed to represent earthly
delights to their best advantage (5, 326–27):

> fruit of all kinds, in coat,
> Rough, or smooth rin'd, or bearded husk, or shell
> She gathers, Tribute large, and on the board
> Heaps with unsparing hand; for drink the Grape
> She crushes, inoffensive must, and meaths
> From many a berry, and from sweet kernels prest
> She tempers dulcet creams, nor these to hold
> Wants her fit vessels pure, then strews the ground
> With Rose and Odors from the shrub unfum'd.
> (5, 341–49)

Raphael later confirms, upon sampling the finished product, that
"God hath here / Varied his bounty so with new delights, / As may
compare with Heaven" (5, 430–32; cf. 5, 329–30). But Raphael has
not seen Eve scramble through bush and brake, ponder fit propor-

tions, gather, crush, and temper ingredients to construct the various dishes that impress him. Nor do I suppose that Raphael has any inkling about the particulars of such labor, though certainly he understands the concepts of labor and service. The labor involved in preparing a feast on earth as opposed to heaven befits the distinction between human (discursive) and angelic (intuitive) modes of reason. Except when God endues Man's "sudden apprehension," humans must ponder and discuss problems, consider evidence, judge of fit and meet, ask questions — scramble through the mental brush (8, 354). Raphael even suggests that God takes pleasure in watching humankind's quaint cogitations (8, 75–84), just as he takes pleasure in watching them gather fruit. Angels, though, depend on no such cumbersome process to attain knowledge; they simply know.

I begin with the example of food and its implications for human and angelic knowledge because the difference between eating and knowing on earth and in heaven is finally inconsequential. It hardly matters that angels apprehend immediately while Man wanders after knowledge. The results are the same. When we shift our focus from food to sex, however, the differences between Adam and Raphael become more consequential.

With ease of complete interpenetration to match the instant apprehension of their intellects, angels understand little of the mysterious rites of the genial bed. The pleasures of philosophical dialogue, or of wooing one's beloved — pleasures closely related by Plato — are unknown in the heavenly realm of instant gratification. It follows that the angels should, as do the birds toward Man, exhibit a relatively uncomplicated, typically "prompt" obedience toward God (8, 240).[3] I am not claiming that humans are better than angels; Adam does, after all, bow low to the "superior nature" represented by Raphael (5, 360). But unfallen Man's analogical relation to God entitles him to a categorical sovereignty that angels do not enjoy. Although angels make a regal appearance as ministers, attendants, guards, and messengers, it is "our Primitive great Sire" who is described in terms of royalty (5, 350ff.). When God speaks to Adam in the Garden, he abandons the peremptory tone that characterizes his proclamations to the angels and that suits the decorum of a king addressing his court. The relationship he establishes with Adam is such that for the most part they talk sire to sire. It is crucial to remember that

Adam and Eve enjoy a God-like, parental glory that the nonpro-creative angels do not share.

Although I reserve consideration of the angelic rebellion for the final chapter, even now it seems clear that their Fall must be ana-lyzed according to the voluntary as opposed to the intellectual side of their relation to God. The physiological aspect of existence symbol-ized by nutrition and food does not perplex them; they intuitively understand how things hold together, where things belong in the cos-mic harmony. But the volitional aspect of existence, symbolized by love and sex, is another problem. A modern might say that angels are goal oriented while human beings are process oriented. Not surpris-ingly, despite his supposed expertise as a marriage counselor, Raphael fails to understand the delicate hesitancy of "sweet reluctant amorous delay" and harps instead on mere design, even though Adam well understands "the prime end / Of Nature" in his marriage (8, 540–41). Northrop Frye agrees that in rebuking Adam, Raphael "goes too far" and that his warning is "insensitively coarse," but he attributes this barbarism to the courtly seraph's anxiety over Man's danger.[4] Yet the generally imperturbable Raphael knows all along that Man's Fall is a foregone conclusion. If his rebuke is "insensitively coarse," it may be because he, as an angel, does not understand human love, a love marked by self-conscious hesitancy. Human love is slower and sweeter than angelic because it must cross a gulf of difference in will and body that is relatively immaterial for the angels.

Adam thus does not need Raphael to remind him of his natural superiority to Eve, nor does his susceptibility to sexual passion en-danger his sense of hierarchy and priority. He most cherishes the humble perfections of his and Eve's voluntary harmony:

> those graceful acts,
> Those thousand decencies that daily flow
> From all her words and actions, mixt with Love
> And sweet compliance, which declare unfeign'd
> Union of Mind, or in us both one Soul;
> Harmony to behold in wedded pair
> More grateful than harmonious sound to ear.
>
> (8, 600–6)

God commands the angels, we should recall, to abide under the Son "united as one individual Soul," terms similarly suitable to wedlock (5, 610). A full third of the angels disobey this command at least in part because they disdain the kind of personal, intimate submission that Eve yields her head.

Nor should Adam's comparison of wedded love to musical harmony be underestimated. Raphael has already informed Adam of the angels that, "in thir motions harmony Divine / So smooths her charming tones that God's own ear / Listens delighted" (5, 625–27). Adam thus implies that human marriage may surpass angelic music as a vehicle for the expression of harmony. In any case, the mathematical intricacies and beauties of music suit the angelic preoccupation with the scheme of things just as the subtle accommodations of one will to another in marriage suit the human preoccupation with voluntary harmony. The minutiae of Adam and Eve's days reveal and lead to the union of two distinct creatures. So also the passage of creation through time reveals and leads to the amorous submission of creatures to God. The "delay" of space and time heightens and lends depth to the wedded bliss of eternal beatitude and apocalyptic glory.

The point is that Man's will is his richest, deepest register for the expression of God's glory, while the intellectually gifted angels excel in natural appreciation and representation of glory. Each species also suffers from corresponding weaknesses: whereas Raphael, at the end of Book VIII, reveals angelic insensitivity to the awe-inspiring power and beauty of "sweet compliance," Adam, at the beginning of Book VIII, betrays human limitations in fathoming the natural order. In presenting the Falls of Satan and of Man, Milton carefully observes the differences in the human and angelic characters. While Adam and Eve never rebel as the fallen angels do, Eve succumbs to a fraud regarding the significance of the forbidden fruit for which no angel would ever fall. Admittedly, I am speaking in terms of tendencies, not hard-and-fast distinctions. Yet the subtle differences between men and angels reveal as much as their basic similarities for an understanding of disobedience in Milton's epic. Put a little crudely, while the rebels' willfulness leads to their stupidity, Man's stupidity leads to his willfulness.

Disintegrating Glory

In reviewing Man's position prior to the Fall, we recall that his goal is to achieve glorious union with heaven by knowingly reflecting God's will in the form that God intends. God himself declares his intention for Man:

> a Creature who not prone
> And Brute as other Creatures, but endu'd
> With Sanctity of Reason, might erect
> His Stature, and upright with Front serene
> Govern the rest, self-knowing, and from thence
> Magnanimous to correspond with Heav'n,
> But grateful to acknowledge whence his good
> Descends, thither with heart and voice and eyes
> Directed in Devotion, to adore
> And worship God Supreme, who made him chief
> Of all his works.   (7, 506–16)

The order of terms in this summary of Man, joined by a variety of adverbs of location and direction, evokes a veritable concourse of motion to and from God and exactly summarizes Adam's own narration of his beginning. Man progresses from raw awareness of existence to self-knowing correspondence with its source. Thus, according to the *OED*, the meaning of the apt verb *to correspond*, includes not only the obvious sense of "to communicate" but also "to be compliant or in accord," and even "to be analogous."

As I noted in the last chapter, trial accompanies every step of Man's way to the intended, final glory. First, Man proves his ability to stand erect and to reason about causation, about a creator. The next test, that of the forbidden fruit, symbolizes the bond of obedience that makes Man at once the servant of the Lord and sovereign of the world. As a condition of life in the Garden, the prohibition of the fruit represents Man's ability to recognize and express the analogy between himself and God. In both cases, the attainment of greater glory is preceded by sleep and followed by an awakening to a new creation and a new trial.

Awakening to Eve should allow Man to continue toward the complete obedience and love exemplified by the Son. Appropriately, the chief, practical issue confronting Adam and Eve is how to reconcile the freedom of unbidden love with the duty of required obedience. As we have already seen, Milton's description of their love stresses the paradoxical character of their relationship, an amorous subjection. Ideally, their love should be yielded and received not out of obligation or privilege but simply because yielding and receiving, as a recognition of their separateness, constitutes the happiness of their marriage. Their love will allow them, like the Garden they govern, to be fruitful and multiply and thus better to reflect the creative potency of God (*kabod*), better to know him as Father (*doxa*), and therefore better to advance toward the glory of union with him. Hence, when Eve requests more distance from Adam, even if only for a morning of work, she rejects the divinely ordained mode of advancement in creation as well as, ironically, the divinely ordained prelude to more thorough gardening. The very substance of their love, as Adam so ably defined it in Book VIII, becomes the rationale for division:

> For while so near each other thus all day
> Our task we choose, what wonder if so near
> Looks intervene and smiles, or object new
> Casual discourse draw on, which intermits
> Our day's work brought to little.   (9, 220–24)

Although Adam replies that the maintenance of their love counts for more than maintenance of the Garden, that in fact the latter is only a reflection of the former, he unwisely relegates his most telling argument to the realm of litotes — "love not the lowest end of human life" (9, 241).

As is commonly agreed, the unfallen dispute between Adam and Eve previews the Fall and its aftermath.[5] Their experiments in dramatic posturing indicate that they have discovered the plastic dimension of language, shifting their attention from what the words themselves say to what they expect to achieve through them.[6] Reacting to the obsequious delicacy of Adam's address, Eve seizes the opportunity to put Adam on the defensive: "his fraud then is thy fear, which plain infers / Thy equal fear that my firm Faith and Love /

Can by his fraud be shak'n or seduc't; / Thoughts, which how found they harbor in thy breast, / Adam, misthought of her to thee so dear?" (9, 285-89). The dismayed "how could you" that all but breaks the surface of Eve's question forces Adam into a squirming evasion — "not diffident of thee," no, of course not, "but to avoid / Th' attempt itself" (9, 293-95).[7] Thrusting past his weak parry, Eve perversely exaggerates the applicability of her current frustration to life in Paradise generally — trapped "in narrow circuit strait'n'd by a Foe" (9, 323). The issues discussed by Adam and Eve clearly do not matter so much as the problem they suddenly find themselves facing — how do perfect lovers manage a conflict in will? One of them must get his or her way — they cannot both stay together and be apart — and as soon as one does, the harmony of their marriage suffers. To Adam's credit, he recognizes this, "thy stay, not free, absents thee more," but he blunders so seriously in condescending to Eve that her stubbornness can hardly be faulted (9, 372).

Eve's departure from Adam at this climactically metamorphic moment Milton in part describes by alluding again to Ovid: "To *Pales,* or *Pomona,* thus adorn'd, / Likest she seem'd, *Pomona* when she fled / *Vertumnus*" (9, 393-95). Fowler reads the allusion as implicitly equating Vertumnus, who approaches the agriculturally minded Pomona in disguise, with Satan.[8] But Vertumnus accosts Pomona in order to persuade her to attend to love rather than to devote herself solely to her garden. The simile is thus better read as a summation of the preceding discussion with Adam than as an anticipation of the subsequent seduction by Satan. Vertumnus insists that Pomona should heed the example of the vine and elm and unite with him in marriage, and this appeal has already supplied a key description of Adam and Eve's agricultural labors as a reflection of their love and spiritual aspirations: "to check / Fruitless imbraces . . . they led the Vine / To wed her Elm; she spous'd about him twines / Her marriageable arms, and with her brings / Her dow'r th' adopted Clusters, to adorn / His barren leaves" (*PL* 5, 214-19; see *Met.* 14, 661-69).[9] Vertumnus' comparison of elm trees and vines with human lovers lies also behind the interpretation of Eve's wanton ringlets as evidence of her dependence on Adam (4, 306-7). Unlike Satan, Vertumnus wishes neither to ravish the object of his desire nor to deceive her, but to gain her hand in marriage (*Met.* 14, 667-83). Fowler reads "fled" in the comparison of Eve to Pomona — "*Pomona* when she fled / *Vertumnus*" — as ironic because Pomona does finally yield to Vertumnus, just as Eve will to Satan. But clearly "fled" here is better read as a straightforward recollection of previous events, when the newly created Eve fled from Adam (*PL* 4, 477f.). The simile implies that Adam and Eve are in danger of regressing to the point where Eve disdains Adam for the sake of her own image.[10]

As Eve parts from Adam, we may also detect an indirect situational reference to Ovid's description of Philomela's departure from her father, Pandion:

> now she
> Hangs on her fathers neck: and what would be
> Her utter ruine, as her safety prest:
> While *Tereus* by beholding pre-possest.
> Her kisses and imbraces heat his blood:
> And all afford his fire and fury food.
> And wisht, as oft as she her Sire imbrac't,
> Him-selfe her Sire.   (*Met.* 6, 476–82)

Philomela as she parts from Pandion, like Eve as she parts from Adam, resembles "the stately *Naiades*, and *Dryad's* . . . / In Sylvan shades" (*Met.* 6, 452–53; cf. *PL* 9, 386–88). Tereus, like Satan in Book IV, lecherously envies the pure embraces innocently enjoyed by the intended victims of his fire and fury (*PL* 4, 502–4). Pandion, like Adam, is reluctant to let his daughter leave him: "all delay / To me is death . . . / . . . Daughter . . . / For pitty leave me not too long alone" (*Met.* 6, 500–3; cf. *PL* 9, 400). Where Pandion "dreads his soules presage," Adam's heart also misgives him, "divine of something ill" (*Met.* 6, 510; *PL* 9, 845). But where Adam begins like the noble Pandion, and Satan like the evil son-in-law, at the end it is Adam who in his sin and punishment recalls Tereus. In both cases the tragic consequence is a Thyestean banquet in which a father becomes the "unhappy tombe" of his offspring (*Met.* 6, 665; cf. *PL* 10, 688).

The great difference between the stories of Philomela and of Eve is that Adam, unlike Pandion, is both husband and father to Eve. The doubleness of these family ties reinforces the great ethical dilemma of life in the Garden. Eve is Adam's partner and lover, yet she owes him the duty and obedience of a child to its parent. Analogously, God at once desires Man's obedience and his love. For Man as for Eve, the problem is to reconcile filial obligation with the romantic desire for union. The simultaneity of father-daughter, husband-wife relations accounts for the gingerly atmosphere surrounding Adam and Eve's discussion at the beginning of Book IX. Eve finds it as difficult to love freely the one whom she must obey as Adam does to require obedience of the one whose free love he desires. Thus Eve must ask Adam's permission to leave him for the morning, without appearing to reject him, and Adam must grant or deny her request, without appearing to force her love.

The complexity of superimposed father-daughter, lover-beloved relations is continued and parodied in Satan's desire to replace Adam as Eve's father and lover. He wishes to make Eve his daughter-mate, to transform her into Sin. That Satan, like a Restoration rake, wishes to occupy Adam's paternal post as our general sire appears in his echo of Adam's response to the creation of Eve: "what pleasing seem'd, for her now pleases more, / She most, and in her look sums all Delight" (9, 453–54; cf. 8, 471–74). What Raphael has difficulty appreciating about Adam's experience of love, Satan himself experiences as Eve's submissive appeal stuns his intellect and volition: "her graceful Innocence, her every Air / Of gesture or least action overaw'd / His Malice" (9, 459–61; cf. 8, 558–59, 600–603). (Paradoxically, her perfect qualifications as a victim render her nearly immune to attack, a paradox fully realized only when Satan encounters the Son.) Satan's response to Eve differs from Adam's only insofar as she represents God's will. The pleasure of her company, ordained for Adam, reminds Satan once more of "pleasure not for him ordain'd" (9, 470). Once he does seduce Eve, however, Satan effectively steals Adam's pleasure, subverts God's will, and becomes our illegitimate father.

Satan appeals to Eve's narcissism in familiar terms so that, despite the strangeness of the circumstances, she will feel comfortable enough to participate in a serpentine conversation.[11] First, the serpent confirms her earliest suspicions: she is the "fairest resemblance" of God (9, 538; cf. 4, 478–80) and should rightfully occupy all creatures' attention (9, 539–42; cf. 4, 657–58). During the dream, Satan exalted her perspective, so that she could see the earth "out-stretcht immense" beneath her (5, 88). Now he builds on that foundation, elaborating on the provincial character of life in the Garden:

> here
> In this enclosure wild, these Beasts among,
> Beholders rude, and shallow to discern
> Half what in thee is fair, one man except,
> Who sees thee? (and what is one?) who shouldst be seen
> A Goddess among Gods, adored and served
> By Angels numberless, thy daily Train.   (9, 542–48)

In describing his own elevation, the serpent speaks with contempt of the lowly traffic that once crossed his mind: "of abject thoughts and low, / As was my food, nor aught but food discern'd / Or Sex, and apprehended nothing high" (9, 572–74). Only after eating the forbidden fruit, says the serpent, did he transcend the banalities of food and sex to consider "all things visible in Heav'n / Or Earth, or Middle" (9, 604–5). Food and sex, the ordained modes and symbols of Man's aspirations to heavenly glory, are sneered at by a snake. No wonder Eve is jolted.

Once Satan gets Eve to the tree, he arouses her indignation by characterizing her obedience as a tether that functions primarily to exhibit the mastery of Adam and ultimately of God (9, 665–66, 692–97, 703–9). Eve, it seems, desires to be free, though just what kind of freedom she wants is not too clear. It may be that she desires freedom from the existential bondage of food, love, gardening, and sleep. Or she may wish simply to be seen and admired by creatures other than Adam and the animals—free to win the glory of fame. To become "as the gods," the serpent suggests, would give her the freedom she now lacks, perhaps even make her the master on occasion. But Eve does not stop to consider that the angels' exalted life in heaven inescapably depends on their residence where God preeminently is. Assuming that she could attain angelic stature merely by eating the fruit, where would she isolate herself from the "great Forbidder" to whom her proximity would only have increased (9, 815)? "I perhaps am secret," she says, far from basking in admiring gazes, "Heav'n is high, / High and remote" (9, 811–12). Eve wishes to be both seen and unseen, to be exalted and hidden, to be glorified and unnoticed. The contradictions of hell have entered Man's world.

Treated as an allegory, Milton's rendition of the Fall aligns Eve with human will, or, more accurately, with the volitional aspect of reason (*ratio*) operating in a world of moral choices. Adam represents, in this view, the angelic half of the human psyche, the intellect (*intellectus*) or, as I have described it, the capacity to understand how things fit together.[12] In these terms, Eve represents Man's will striving after higher status in what the intellect would recognize as a contradictory fashion. Consequently, despite the popular conception that Eve, more than Adam, resembles Satan (because her Fall involves aspiration), Adam, as is appropriate to his more exalted intellectual status, actually resembles Satan more closely.[13] Unlike Satan, Eve has to be tricked into disobedience; her original point of vulnerability is her intellect. Adam, like Satan, simply and almost immediately refuses to obey, even though he knows that he should. His original point of vulnerability, like Satan's, is his will, not his intellect. Moreover, his decision, like Satan's, is at bottom selfish. He feels that he cannot survive without the woman, who is all but equal to him, recognizes his authority and stature, admits her duty to obey him, but yields to him because she loves him. Having lived in the perfection of human harmony, he now is confronted with the likelihood of a drastic change and chooses the human reflection of glory over its source. Similarly, Satan, confronted with the likelihood of a drastic change, preferred the angelic reflection of glory to its source.

In "submitting to what seem'd remediless," Adam behaves as if the situation were identical with the only truly unalterable thing, God's absolute will (9, 919). Adam ignores the metamorphic potential of a creation that above all else reflects God's infinite resourcefulness. As one writer on metamorphic literature has put it, "the bad is what arises when the good can think of no escape or alternative, when it is forced to confront existence as single."[14] Adam's proper course would be simply to wait, to endure what God wills and not to abet what God abhors. But Adam, misconstruing the situation, chooses rather to burn in lust than mourn in bliss.

The metamorphic progress that Man has already made toward God is immediately reversed after the Fall. Man's next awakening, after a restless sleep, reveals the world remade again: "up they rose / As from unrest, and each the other viewing, / Soon found thir Eyes how op'n'd, and thir minds / How dark'n'd" (9, 1051–54). There is a fearful symmetry here as Adam and Eve, for reasons both moral and natural, first begin an endless argument, then lose dominion over the creatures, and finally exit from the Garden (9, 1067ff.; 11, 181ff., 259–62). No longer able on his own to cooperate with creation's movement toward final harmony, Man must now await God's "motions in him" (11, 91). Now Eve, not Adam, sleeps and dreams as the history of God's grace contending with Man's loss, a history born of Eve, is revealed to her husband.

Because Adam's "higher intellectual" easily detects the fraud to which Eve succumbed, no-nonsense critics blame Adam for not sending his wife packing.[15] One can, in fact, support this position by resorting again to Ovid and comparing Adam to Minos, whose unerring judgment won him the post of judge in Hades. Tempted by Scylla, who betrayed her father on Minos' behalf, he rejects her love and earns his reputation for moral excellence:

> she
> Presents the gift with wicked hand. But he
> Rejects her proffer: and much terrifi'd
> With horror of so foule a deed, reply'd:
> The Gods exile thee.   (*Met.* 8, 94–97)

Compare Adam's response to Eve:

> She gave him of that fair enticing Fruit
> With liberal hand: he scrupl'd not to eat
> Against his better knowledge, not deceiv'd,
> But fondly overcome with Female charm.
>   (*PL* 9, 996–99)

Ovid abounds with tales of daughters who betray fathers on behalf of their lovers, and generally these women come to evil ends. But Minos' piety in immediately rejecting the romantic love of a disobedient daughter is exceptional. Surely, Adam suffers by this comparison.

Yet, to be fair, Adam's temptation is more difficult and complex than Minos'. Adam, after all, not only resembles Minos, to whom Scylla is a stranger, but also Pygmalion, to whom the gods give a woman who perfectly fulfills his own idea and desire. Moreover, as opposed to Satan's enjoyment of Sin, Adam's love of his image is sanctioned by God to instruct humankind as an image about its relation to God. We should, therefore, neither judge Adam according to the standards of Minos nor absolve him as if he were Pygmalion confronted with the loss of his and the gods' creation. To the extent that we condemn or absolve Adam and Eve, and this perhaps is Sin's most ironic surprise, we ignore our status as splinters — like Minos or Pygmalion — of that original coherence, "that first naked glory."

9

THE NECESSITY OF GLORY

THE PRECEDING CHAPTERS detailed the natural and moral metamorphoses by which Milton characterizes good and evil creatures. Nutritional and sexual metaphors express the epistemological and volitional progress of creatures toward glory or shame. Recognition and desire are the two components of an inherent metamorphic capacity that can, given God's substantial presence in creation, refine rational beings and advance them toward the apotheosis of final glory. Innocent creatures exhibit a simple clarity of perception and purity of desire, as opposed to fallen creatures, who suffer confusion and perversion, intellectual and sexual frustration.

Thus, for example, when Adam beholds Eve fallen, he lapses immediately into the rhetorical questions of hell, questions that become exclamations of wonder and ignorance:

> How art thou lost, how on a sudden lost,
> Defac't, deflow'r'd, and now to Death devote?
> Rather how hast thou yielded to transgress
> The strict forbiddance, how to violate
> The sacred Fruit forbidd'n!   (PL 9, 900-4)

The loss naturally appears first in Eve's face, and, ironically, Adam describes her as having yielded to disobedience — a yielding that is a failure to yield. The fallen pair awaken "in face / Confounded," and like the demons in Book I, find themselves changed (9, 1063-64):

each the other viewing,
Soon found thir Eyes how op'n'd, and thir minds
How dark'n'd.   (9, 1052–54)

O how unlike
To that first naked Glory.   (1114–15)

"Of Honor void" — emptied of *kabod* — "naked thus," Adam and Eve now reflect the confusion and uncertainty of hell (9, 1074).

Adam and Eve failed to glorify God and consequently have lost their original glory. In order to assess the justice or injustice of their fate, I must turn from a consideration of particular creatures to focus instead on the relation between God's reason and will and the reason and will of his creatures. This chapter and the next examine the success or failure of Milton's theodicy in terms of glory. My intention now is to construct as strong a case against God as possible, though not exactly from the romantic perspective, which sees in Milton, and in Satan, a grand foe of tyranny — whether political or rational. I ask for patience if this chapter seems one-sided. The next chapter will address the same issues from a different perspective. For now, however, I wish to consider the grounds for a case against God in terms of glory. It is thus not the rationalism or cosmic absolutism of Milton's God that I wish to criticize, but rather their service in his pursuit of glory. The fatal necessity of *Paradise Lost* is that God's glory must be seen to excel in heaven and Earth. Can we help but question the justice of a system that stresses the complete mastery of God and the utter subservience of his creatures as the controlling pattern for testimony to divine splendor?

William Empson has argued that interpretations of *Paradise Lost* depend ultimately on their authors' reactions to Christianity and particularly to the Christian God: "The subject cannot be viewed in a purely aesthetic manner, as Milton himself would be the first to claim."[1] Some critics have perhaps attempted to assume the point of view of a typical seventeenth-century Christian for the purposes of interpreting the poem. But the effect described by Empson remains the same. Such critics simply claim that *Paradise Lost* reflects their version of seventeenth-century Christianity. We cannot escape the fact that when we assess *Paradise Lost* as a theodicy, we are also assessing Christianity, or at least Milton's version of it. The barbarous dissonance let loose by certain Miltonists in response to Empson's brilliant book indicates just how personally scholars do respond to an interpretation of *Paradise Lost* that is critical of Christianity. There is more riding on one's analysis of Milton's theodicy than the simple formation of a scholarly opinion, and everything we know about Milton indicates that he intended his art to have this effect.

Indeed, Stanley Fish has argued in *Surprised by Sin* that Milton takes advantage of his declared epic intention in order to tempt the reader: realizing that readers will at certain junctures make deficient responses to the action — indeed tempting readers to do so — Milton builds into the plot a scornful rejection of that encouraged response. As Lester A. Beaurline remarks about Jonson's *Epicoene*, "Nothing is more titillating . . . than to build the stage illusion into the plot":

> You are carried along with the pretense; your passions are moved "by such insinuating degrees that you shall not choose but consent and go along with them" while at the same time you "stand admiring the subtle tracks of your engagement."[2]

According to Fish, much the same process occurs within acute readers of *Paradise Lost*. Fish reveals the "subtle tracks" of our "engagement" with the devil and thus aligns himself with the author, who is, according to Fish, aligned with God. The "stage illusion" of a justification of God's ways becomes merely an ironic invitation to assume the fallen perspective: "The search for cause and for a rational justification is an attempt to confine God within the limits of formal reasoning, and is thus a temptation."[3] Milton allegedly employs readers' false expectations (which he himself has fostered) in order to educate them.[4]

Empson, on the other hand, sees the poem as a fairly straightforward attempt to do what it says it will do. Borrowing from Nietzsche's analysis of Christianity, Empson argues that the "traditional God of Christianity" is "very wicked."[5] He credits Milton for struggling with the Christian concept of God and for not blindly embracing the orthodoxy of his time.[6] He concludes that Milton finally failed in his project because of the "Neolithic craving for human sacrifice" implicit in the "basic structure" of Christianity.[7] Milton could not side with the sadist who governs such a structure. Thus the Romantics were correct. Even though he could not admit it consciously, Milton, too, rebelled against the Father and consequently depicted a sympathetic Satan and a reprehensible God. Empson at once attacks critics who see *Paradise Lost* as a triumph of Christian orthodoxy and praises Milton for making God "so bad," for telling the truth about the divine desire to torture.[8]

Empson's insistence that *Paradise Lost* cannot be viewed simply in an aesthetic manner would seem to undermine his own indictment of Milton's God. After all, if one believes the Christian God to be wicked and indefensible, then one will find it difficult to evaluate fairly the success of a poem whose purpose is to justify him. Yet, the fact of the matter is that over the centuries many sensible readers and respected scholars notable for their Christian faith have also taken exception to Milton's God. For example, C. S. Lewis, widely considered a champion of *Paradise Lost* as a sincere and effective expression of mere Christianity, nevertheless thought divine derision offensive:

> Milton has imprudently made his Divine Persons so anthropomorphic that their laughter arouses legitimately hostile reactions in us — as though we were dealing with an ordinary conflict of wills in which the winner ought not to ridicule the loser.[9]

As we have seen, however, the anthropomorphic presentation of God derives directly from Scripture, and Milton insists — as a fundamental, hermeneutic principle — that God offers himself to our imaginations in precisely the fashion that he would have us think of him. To discount the side of God that makes him appear like a poor winner is presumptuous and sinful. God chooses to torment losers with unremitting and eternal consciousness of their loss. This is justice.

The fact is, the Bible offers various pictures of God, which, like the limbs of Truth, presumably belong to a single, coherent whole. Milton will not discard a piece of the truth because it might offend his readers. If one wished to organize the diversity of Milton's scriptural God, one might divide him into two component deities: one, the loving, forgiving God of the Evangelists; the other, the harsh, egomaniacal God of Pharaoh and Satan. The first God appears in the comforting verse from the Gospel of John declaring that "God so loved the world that he gave his only begotten Son, that whosoever believeth in him should not perish, but have everlasting life" (3:16). This verse occupies a prominent post in any Evangelist's scriptural repertoire because it paints a sympathetic portrait of a Father giving up his Son and because it makes Man the chief factor in God's motivation. One cannot choose but be grateful to a God whose love persuades him to sacrifice his son for one's sake.

Man does not enter the picture at all, however, when Isaiah represents God as declaring, "For mine own sake, even for mine own sake, will I do it: for how should my name be polluted? and I will not give my glory unto another" (48:11). This God repeatedly hardens the heart of Pharaoh, even though Pharaoh himself appears willing to relent, simply so that he might display his glorious power in ever more spectacular ways. Milton admits that "God often hardens the hearts of powerful and arrogant world-leaders to a remarkable degree so that through their pride and arrogance his glory may be more clearly seen" (*CP* 6, 337). Indeed, God so toughens Pharaoh's already stubborn heart that it appears justifiable to send the angel of death to slaughter the firstborn of Egypt, an event annually celebrated as an instance of divine mercy over the last thirty-odd centuries. To magnify his power even further, God inspires Pharaoh's pursuit of the Hebrews so that he might perform the glorious parting of the Red Sea, along with the drowning of untold Egyptians. These glorious acts begin forty years of wilderness wandering for the chosen people, a period fondly recalled by later generations who believed that Man stands right with God only when he incessantly recognizes that he owes everything to God. In this respect, the nomadic Hebrews lived under ideal conditions, utterly and undeniably dependent on God for food, water, protection, and guidance. Hence the best of the prophets, from Elijah to John the Baptist, reveal the divine will not only through their words, but also by the "true poems" of their lives: they wear animal skins, walk in the wilderness, suffer in the desert for God. These men worship an absolute sovereign, a potentate of the oriental cast whose pride and privilege, whose desire to manifest his own glory, determine all that he does.

In terms of this perspective, Christ must die not only to ransom Man but also because his gruesome death will best testify to the glory of God. The Gospel of John quotes Isaiah to explain why men refused to believe in Christ and crucified him despite all the wonders he performed (just as Pharaoh refused to believe even after all the signs and wonders performed by Moses): "He hath blinded their eyes and hardened their hearts; that they should not see with their eyes, nor understand with their heart, and be converted, and I should heal them" (John 12:40; see Isa. 6:19). If men had believed when Christ performed miracles or taught in parables, the glory of Easter morning would never have occurred. The blood sacrifice and the subsequent delivery from bondage are two movements on the same theme. It seems that the latter cannot happen without the former. The Cambridge Neoplatonist John Smith all but equates Man's salvation and the glory of God:

> I doubt we are too nice Logicians sometimes in distinguishing between *the Glory of God* and *our own Salvation*. We cannot in true sense seek *our own Salvation* more than *the Glory of God*, which triumphs most and discovers itself most effectually in *the Salvation* of souls.[10]

Man's need for salvation allows God to manifest his glory in a particularly striking fashion.

In order to understand the link between glory and salvation, it will help to recollect what Smith and Milton meant by glory. Smith makes a particularly useful point of reference because his thought, like that of other Cambridge Platonists, so closely resembles Milton's that scholars have generally been persuaded to see more Plato in Milton than is in fact warranted. In this case, while the similarities between Smith and Milton will further verify the meaning of glory as articulated in this book, a key difference between them will help to clarify the issues involved in Milton's theodicy.

Like Milton, Smith describes the activity of creation according to a Neoplatonic framework of emanation and return. Accordingly, he defines religion as "Life and Spirit, which flowing out from God . . . that hath life in himself, returns to him again as into its own Original" (p. 157). Although not a materialist, Smith nevertheless argues, like Milton, that God forms out of himself a creation that naturally expresses him and desires to reunite with him:

> He derived himself through the whole Creation, so gathering and knitting up all the several pieces of it again; that as the first production and the continued Subsistence of all things is from himself, so the ultimate resolution and tendency of all things might be to him.   (p. 162)

"The nearer any Being comes to God, who is that Infinite fullness that fills all in all," writes Smith, "the more *vast* and *large* and *unbounded* it is; . . . the further it slides from him, the more it is streightned & confined" (p. 158).

Like Milton, Smith opposes the glory of the good man to the vanity of the wicked in terms that suggest the solidity and substantiality of divine glory:

> Wicked men converse with nothing but their *Lusts* and the *Vanities* of this fading life, which here flatter them for a while with unhallowed delights and a mere Shadow of Contentment; and when these are gone, they find both *Substance* and *Shadow* too to be lost Eternally. But true Goodness brings in a constant revenue of solid and substantial Satisfaction to the Spirit of a good man.   (p. 157)

Smith and Milton choose the same biblical character to exemplify false glory: "that *bravery* and *gallantness* which seems to be in the great *Nimrods* of this world is nothing else but the *swelling* of their own unbounded pride and *vain-glory*" (p. 164; see *PL* 12, 24–62).

Moreover, Milton agrees with Smith's assessment of evil as involving illegitimate ambition. Smith insists that "the Seed of the Evil Spirit" wars with "the Seed of God and the Heaven-born Nature" because it wants "with a Giant-like pride to climb up into the Throne of the Almighty, and to establish an unbounded Tyranny in contradiction to the Will of God, which is nothing else but the Issue and Efflux of his Eternal and Unbounded Goodness" (p. 162).

Smith, like Milton, identifies God's will and the glory it seeks with the extension of his goodness in and through creation:

when God *seeks his own Glory*, he does not so much endeavor anything *without himself*. He did not bring this stately fabrick of the Universe into Being, that he might for such a Monument of his mighty Power and Beneficence gain some *Panegyricks* or Applause from a little of that fading breath which he had made. Neither was that gracious contrivance of restoring lapsed men to himself a *Plot* to get himself some Eternal *Hallelujahs*, as if he had so ardently thirsted after the layes of glorified spirits, or desired a Quire of Souls to sing forth his praises. Neither was it to let the world see how *Magnificent* he was. No, it is his own *Internal Glory* that he most loves, and the Communication thereof which he seeks.   (p. 169)

The Son makes the same argument in *Paradise Regain'd:*

> his word all things produc'd,
> Though chiefly not for glory as prime end,
> But to show forth his goodness, and impart
> His good communicable to every soul
> Freely; of whom what could he less expect
> Than glory and benediction, that is thanks,
> The slightest, easiest, readiest recompense
> From them who could return him nothing else.
>
> (*PR* 3, 122–29)

The Son here presumes, properly, that when Satan says "glory" he means only "praise," and he responds accordingly (but see *PL* 3, 164). As has been noted throughout this study, however, Milton generally agrees with Smith that, primarily, "the glory of God" implies the communication and display of the divine goodness in creation.

Smith, however, goes further than Milton would in dismissing God's desire for Satan's partial version of glory. God's alleged desire to reap his creatures' submissive praises, says Smith, is simply a matter of evil Man's projection: "Some are apt to look upon God as . . . *Peevish* and *Self-will'd* . . . because themselves are such" (p. 241). Smith's reasoning resembles that which lies behind the interpretive doctrine of accommodation. Humankind's limitations — and in this case, perversions — account for a misconception that Scripture only appears to warrant. But Milton's Christ, even in the passage cited above, admits that God expects at least "glory and benediction" from creatures "who could return him nothing else." Unlike Smith, Sir Thomas Browne, in *Religio Medici*, accepts God's desire for praise in terms that recall Milton's picture of the deity:

> God made all things for himself, and it is impossible hee should make them for any other end than his owne glory; it is all he can receive, and all that is without himselfe: for honour being an external adjunct, and in the honourer rather than in the person honoured, it was necessary to make a creature, from whom hee might receive this homage, and that is in the other world Angels, in this, man; which when we neglect, we forget the very end of our creation, and may justly provoke God, not only to repent that hee hath made the world, but that hee hath sworne hee would not destroy it.[11]

God listens with delight to the angels' hymns of praise and appreciates Man's adoration pure. Creatures *can* give glory to God, glory that God does *not* possess on his own, and the enabling condition for that gift is the free will.

Milton's God desires the voluntary, personal submission of his creatures to his will; he takes pleasure in it (*PL* 3, 107). Thus, in the Christian religion, "the essential act of life is the surrender of the will."[12] Loving obedience to God is the highest priority in Milton's religion — not rational pursuit of the good. If God had not forbidden it, the apple would merely have been another fruit, eating of it another good act. But God challenges his creatures, and reveals where his priorities lie, when he outlaws a good. Obedience comes first, and it comes first because, as Browne reasons, it manifests something outside of God conforming to what God wants and thus voluntarily praising him. God, sometimes in a notoriously provocative fashion, confronts his creatures with opportunities to disobey him. Presumably he does so because he wishes them to develop into even better, more perfect creatures. But presumably he does so also because the more difficult the problem for a creature's will, the greater the glory to God if obedience is preserved. In order to win a part of final, apocalyptic glory, one must play for high stakes. The game is in earnest, and the consequences are staggering. At the first moments of the epic action, Satan encounters a test of obedience that, for him, transformed all God's goodness into ill "and wrought but malice" (4, 49).

Satan is doomed forever to oppose God and thus to serve as the chief instrument for the display of God's glory. The emotional power of Satan's false heroism — so carefully undermined by the didactic narrator — originates in the God who, as we have seen, "hardens the hearts of powerful and arrogant world leaders to a remarkable degree so that through their pride and arrogance his glory may be more clearly seen." Satan no longer enjoys inviolable freedom of the will. His psyche undergoes an uncanny, mechanical cycle of sorrowful remorse succeeded by hardened enmity that in a different context would be comic. When, for example, Satan observes his collected troops fresh from the fiery deluge, "his heart / Distends with pride, and hard'ning in his strength / Glories" (1, 571-73). The responsive reader understands that God hardens Satan's heart and that God stands to "glory" by Satan's renewed strength, just as such a reader will recall that Satan and Beelzebub "glorying to have scap't the *Stygian* flood / . . . by thir own recover'd strength" in fact owe their glory and strength to "the will / And high permission of all-ruling Heaven" (1, 239-40, 211-12). One of the chief ironies of the simile comparing Satan and his followers to Pharaoh and his troops is that the "floating Carcasses" of the historical "Memphian Chivalry" are not salvageable. Pharaoh is finally beaten. But the pitiable Busiris of *Paradise Lost* stands eternally subject to the divine infusion of adversarial will and power — a devil of the motions, to paraphrase *Areopagitica.*

Against so potent an adversary, God can manifest the metamorphic power of his omnipotence and omniscience in ever more glorious ways. Foreseeing our Fall, God decides to allow humankind mercy where he would not allow it to the fallen angels: "in Mercy and Justice both, / Through Heav'n and Earth, so shall my glory excel" (3, 132-33). As Smith argued, there is no real distinction between our salvation and the glory of God. Once God announces his intention to show mercy, the Son applauds him, emphasizing both God's love for his creatures and his concern for his own glory:

For should Man finally be lost, should Man
Thy creature late so lov'd, thy youngest Son
Fall circumvented thus by fraud, though join'd
With his own folly? that be from thee far,
That far be from thee, Father, who art Judge
Of all things made, and judgest only right.
Or shall the Adversary thus obtain
His end, and frustrate thine, shall he fulfill
His malice, and thy goodness bring to naught,
Or proud return though to his heavier doom,
Yet with revenge accomplish't and to Hell
Draw after him the whole Race of mankind,
By him corrupted? or wilt thou thyself
Abolish thy Creation, and unmake,
For him, what for thy glory thou hast made?
So should thy goodness and greatness both
Be question'd and blasphem'd without defense.

                                                    (3, 150–66)

To blaspheme means to defame God, to say something false or slanderous about him, and the Fall brings creation to the point where
it appears that God's every option justifies such defamation. God
could erase the perverted creation and abolish what he has made
for the sake of his own glory. But God cannot act against his own
glory. Thus creation and Man with it will be redeemed. The Son's
riddling exposition of God's alternatives points to the only necessity
in all of *Paradise Lost*, that God be who he is and that all events
in creation build toward his greater glory — that is, toward a fuller
display of his essential character and toward creatures' correspond-
ingly more articulate praises. I use the word *riddling* because riddles
typically point to the identity that underlies apparently irreconcilable states of affairs. An almost Darwinian principle informs the action of Milton's epic, a kind of natural selection invisibly shaping
every creature's life — no matter how inconsistent or contradictory
those lives seem — toward a single goal, the final, triumphant glory
of God. Just as Milton denies the accommodating paraphrases that
fit Scripture to Man's expectations, so also he insists that history's

crushing, inevitable movement from misery to misery be accepted as another one of Luther's masks of God.

Given that, at the very least, God rules out alternatives that seem inconsistent with his glory, does he also favor the adoption of alternatives that most profit it? "In Mercy and Justice both," says God, "so shall my glory excel," and this declaration means that not only will he bring good out of Satan's evil, but also he will outdo Satan in the competition for glory instituted by Satan. Certainly Milton recognizes that "to excel" means literally "to rise upward," "to tower" — the very motion and image that characterize Satan's version of glory. Apparently, God abides by Satan's definition of the terms of battle: "The strife which thou call'st evil, but we style / The strife of Glory" (6, 289–90).

"God needs the Fall," says Lovejoy, "to elicit his divine attributes and power."[13] God, says Milton, "PRODUCED EVERYTHING THAT EXISTS BY HIS WORD AND SPIRIT, that is, BY HIS WILL, IN ORDER TO SHOW THE GLORY OF HIS POWER AND GOODNESS" (*CP* 6, 300); his redemption of Man even more clearly displays his glory. John Robinson, an influential Separatist and precursor of the revolutionary Independents, recited the Christian commonplace that though we receive a "glimpse of the Divine light by the creatures," we perceive "the more glorious light" by witnessing the redemptive acts of God in the gospels.[14] As we have already seen, in charting creation's perilous course between logically exclusive extremes — mercy and justice, salvation and damnation, victory and defeat, vengeance and forgiveness, glory and blasphemy — God reveals his ability to reconcile the paradoxical demands of his own infinite being. On the first battleground, when Satan mounts his rebellion, God's might appears before all heaven: "till then who knew / The force of those dire Arms?" (1, 93–94). In seducing Eve, Satan has set the stage for an even more complete revelation of God's supremacy. The battle in heaven demonstrates only God's superior force, but his salvation plan will manifest his glory as the supreme strategist, the dramatic victor in a cosmic game of chess. On the new battleground, "covert guile" will be the chief weapon (2, 41), and the second victory will better satisfy, to use Burckhardt's phrase, God's "sense of fame."[15]

A comparison to the most famous chess game of the twentieth

century will help to explain the sheer dramatic power of God's victory. A fourteen-year-old Bobby Fisher, while playing a grand master, lost his queen so early in the match that defeat seemed inevitable. But Fisher continued to play, and move by move it became clearer that, even though Fisher had left his queen exposed, he had also poised his other chessmen so that the grand master was the one who in fact faced an inevitable, piece-by-piece slide into defeat as soon as he went for the vulnerable queen. The grand master could never have suspected so extraordinary a variation on the poisoned pawn gambit. After all, who would risk the queen, the piece that carries the fate of all the rest of the chessmen with her? The grand master simply saw the unguarded queen and leapt at the opportunity. How keen a sense of triumph Fisher must have enjoyed. One wonders if anyone had ever before seriously considered such a ploy. Fisher won the game in the most striking and dramatic fashion possible. His opponent's expectation of victory at the moment he took Fisher's queen must have been absolute; his growing sense of defeat, as the manifestly brilliant Fisher captured piece after piece, absolutely crushing.

A queen sacrifice occurs also in *Paradise Lost*. When Eve is left exposed, the expectant Satan captures her and in so doing appears to have captured the entire human race, triumphing over God himself. But this apparent victory actually insures Satan's redundant damnation and allows an occasion for a crushing display of God's providential brilliance. God, it seems, reaps more glory from a creation perverted by Man's Fall than he would from either an annihilated creation or an innocent one. A discriminating Dennis Burden has rightly stressed that fallen humanity does not gain a destiny better than the one originally intended.[16] From a human perspective, this resolves the paradox of the fortunate Fall; the loss is real. Fallen life surely suffers in comparison with unfallen, and those who never find salvation are infinitely worse off than they would have been in an unfallen world. Satan, too, suffers an even more horrible hell thanks to his apparent triumph. But God profits from the Fall, and the profit consists of glory. This is not to say that God would not reap glory from an unfallen order in which man works his way up to heaven. All good versions of creation reflect God's glory. But the extreme difficulty of saving fallen humankind reflects God's glory more fully than the relative ease of materially enabling the advance of obedient creatures.

The sad irony of *Paradise Lost*, therefore, is that the goal of creation — to give glory to God by revealing him as fully as possible — is better met in a fallen than in an unfallen world. If Man had not sinned, he could have thanked himself for his *continuing* happiness (5, 521). Adam and Eve would have merited their own glory for their steadfastness, just as Abdiel, say, does. But after the Fall, those who are saved must recognize that they owe to God not only their existence, but also any chance for an escape from never-ending misery:

> Upheld by me, yet once more he shall stand
> On even ground against his mortal foe,
> By me upheld, that he may know how frail
> His fall'n condition is and to me owe
> All his deliv'rance, and to none but me.   (3, 178–82)

The "me" that punctuates each proposition in this passage insists that Man can no longer attribute any bit of goodness to his own account. The only thing left Man to do on his own is to recognize his fallenness and to resolve to obey God, and only by God's grace is Man capable of doing even that. Before, Man could at least tend his garden and resist temptation independently. Now, everything that Man does ends in disaster and serves simply as a backdrop for his recognition of the creator and for his resolution to obey him. Given that humankind cannot even recognize the way to salvation on its own, the only independent faculty left fallen Man is the capacity freely to glorify God by sincerely endeavoring "Prayer, repentance, and obedience due" (3, 191). From God's perspective, the "Sighs / And Prayers" that accompany Man's repentance are "fruits of more pleasing savor . . . / . . . than those / Which his own hand manuring all the Trees / Of Paradise, could have produc't, ere fall'n / From innocence" (11, 23–30). The bloody misery of history reiterates a single lesson; Man can do nothing on his own except praise God. It seems as if Man's subservience glorifies the creator, and the Fall increases Man's subservience.

In sum, a creature is glorified by God, and God achieves the glory for the sake of which he creates, when that creature accepts nature and history as symbols of God — the transmission of the infinite through the finite. Ultimately, a creature must accept even itself, a natural and historical phenomenon, as a symbol of God. Only then does it participate in the goal of creation — the glory of God. In Milton's version of the apocalypse, such a creature has in effect become an essential participant in God, and vice versa. But a creature must choose whether or not to become identified with its creator. A creature must elect either to accept or to refuse what God wills. Those who choose what God wants lead an existence of clarity, pleasure, and happiness. Those who reject God's will suffer in obscurity, pain, and misery. God's glory appears with greatest dramatic force in creatures whose only efficacy lies in their power of choice, their power to glorify God — regardless of their capacity to translate their choice into effective action. Indeed, the sincere sorrow of those who honestly choose what God wants but fail to act accordingly, is an even more pleasing variety of praise than the joyful love of inviolate obedience. The worse a creature feels about offending his creator, the more glory to God. Furthermore, the rescue of such sinners, the triumph of good in a creation dominated by both unintentional and intentional evil, displays God's omnipotence and omniscience in the most striking fashion imaginable. It seems, therefore, that if God's glory is to be fully revealed in creation, a confrontation must occur, even if God himself must set it up. Even in an innocent creation, the best of the new creatures engages in a dialogue where God playfully takes the role of straw man so that Adam can learn adversarial behavior and, by the way, assert some of the glories of the infinite, perfect, and absolute divine character. Milton repeatedly tells his readers that only through darkness shines the glory of God (2, 263–67; 3, 375–82). "Who seeks / To lessen thee, against his purpose serves / To manifest the more thy might," sing the angels, and of all God's creatures, Satan contributes most to the manifestation of God's glory (7, 613–15).

Despite all of the implications of wickedness contained in this chapter, I nevertheless think that Milton achieves a limited success in his justification of God. But we can only appreciate the subtlety of that justification if we understand more about Milton's ideas concerning God's will. My intent in the following chapter is to demonstrate that, though Satan's desire for his own glory is appealing and powerful, he finally must be seen as self-defeating and obstinate. One word of caution. I do not intend to argue that Milton's God is "good" in any sentimental sense of that word. He is not a God with whom I can sympathize. The masks that express him are sternly paternal, and the love that flows through them provides comforts only of labor and resignation. He is wild, unpredictable, and dangerous. Most of the religious people whom I know do not worship a God like Milton's.

10

THE GENEALOGY
OF MORAL GLORY

G IVEN ITS POSITION, this chapter may seem intended to refute some of the more frightening observations about Milton's God made in the last chapter. But those observations must stand.
Milton's God is best glorified by the anguish of a sinner who would
rather not sin and who begs forgiveness for his offense. The manifestation of glory required to save such a divided creature from the
evil in and around him is dramatically satisfying in a way that the
proposed natural metamorphosis of innocent creatures into heavenly beings is not. Furthermore, in a fallen world, God gets all the
glory — which is not to imply that glory is finite, but only that God
prefers not to share it. Man must satisfy himself only with having
formed a meritorious intention — and that only after God has forced
him to recognize his true alternatives. For Man to form that meritorious intention is simply to glorify God.

I realize that counterarguments in defense of Milton's God are
possible. But rather than debate the conclusions of the previous chapter, this one instead explores the genealogy of an order that must
be described as specifically moral. Earlier, I observed that life in the
Garden united the moral and natural realms — not that the two could
not be distinguished, but that they were for the most part coinciden-
tal. As a consequence of the Fall, according to commonplace Christian beliefs, the moral and natural in Man's world are often at odds.
Indeed, this division generally accounts for the inner division that
is the basis of God's greatest pleasure (our contrition and repentance)
and the most striking expression of his glory (our salvation). The

origins of the moral order, and thus of the kind of glory that is the final cause of creation, Milton traces to the events surrounding Satan's rebellion.

The episode of Satan's Fall (*PL* 5, 563–907) must occupy any interpreter of *Paradise Lost* because it presents the first instance of evil in a poem concerned with its origins. Also, in this scene Milton is at his most original, as J. M. Evans has pointed out:

> Although very many reasons had been offered for the Satanic revolt, nothing quite like this had ever appeared before. Milton's analysis of it is one of the most genuinely original things in the whole poem. Why, then, did he find it necessary to invent a new version of the episode?[1]

Milton's invention has ramifications for our understanding of Satan's motives and of Milton's theology as it involves the relations between God and the Son.[2] I contend that, in begetting the Son, God inaugurates an ethical order that allows discrimination between natural and moral excellence. In order to explain the transition between natural and moral orders, this chapter employs reasoning of Duns Scotus regarding the play between the wills of God and his creatures. I do not propose to prove that Milton borrows from Scotus, although I suggest that Milton studied him. Regardless of whether or not Scotus actually influenced Milton, the famed subtlety of Scotus' metaphysical and ethical distinctions clarifies what exactly happens in heaven at the unprecedented beginning of the epic action.

Milton mentions Scotus in the oft-quoted passage from *Areopagitica* which proclaims Spenser's superiority to Scotus, as well as to Aquinas, as a teacher (*CP* 2, 516). The passage does not denigrate Aquinas or Scotus, however, so much as it praises Spenser by exalting him over two philosophers eminent for wisdom and influence. Still, no one will deny Milton's antipathy for the schoolmen. His objections to them and their methods appear most clearly, if in an exaggerated form, in Prolusion 3, where he attacks Scholastic philosophy as tedious foolishness and compares his intellectual encounter with it to Hercules' more physical one with the Augean stables (*CP* 1, 241–42). Anyone who has looked at, or even lifted, the enormous Wadding edition of Scotus' works, in twelve folio tomes averaging over a thousand pages each, will sympathize with the young Milton's lament. The only other passage in which Milton refers specifically to Scotus occurs in *Tetrachordon* and also registers Milton's ostensible agreement with popular opinion of him as the primal dunce (*CP* 2, 621). As early as 1600, however, Cambridge libraries held over twenty-five titles attributed to Duns Scotus, and the Cambridge dons looked upon the Scholastics, and Scotus in particular, with great respect, so that Milton may have had more access to Scotus' work than he wished.[3]

A demonstration of Milton's acquaintance with the medieval schoolmen seems almost redundant in light of the evidence of Prolusions 4 and 5 and Milton's characteristic mode of argumentation (see McEuen's incisive note, *CP* 1, 240). Yet scholars generally associate Milton more with classical than with medieval authors and accept his contempt for Scholastic excesses as a rejection of their methods and ideas. Admittedly, what we like best about Milton's poetry — its assurance, formal variety, and architectonic splendor — reminds us more of classical than medieval literature (with the obvious exception of Dante). But as a thinker and a theological poet, Milton traveled in lands that the schoolmen had conquered and divided. Their charts and guides saw him through his journey in the golden realms, and though they sometimes hindered him, and though he sometimes ventured beyond their provinces, his perceptions and impressions mainly took shape within their categories.

Roughly speaking, Milton attributes to matter what Scotus affirms of being — that it underlies everything that is or that *could be*.[4] Keeping in mind this fundamental difference in the nature of their first principles — "one first matter all" versus "one first being all" — we may note that both understand God to be the necessary source and sustenance of everything that partakes of existence.[5] Scotus inherits from Avicenna a broadly Neoplatonic understanding, which Milton shares, of the hierarchical disposition of the first principle — be it matter or being — into degrees or grades of eminence.[6] Unlike many Neoplatonists, however, whose God can scarcely help but pour forth his goodness, Scotus and Milton insist that the divine will is the prime requisite of creation.

As we have already seen, Milton's insistence on the primacy of the divine will appears most prominently just prior to his description of the creation: "Though I uncircumscrib'd my self retire," declares God, "and put not forth my goodness, which is free / To act or not, Necessity and Chance / Approach not mee, and what I will is Fate" (*PL* 7, 170–73). We need not enter the debate on this controversial passage to hear in it God's claim that the only limits he observes are self-imposed. For a Neoplatonist such as John Smith, as was observed in the last chapter, "God's *Unchangeable Goodnes* . . . is also *The Unchangeable Rule of His Will*; neither can he any more swerve from it, then he can swerve from himself."[7] For Smith, it seems, God cannot help but create what he creates; his goodness simply exudes from him in the shape that it does. For Milton, however, creation displays the definite selections of an arbitrary sovereign, not the emanations of a divinity who creates as a hemophiliac bleeds. Nothing is more essential to Milton's God than his sovereignty; his glory consists in his absolute ability to decide when, where, and how to put forth what portion of his goodness it pleases him to put forth. As Milton insists at various points throughout *Christian Doctrine*, God's "decrees and still more his actions, whatever they may be, are absolutely free" (*CP* 6, 159).

Scotus' similar insistence on God's absolute sovereignty led him to distinguish between two kinds of divine power. Following Augustine, medieval thinkers generally concurred that the continuation of the present order, despite its apparently fixed nature, depends entirely on God's willingness to let it be as he made it. But the essential precariousness of things did not much enter into their elaborate theological systems, which they based on the way things in fact are. Beginning in the late thirteenth century, however, with the work of Henry of Ghent, the distinction between 1) what God in fact does, and 2) what he could do figured prominently into Scholastic argument. By the early fourteenth century, Scotus had elaborated this renewed awareness of the subjunctive mood into a division between two realms of power. Leff defines the two kinds of power as God's "ordained power (*potentia ordinata*), . . . his law for this world, and his absolute power (*potentia absoluta*), . . . his omnipotence pure and simple, regarded solely in itself and expressed in the creed of . . . God limited by nothing save logical self-contradiction."[8] Scotus himself puts it this way: "God, being able to act according to those upright laws — just as they were set up by him — is said to act according to his ordained power; as he is able to do many things which are not according to those same laws, but beyond them, his power is said to be absolute. . . . The many other things . . . possible to be done . . . do not include contradiction."[9]

In *Christian Doctrine* Milton similarly maintains that "God has not absolutely decreed all things" (*CP* 6, 156). God, for example, creates the "Lights / High in th' expanse of Heaven" and exhorts them to "be for Lights as I ordain / Thir Office" (*PL* 7, 339–44). God's decree thus sets the division and duration of years, seasons, days, and nights. But God can and, according to Scripture, does intervene in the regular operation of his ordinance, and this exemplifies the differences between what Milton calls God's "ordinary" and "extraordinary" providence (*CP* 6, 340–41). Miraculous violations of the natural order, however, provide only specific instances of Scotus' fundamental distinction, and they can mislead us into thinking that the point of the dichotomy is to shock men with amazing spectacles of divine whimsy.

In fact, the contingency of the present order pervades and shapes the thinking of Scotus and Milton and is the logical basis of Milton's theodicy. God can change what he has already made because "the Almighty Maker," as Chaos understands, also pervades the realm of possibility. The elements of Milton's primal matter remain potent confusion only so long as God does not "them ordain / His dark materials to create more Worlds" (*PL* 2, 915–16). Like Scotus, Milton attributes being to a realm of absolute possibility out of which reality takes shape. In effect, each distinguishes between ontological and metaphysical first principles: what can or could be provides an infinite background of being for what in fact appears. Anything or any person that is or is not could be otherwise. God can, at his pleasure, as Adam remarks, "raise thy Creature to what highth thou wilt / Of Union or Communion, deifi'd" (8, 430–31). Scotus agrees that God can elevate a creature even unto union with himself or award it "some Godlike form" so that it "is loved in a special way."[10] Satan recognizes, and in his Fall exemplifies, the reverse, as he wishes that God had "ordain'd / [Him] some inferior Angel" so that he would not have led, at least, the rebellion (4, 58–59).

Scotus' speculation regarding "the interplay between God's ordained and absolute power," as Leff describes it, licenses neither theories on the likelihood of rectilinear planetary orbits nor the manufacture of subtleties for subtlety's sake — though both abuses resulted from it.[11] Rather, Scotus' thought on this interplay involves "questions of moral theology: justification, predestination, merit, free will, and sin."[12] Although Milton damns the intricate quibbling that often attends these questions, he obviously considers them of great importance. In the absolute contingency of creation rest the possibilities both of ultimate happiness and of tragedy: "God has not decreed that everything must happen inevitably" (*CP* 6, 164). Hence, although God ordains all of creation for man's pleasure (*PL* 3, 664), once man has fallen, he removes him from the Garden and alters the entire creation (11, 48–57; 10, 649–715). Everything changes.

From our viewpoint, these "changes" in the ordained order are not changes at all. Because things have always been this way for us, we cannot help but look at the events leading up to the present order as pat. I suggested in the last chapter that God appears to direct events to the conclusion that will most benefit him, increasing his glory, Man's subservience, and Satan's damnation. But we must not forget that God *shares* events with his creatures. Even Fisher would not have been able to execute a queen sacrifice if it were not for the blind arrogance of the grand master chasing Fisher's queen. Events have a way of bringing more glory to God only when creatures have permission to shame themselves and then proceed to do exactly that. For then God must exercise his infinite goodness in a fashion that will snatch victory from their defeat. Far from intending us to suspect a divine setup, Milton would have us go to the other extreme. It is almost as if his God *improvises* the action of *Paradise Lost.* Milton warns us that describing God's behavior with a word like *improvise* can be misleading and that we should discount its association with human imperfection (*CP* 6, 134–35). Perhaps *extemporize* would better suit the case. So long as we get a sense of an unrehearsed performance and spontaneous response, however, we understand more accurately even the obvious events in the epic, events which have become so hackneyed in criticism that we tend to ignore them altogether.

But the fact that the action of the poem is unrehearsed and spontaneous does not mean that it is completely random or silly. God will not contradict himself, and he must will the good. Here we see the influence of Scotus on Milton, and on the Reformation, at its most seminal point. Maurice Kelley says that the doctrine of non-contradiction "is a theological commonplace" (*CP* 6, 148), but this convention derives from Scotus' fourteenth-century innovation.[13] For neither Scotus nor Milton does this doctrine satisfy a desire merely for logical coherence. Rather, it expresses their conviction that at the basis of all thought and action lies a single, independent, necessary tautology, "I am that I am."

Necessity and freedom coincide for Milton's and Duns Scotus' deity on the most general ethical distinction, that between good and evil. The premise that goodness constitutes the divine essence, in combination with the certainty that God must be who he is, guarantees for Scotus and for Milton that whatever an omnipotent God does is good. Scotus thus argues that "the divine essense is identical with its volition"; hence, "the divine will necessarily wills its own goodness, and yet is free in willing this."[14] Milton put it: "in God a certain immutable internal necessity to do good, independent of all outside influence, can be consistent with absolute freedom of action. For in the same divine nature each tends to the same result" (*CP* 6, 159). The underlying premise appears in *The Response of John Phillips:* "goodness is just as much of the essence of God as the will itself of God" (*CP* 4, ii, 940).

Milton's belief that perfect freedom and a necessity to will the good coexist in God is labeled "compatibilism" by Dennis Danielson, who appropriately links the belief with Milton's dismay at the prospect of a voluntarist deity.[15] My claim is that God's perfect freedom is a function of his control over the realm of absolute power. In other words, there is an infinity of good latent in existence that God draws on as he sees fit. No matter how certain it appears that reality has posed a dilemma requiring God to contradict himself, his infinite goodness allows a solution that may stretch the divine tautology almost to the point of contradiction but nevertheless preserves the identity of God.

One event that Milton presents as necessary and eternally irrevocable is Satan's expulsion from heaven. One might insist that God "Ordain'd without redemption, without end" the exile of any disobedient angel, and that, therefore, once an angel disobeys, God finds himself eternally bound by the law of noncontradiction to make

good on his threat (*PL* 5, 615). This "merely logical" attitude underlies Belial's willingness to endure God's sentence: "fate inevitable /
Subdues us, and Omnipotent Decree, / The Victor's will. To suffer,
as to do, / Our strength is equal, nor the Law unjust / That so ordains" (2, 197–201). We find this attitude attractive because it resembles Milton's characteristic mode of heroism – a patient readiness to enact the divine will. Belial's heroism, however, aspires only
to a diminution of the anguish attendant on active disobedience.
Belial does refute the Calvinist sentiments of Moloch's camp, that
the devils were "decreed, / Reserv'd and destin'd to Eternal woe" (2,
160–61). But even though hell is the "Prison ordained" for the damned
by "Eternal Justice," Belial still errs in thinking of himself and the
rest of the rebels as crooks who got caught and are now doing time –
all of it (1, 70–71).

God's enforcement of his decree is actually a matter of crime and
punishment more as Dostoevsky portrays it, or as Tolstoy does in
Anna Karenina, than as Belial's speech implies. Hell, as I have argued, naturally objectifies the ethical relations between fallen angels
and God. That God recognizes this state of affairs before it in fact
occurs does not make his recognition a threat, nor even, in the usual
sense, a law. The fundamental unity of logic and ethics undercuts
the artificial distinction between crime and punishment. As Ludwig
Wittgenstein would later contend,

> When a general ethical Law of the form "Thou shalt . . ." is
> set up, the first thought is: Suppose I do not do it?
>   But it is clear that ethics has nothing to do with punishment
> and reward. So this question about the consequences of an ac-
> tion must be unimportant. At least these consequences cannot
> be events. For there must be something right about that ques-
> tion after all. There must be a *kind* of ethical reward and of
> ethical punishment but these must be involved in the action
> itself.[16]

Simply if mysteriously put, "the world of the happy is a *different*
world from the world of the unhappy."[17] We have already seen that
Milton illustrates this mystery in his depiction of the correspondence
between Hell and its denizens.

Seeing "undelighted all delight," Satan further verifies Wittgenstein's dictum in what seem laboratory conditions designed to disprove it (*PL* 4, 286). His soliloquy delivered on the verge of Paradise reveals why perdition is by definition perpetual and inescapable. His contrary will — "Evil be thou my Good" — is as necessary and as free as God's tautologous one (4, 110). Absolutely speaking, God could, by "Act of Grace," restore a repentant Satan to his "former state" (4, 94). But Satan recognizes that he cannot repent, nor can he offer sufficient reason for his evil will other than the fact that he is the Adversary, possessing a will contrary to heaven's. Iago says it best when he proclaims to Roderigo, "I am not what I am" (*Othello* 1, 1, 65).

We must describe Satan as contradictory, rather than as tautological in his own way, because in accord with his origins, he intellectually recognizes and naturally inclines toward the good. In a sense, Satan's choice of evil manifests the essentially free condition of the will — its ability to choose against its own predisposition. Satan, recognizing the good, chooses evil, indeed, irreversibly commits himself to evil even as God is irreversibly committed to good. Milton and Marlowe thus agree in their presentation of damnation; hell means never being able to admit you're sorry, even though you are (cf. *CP* 6, 195). If we find this condition as baffling as the tautological one of God, it is because between them God and Satan constitute the limits of our ethical and logical world. Our lives make sense because of the senselessness of their conditions.

The moment in *Paradise Lost* with which I am now concerned is the moment when the angel become the Adversary. Milton cannot present directly the origin of evil; we never are shown who Satan was before. By the time we get a look at the precipitous decline of Satan's thoughts in Book IV, the essential change has already occurred. Milton nevertheless conveys the absolute character of the change in a number of ways, one of the most obvious being Satan's change in name (*PL* 5, 658–59). The allegory of the birth of Sin is another attempt to express the sudden accomplishment of so prodigious a transformation. Although Milton does not directly represent Satan's transition from unfallen to fallen, this primal moment in Milton's moral theology evidently depends on the interplay between God's ordained and absolute power.

By way of background, we note that prior to the rebellion, the angels live according to what might be called a fame culture, one which Milton concocts out of Christian angelology and which evokes images of something like the Roman army.[18] At God's request, the "Empyreal Host / Of Angels" gathers and lines up according to distinctions of rank and function. Streaming pennants mark various "Orders and Degrees" and bear "Holy Memorials, acts of Zeal and Love / Recorded eminent" (5, 593–94). This picture suggests that just as some angels enjoy a higher status than others, so also some good actions are more prized than others. Raphael testifies to Satan's immense stature as "of the first, / If not the first Arch-Angel, great in Power, / In favor and preeminence" (5, 659–61).

According to Milton, God allows the angels realms of power and influence where they govern according to the good indicated by their own intelligence (cf. *CP* 6, 346–47). An analogous arrangement pertains in Paradise where Adam and Eve reign and live, as Eve says, "Law to ourselves, our Reason is our Law" (9, 654). Reason and will coincide in the natural lives of unfallen creatures — "Reason also is choice" (3, 108) — as they themselves freely choose to conform to the good indicated by the intellect. Morally, however, reason also allows the possibility of voluntary nonconformity; God made man "sufficient to have stood, though free to fall" (3, 99). We have already seen the distinction between reason and will in Satan's rational recognition that it would be good to repent and in his decision not to. Scotus analyzes the relation of reason and will in this way: "the free power of the agent involves both intellect and will," but "only the will . . . can completely account for the indeterminacy as regards the alternative."[19] Reason and will, in their supposed harmony and potential opposition, are thus the source of ethical tautology and contradiction.

When Satan insists that "Orders and Degrees / Jar not with liberty, but well consist," it appears that he uses double-talk in order to justify his own high rank while inciting rebellion on behalf of equality. But there is a certain consistency in what Satan says. The greater the intellect of a creature and the more self-motivated, the greater his knowledge and volition of the good. The good, being infinite, offers variety and profundity enough for an inspired genius, however bold his initiative, as well as constancy and accessibility enough for the workaday performer, however perfunctory his efforts. The former merits higher status than the latter, nor does the recognition afforded him impinge on the equal liberty of others to pursue the good in their own ways. Uriel, for example, praises the alleged cherub who says he wanders in creation to seek greater acquaintance with the good. He compares him favorably with other, not so self-motivated, spirits (3, 695–701). Uriel does not mean to condemn the relatively lethargic angels by his comment, but rather to praise the superior ambition of the cherub. Ironically, the greatest of creatures and most independent is most vulnerable to the temptation to exceed his limits. We might distrust a system that ordains this apparent injustice if Satan himself did not answer our objection (4, 58–65).

It appears that from the beginning of time until the moment at which the action of *Paradise Lost* begins, the more autonomous the angelic will, operating naturally in accordance with right reason, the more perfect its obedience to God. In introducing "Law and Edict" to creatures accustomed to neither, and who "without Law / Err not," God thus confronts them with a moral problem of discrimination and value (5, 798–99). In calling them to order by their "magnific titles" – "Thrones, Dominations, Princedoms, Virtues, Powers" (5, 772) – God reminds them of their independent functions in creation at the same time that he exercises his sovereignty over them. If, as Fowler remarks, "the angels, symbolically considered, are no less than the operations of providence throughout the universe of secondary causes," then God here insists that they have been autonomously exercising their powers in what is eminently his domain.[20] Though until now autonomy has coincided with service, it apparently should never have been identified with it. The invisible hand of this previously laissez-faire ruler has suddenly become manifest in the person of the Son. The angels must either choose continued independence or sacrifice it on behalf of continued communion with a king who heretofore has not asserted his will except by letting them assert theirs. Until this moment, in other words, sin was, though perhaps possible, quite out of the question for the angels. The internal law of right reason infallibly identified and chose particular goods in a perfect natural realm filled only with natural goods.

God's decree in Book V thus marks the transition from a primarily natural order to a discernibly moral one. The institution of a moral order presumes a distinction between 1) the will as inclined to promote the advantage of the creature doing the willing, and therefore subject to a natural predisposition; and 2) the will as desiring the good for its own sake, and therefore relatively disinterested or morally free. Milton assumes such a distinction when in *Christian Doctrine* he notes that the angels "desire to contemplate the mystery of our salvation simply out of love, and not from any interest of their own" (*CP* 6, 345). Scotus defines the will as acting according to natural inclination "when the soul . . . actually loves itself or actually loves what is advantageous," but he claims that the true nobility of the will resides in its ability objectively "to pass judgment, properly speaking, upon the appropriateness of the action."[21] Obviously, many good actions could satisfy the definition of either category. In my opinion, before the time represented at the end of Book V, one would not be able to distinguish between actions appropriate to one category or the other:

> Man was made in the image of God, and the whole law of nature was so implanted and innate in him that he was in need of no command. It follows, then, that if he received any additional commands, whether about the tree of knowledge or about marriage, these had nothing to do with the law of nature, which is itself sufficient to teach whatever is in accord with right reason (i.e., whatever is intrinsically good). These commands, then, were simply a matter of what is called positive right. Positive right comes into play when God, or anyone else invested with lawful power, commands or forbids things which, if he had not commanded or forbidden them, would in themselves have been neither good or bad, and would therefore have put no one under any obligation. (*CP* 6, 353)

What Milton here leaves implicit, Scotus made explicit, that because God created the natural order, the intrinsic good indicated by nature is also contingent on his will.[22] From the point of view of God's absolute power — which includes in its sway the infinity of possible worlds and all their natural orders — the actually existent state of goodness is arbitrarily determined and ultimately a matter of "positive right." Although one may correctly observe that for Milton God's goodness itself is not arbitrary, the shape his goodness takes *is*. Thus, from a creature's point of view, what may be a good action in one order could be evil in another because, as Milton and Scotus agree, the goodness that does exist is largely a function of the order God does in fact choose to create (*CP* 6, 351–53).[23] Love of God is the only absolute good; not even God can command a creature to hate him, and he certainly must punish it for doing so.[24]

The fact is, overtly "positive decrees," decrees at variance from the dictates of the natural order that God has indeed ordained, seem designed by God to prove and improve the love between God and creatures, insomuch as this love tends toward communion and mutual identity. As I have already argued, the commands regarding the forbidden fruit and marriage concern parts of Man's existence particularly responsible either for moving Man closer to God, or for alienating Man from him. The same double edge characterizes the positive decree regarding the Son. We know how Satan views it, but Abdiel interprets the exaltation as a strategy both to increase unity and to glorify the angels even further: "far from thought / To make us less, bent rather to exalt / Our happy state under one Head more near / United (*PL* 5, 828–31).

Whether or not God himself had ever levied a positive decree prior to the exaltation of the Son we cannot with certainty say. Errands and behests of state, which might have preceded and clearly follow the decree, apparently did not fundamentally alter the order under which the angels led a relatively autonomous existence. It bears repeating that under such an order, though an angel was not necessarily free to do whatever he might choose, whatever he did choose was naturally in harmony with what God wanted. It would take something like the exaltation of the Son to test the angels according to their moral freedom rather than according to their natural inclination. Raphael's narrative diction and Satan's speeches indicate that God's decree divides what is customary and wonted from what is new and unprecedented (see 5, 602–5, 618, 658–59, 662–63, 677–82, 704–5, 790–91; 6, 91–96). God now insists that the angels predicate the pursuit of their own interest on their service to the Son. One can detect Satan's pained indignation in the ironic pretext that he gives for his troops' assembly:

> to prepare
> Fit entertainment to receive our King
> The great *Messiah*, and his new commands,
> Who speedily through all the Hierarchies
> Intends to pass triumphant, and give Laws.
>
> (5, 690–94)

The exaggerated emphasis of the plural "*Laws*," coming as it does at the end of Satan's speech and thus in the position of greatest rhetorical and metrical stress, leaves little doubt as to how Satan interprets the new order. Satan's outrage at the violation of his autonomy appears also in the coordination of "*Messiah*" and "commands" in line 692 and is further suggested by the omission of a comma between "our King" and "the great *Messiah*." In Milton's practice as in modern punctuation, the absence of this comma implies that the Son is only one of potentially any number of kings who could be elevated over the angels. God is king, and now the Son is also king; who will be next? God can do as he pleases, and it is to this principle that Satan objects.

As Empson suggests, we may understand Satan as having always operated according to aristocratic assumptions.[25] The transition between old and new, which throws the angels into discord, effects a transition between the mores of primary and secondary epic as described by C. S. Lewis.[26] Primary epics present aristocratic heroes, such as Akhilleus and Odysseus, who pursue their own excellence. Secondary epics present pious heroes, such as Aeneas, who pursue a goal distinguishable from their own advantage. A more appropriate approach to the transition represented in Book V, however, would be to consider the difference between the Book of Judges, when "there was no king in Israel," when "every man did that which was right in his own eyes" (Judg. 21:25), and 1 and 2 Samuel, which trace the monarchical ascent of the Son's human progenitor.

Like Akhilleus with respect to Agamemnon, then, or like the northern tribes of Israel with respect to the idea of monarchy, Satan calls his followers together, using the same sonorous roll call by which God had addressed them earlier, and declares that these "Imperial Titles . . . assert / Our being ordain'd to govern not to serve" (5, 801–2). Aside from acting as an auxiliary verb for "ordain'd," "being" also suggests that the ontological status of these creatures is that of governors. The fear voiced by Satan is that God, by placing the angels under the Son's command, has left them only their great names, that with the Son in charge, their dominion will be "merely titular" (5, 774). Existentially threatened by the implications of the "knee tribute" that now has been extended to the Son, Satan finds it revolting, "prostration vile" (5, 782).

Milton could scarcely damn Satan for truculence regarding either the installation of a king or the limitation on freedom that it entails. We are not dealing with some servile slug whose morality goes by rote, but with the noblest of noble creatures. "Possest before / By none," the rebels perceive God's decree as an assault on their identities as "Natives and Sons of Heav'n" (5, 790–91). Unlike Man, the angels have lived for untold ages without such a provocative object. As William Hunter has remarked:

> The exaltation of the Son has never been related to Satan in this way by any Christian tradition. Furthermore, to consider that Milton has the Father beget the Son by elevating him above Satan may imply to some degree the Arian view that the Son was created inferior and then raised to a superior position by divine fiat. The Arian position does nicely fit in with the motivation of Satan's rebellion . . . , but I do not believe that Milton was an Arian.[27]

Despite Hunter's skepticism, God's exaltation of the Son does indicate a fundamental change in the customary order, one that allows us better to understand Satan's motivation and one that presumes that Milton's understanding of the Son is categorically Arian.

Aside from a reluctance to ascribe to Milton's "subordinationism" its exact theological label, Milton scholars have also been unwilling to recognize Satan's obvious motivation for the very good reason that it seems to imply, as Hunter puts it, "that the Son was created inferior and raised to a superior position."[28] The Son does begin as God's inferior, and he remains that way, though certainly he has never been inferior to the angels. Yet, his relationship to both God and the angels does change. The change in the Son's status marks the transition from a merely natural order to a specifically moral one. God institutes the new order by presenting the Son and demanding that the angels make a moral decision. Abdiel claims that the Son has previously acted and been known as God's Word, but no mention is ever made of any previous appearance or activity of this creature *as the Son.* Milton himself writes that "the Son existed in the beginning, under the title of the Word or Logos," and that "in the beginning he was the Word" (*CP* 6, 206, 419). He thus distinguishes between the role of the *Son* as the "image . . . by which God becomes visible," and the role of the *Word* as "the word by which God is audible" (*CP* 6, 297). This distinction holds in *Paradise Lost.* Satan objects to the doubled submission to the Father and "to his image *now* proclaim'd" (*PL* 5, 784; italics mine). God has in effect created a new rank, "the head of the angels," and has appointed to it the image of himself, newly begotten at least in terms of his visibility to the angels:

> *This day* I have begot whom I declare
> My only Son, and on this holy Hill
> Him have anointed, whom ye *now behold*
> At my right hand.   (5, 603–6; italics mine)

The begetting of the Son in Book V may be considered metaphorical in that it does not mean that the being now entitled the Son never existed previously. He did, but he existed as the Word and was otherwise unapparent.

The begetting of the Son is best understood as the unfolding of God's intention, represented by the Son, to transform a naturally good order into a morally good one. Milton's second divinity enjoys a special status as the personified link between God's intent and its realization. He is the living representation of the glory for which God creates. In Book V, God presents the tool by which he created heavenly reality — the Word — as a person with free will — his Son. The implication is that God's intention in creation — the manifestation of his glory — will now be accomplished by the voluntary, moral actions of his creatures, actions performed first and foremost because they are what God wants, not because they promote the advantage of the creature.

As we have already seen, Abdiel offers an answer to objections based on the angels' natural desire to pursue their own advantage. God's decrees can be construed as being consistent with angelic interests. But Abdiel also implicitly disputes the assumption that the "lawless," natural good, which the angels have previously known, is necessarily the most appropriate, decorous, or just form of the good. In other words, he raises the possibility that God's higher knowledge of the good might properly require the angels to choose against their own inclination. God's disinterested understanding of how things best are should in any case take precedence over one's own interest — even if the two happen to coincide. As Allan Wolter writes of Scotus' ethics, "actions taken in accordance with 'natural will' are morally indifferent — good though they may be — unless the agent recognizes them as actions in accordance with the will of God."[29] In effect, Abdiel argues on behalf of what I have described as a moral, as opposed to a natural, order.

Abdiel explains that the "begotten Son" is the same being "by whom / As by his Word the mighty Father made / All things" (5, 835–37). God's decree, Abdiel's logic goes, is therefore just, and the exaltation of the Son is decorous, regardless of how the angels construe its effect on their interests. The Son is "by right" and with "honor due" exalted as "rightful" king over the angels (5, 814–18). Although Abdiel has managed to discern the equation between the Word and the Son, the rebel angels either have not or have chosen not to. When confronted with the fact that the creative Word has metamorphosed into the exalted Son, the rebels deny their creation by him, deny their creation by anyone but themselves. Given that the Word and the Son are essentially the same, Satan's rejection of the Son, and hence of the new, moral order, must lead to his rejection of the Word and hence of the natural order that created him. Every point that Satan wants to argue Abdiel blocks with contradiction: as a creature, Satan cannot dispute with the creator about the just status of the king of creatures, and if he goes against what is right and just in order to pursue his own advantage, he will have given birth — at practically the first possible moment to do so — to Sin.[30] By the end of Book V, it has become clear that God's decree demands that the angels enter a moral awareness of their contingency.

The Son enjoys the special role, according to Milton, of being the finite mode or symbol by which God realizes his intent in creation—thus his dual nature as a divine creature. The magnific titles that resound through the opening act of Raphael's narration actually allude to the Word's position as the common denominator of created being (5, 835-41).[31] In declaring his Word to be Son and heir, God personifies and moralizes the natural efficacy by which he formed the hierarchies and autonomous functions that Satan prizes. The Son will fully exemplify the freedom to choose without regard for oneself, but simply in conformity to what is right and just. Abdiel first invokes the new principle of freedom as he confronts Satan prior to their armed conflict (6, 174-85). But the new order best appears in the Son's own words to the Father as he prepares to rout the rebels: "this I my Glory account, / My exaltation, and my whole delight, / That thou in me well-pleas'd, declar'st thy will / Fulfill'd, which to fulfill is all my bliss" (6, 725-29). As Hunter has observed, the events following God's exaltation of the Son typologically anticipate the events of Passion Week.[32] And indeed, the Garden of Gethsemane and Calvary are the excruciating culmination of the distinction between a creature's natural inclination to pursue his own interest and his moral obligation to submit to the will of the creator no matter what the cost.

The unorthodoxy of Milton's version of the Son's role in creation strikes us with fresh force when we consider that Milton makes the Son the exemplar of the ordained order and therefore of contingent being: "however the Son was begotten, it did not arise from natural necessity . . . but was . . . a result of the Father's decree and will" (*CP* 6, 208). The relegation of even the Son's existence to the realm of contingency means that his actions are voluntary and, strictly speaking, unnecessary. Particularly regarding assumption of human nature and redemption of the faithful, the Son could have chosen otherwise. In Book III, God asks, "Which of ye will be mortal to redeem / Man's mortal crime, and just th' unjust to save?" and the narrator remarks that "now without redemption all mankind / Must have been lost, adjudged to Death and Hell / By doom severe, had not the Son of God, / In whom the fulness dwells of love divine, / His dearest mediation thus renew'd" (*PL* 3, 214-15, 222-26). The narrator makes it clear that things could have gone differently. Furthermore, throughout the relevant chapters of *Christian Doctrine*, Milton repeats that the Son freely chooses to assume the burden of

Man's salvation: "HE PAID VOLUNTARILY"; "HE WILLINGLY PERFORMED"; "CHRIST . . . SUBMITTED HIMSELF VOLUNTARILY" (*CP* 6, 415–16, 430, 438). It is difficult fully to appreciate the daring of Milton's God in creating a second divinity who perfectly represents his Father's natural will in creation, but who could choose to forsake his Father's moral will rather than be forsaken according to it.

Here lies the key difference between Milton and Scotus concerning the role of the Son.[33] As an orthodox Trinitarian, Scotus maintains that the Son equals the Father and thus shares the Father's will and status as necessary being.[34] Milton, on the other hand, claims that "God cannot generate a God equal to himself" and that, consequently, "the Father's will is distinct from and greater than the will of the only begotten Son" (*CP* 6, 263, 276). While Scotus understands the Father's "unique production" of the Son as "absolutely and in every way necessary," Milton sees the Son as the ultimate instance of the Father's perfect freedom: "God always works with absolute freedom" (*CP* 6, 209).[35] Even if the Son had not offered to redeem Man—though God, of course, foresees that he will—we must presume that, given his gracious intent, God would have found a way to show mercy.[36]

The unfolding of the Son in *Paradise Lost* does faintly recall the structure of the two-stage logos theory, which Hunter has argued informs Milton's idea of the Son.[37] The change from invisible Word to manifest Son, however, involves an ethical more than a metaphysical development. Even in his role as the Word, the second divinity cannot be thought to have existed from all eternity, not even in the mind of God. Milton baldly states in the *Art of Logic* that a thing that exists only in the mind of a subject cannot in fact be said to exist at all (*CP* 8, 236). Even if Milton had believed that mental phenomena could be said to exist in fact, we still would not be able to distinguish, on the grounds of mental existence, between the Son and the rest of creation, which certainly must also have preexisted in the mind of an omniscient creator. Moreover, if the presence of a being or its actions in the mind of an omniscient God could be said to constitute its or their *existence*, the careful distinction that Milton draws between foreknowledge and predestination would seem to crumble. With respect to other creatures, the Word or Son has always been and will always be, in one form or another, summing up the created order in himself. He is the principle of finitude in Milton's theology: through him the Father defines, circumscribes, forms, that is to say, creates essences apart from himself so that he may be glorified by them and express his glory through them. But with respect to all that *could* be, the Son represents only one alternative, the one that God happens to have chosen.

The hopelessness of Satan's stand and the source of his heroic appeal thus rest in the same state of affairs. God has not asked whether or not creation will accept domination by the Son, of "right endu'd / With Regal Sceptre" (*PL* 5, 815–16). He simply has changed things, and Satan too must change if he wants to join in the shape of things to come. But Satan remains obsessed with his old place and position, addicted to them, we might say. Satan mourns the "state" from which he fell, not the loss of heavenly communion (4, 38). His debt to the creator is for creating him, as he says, "what I was / In that bright eminence" (4, 43–44). Repentance and grace he comprehends only insofar as they might win for him once again his "former state" (4, 94). But the order that Satan refuses to give up no longer exists. Creation has undergone an essential, metamorphic development in the revelation of the audible, natural Word as the visible, moral Son. Rather than heroic autonomy, the newly ordained mode of existence demands humble obedience — even unto crucifixion. Satan's old place no longer exists. Like an absurd Peter Pan who refuses to grow up and is consigned to never-never land, or like an archetypal rebel without a cause, Satan pays his allegiance to what no longer is, and hence he becomes a has-been who will not be.

CONCLUSION

who Gods before
Receiv'd, be such: adorers we adore.
— Met. 8, 722–23

CHAPTER 1 of this book discussed the Hebrew word for glory — *kabod* — and the implications of its original reference to weight, a reference that may underlie Milton's association of true glory with solidity or gravity and of false glory with lightness or levity. The biblical man of *kabod* is notable for the gravity of his bearing and for the possession, typically, of wealth and family. A household heavy in land, goods, and children further suggests durability and consistency. God's promises to Eve, Abraham, Isaac, Jacob, and David appeal to precisely this sense of *kabod*, and the terror of the Book of Job lies in the fact that just such a household is, in no time at all, effectively demolished. No doubt the tangibility of glory in the Old Testament appealed to Milton's materialist sensibility and in *Paradise Lost* influenced his unique representation of the substantial facts of life.

Homeric glory, on the other hand, focuses attention more on subjective consciousness than on objective material circumstances. The *Iliad* exemplifies epic's characteristic fascination with human consciousness of free choice versus the objective certainty of an immutably foregone conclusion. As Tolstoy explained it, on the one side lies the exalted perspective of rational observation, which, like the vision of God in Book III, witnesses the inevitable sequence of history. On the other side lies the consciousness of freedom:

The fact that, from the point of view of observation, reason and the will are merely secretions of the brain, and that man

[167]

following the general law may have developed from lower animals at some unknown period of time, only explains from a
fresh side the truth admitted thousands of years ago by all the
religious and philosophic theories — that from the point of view
of reason man is subject to the law of necessity; but it does
not advance by a hair's breadth the solution of the question,
which has another, opposite, side, based on the consciousness
of freedom.[1]

In the *Iliad*, inevitability is synonymous with death, and the warrior stands out from the rest of his society because his job is to face
death at the hands of other men. The second chapter thus contended
that the valor of Akhilleus, though certainly tied to simple prowess
or battle strength, is fundamentally apparent in his great-souled encounter with his own mortality.

Milton also believed that glory for humankind requires intimacy
with death: the fortitude to accept the inevitable and to become a
voluntary participant in it. Samson is perhaps the most emblematic
example and the one closest to Akhilleus in character, but the Son
of Book III perfectly reveals the essential unity of soaring life and
implacable death in the ideal of glory. For many readers Adam's
heroism similarly rests on his ability to acquiesce in the fatal history
that inevitably proceeds from his ruin and ultimately redresses it.
Indeed, it almost seems as if his heroism equals his willingness to
procreate, to *consort* with death as per Milton's insistent, metaphysical pun on the Latin for fate (e.g., 9, 953–54). Though borne out
by action, such heroism originates in the subjective realm of light
opinion (*doxa*), the epistemological battlefield where for Milton
human glory truly resides.

Chapter 3 accordingly examined Milton's Christian synthesis of
Greek (light) and Hebrew (weighty) versions of glory. Its argument
may be considered revisionist in that it insists on an Akhillean side
of Milton that does not currently enjoy much scholarly notice. Despite his quotidian pacifism, Milton consistently speaks of virtue as
the product of a battle on behalf of truth and recognizes Akhilleus
as a model in conducting his own life. The nearly debilitating horror Milton appears to have felt at the prospect of death, and at the
cavalier treatment of one's corpse by a ferocious, at best oblivious

world, similarly suggests the strong Homeric tenor of his pursuit of glory. But Milton accepts Homeric glory precisely in the sense that it anticipates, or may be reconciled with, the idea of glory implicit in the Book of Job or in the Gospels. In this respect, human glory begins with subjective acknowledgement of the inescapable premise that, as Simone Weil said, "All men, by the very act of being born, are destined to suffer violence."[2] In *Paradise Lost* Milton symbolizes the violence to which men are ever subject by Death, who appears in the guise of an exultant Homeric warrior: "over them triumphant Death his Dart / Shook, but delay'd to strike" (11, 491–92).

We may feel tempted to dismiss the light/heavy ambiguity of glory as idiosyncratic to Milton's work, but the mystery of this cleaving opposition winds its way through the Western tradition from ancient to modern times. As Milan Kundera observes in *The Unbearable Lightness of Being*, the ancient Greek Parmenides saw lightness as positive and weight as negative.[3] The modern German composer Beethoven, however, was inclined to see value only in weight, a predisposition that Kundera suggests most share: "We believe that the greatness of man stems from the fact that he bears his fate as Atlas bore the heavens on his shoulders" (p. 33). The apparent inevitability and irrevocability of events — proceeding like the steps of a sombre dance we have danced a thousand times — accounts for this sense of fateful heaviness, which Kundera expresses through Nietzsche's myth of eternal return:

> If every second of our lives recurs an infinite number of times, we are nailed to eternity as Jesus Christ was nailed to the cross. It is a terrifying prospect. In the world of eternal return the weight of unbearable responsibility lies heavy on every move we make. That is why Nietzsche called the idea of eternal return the heaviest of burdens. (p. 5)

The alternative to supporting this burden is to approach the events of life as if they occurred once and were over, leaving not a rack behind. Kundera refrains from judging between these opposed though curiously interwoven views of life — "the only certainty is: the lightness/weight opposition is the most mysterious, most ambiguous of all" (p. 6).

But why do I say that these apparently mutually exclusive views are interwoven, and what makes Kundera insist that the lightness/weight opposition is "most mysterious, most ambiguous?" I would suggest that part of the mystery lies, as Tolstoy might agree, in the disposition of the subjective consciousness toward the world. For some, the idea of a world of lightness, and the image of sheer inconsequence that accompanies it, is as Kundera's title suggests, insupportable. For others, the idea of weight, and its association with irresistible fate, actually alleviates the ponderous burden of human responsibility. Milton's sense of glory, encompassing the extremes of ephemeral opinion (*doxa*) and substantial being (*kabod*), includes both sides of the lightness/weight opposition, as well as the subjective perspectives appropriate to either side. God witnesses all events and actions *sub species aeternitas,* a viewpoint approximated in Nietzsche's myth of eternal return, while Satan, who undergoes ceaseless and senseless oscillations, appears to suffer the unbearable lightness of being.

Yet, and here again we find ambiguity approaching paradox, the lightness of being readily applies also to Milton's eternal, all-powerful God. His infinite material potency, in the allegorical guise of Chaos and Night, constitutes a state of being so light that it never occurs at all in created reality. As argued in chapter 4, which set forth Milton's concept of substance as an Aristotelian elaboration of Hebraic *kabod,* God's material potency is a realm of infinite possibility that substantiates created reality. Indeed, unlike created reality, chaos exists necessarily and absolutely as an essential dimension of divine being, and its lightness is fundamental to the inexpressible weight of divine majesty. In fact, in the context of such unlimited existential possibility, the actual created world appears as a rather whimsical state of affairs. Things could be otherwise, infinitely so.

Given the theoretical claim of chapter 4 that an infinite potential for otherness permeates (and at bottom is) substance, chapters 5 through 8 described the respective stations of Milton's epic characters according to their metamorphic and metaphorical natures. In *Paradise Lost,* creatures *must* change in order to participate in the ultimate apotheosis of creature with God, and such change occurs primarily through rational and volitional processes that Milton expresses through metaphors of food and love. Combining alchemical and Ovidian perspectives to render the simultaneously material and psychological nature of these processes, chapter 5 reconstructed the nutritional and sexual dynamics of Milton's cosmos.

The horror of Satan's lot — and of damnation generally as described in chapter 6 — lies in the fact that those in hell cannot be otherwise. Enjoying none of the gustatory or sexual pleasures of unfallen creatures, Satan lives only as the eternal adversary. Despite his many changes, he remains fixed in his opposition to God's creation, its variety determining his ceaseless oscillations. From an ironic perspective, it is therefore Satan who suffers the weight of unalterable being, though mere contradiction defines his inescapable fate. The heaviness of his existence indeed takes much the shape of Nietzsche's myth of eternal return; all his changes, far from providing refuge from his burden, simply track his unending opposition to God's metamorphic creation.

With God representing the perfect fulfillment of being and Satan striving for its contradiction, humanity seems designed to strike a balance between the giddy weight of boundless divine sameness ("I am that I am") and the heavy changes of Satanic difference ("Evil be thou my Good"). I argued in chapter 7 that Adam and Eve are created in Satan's image as well as in God's and that through Man God offers to heal a great division in the fabric of being, one first symbolized by the "discontinuous wound" that Michael inflicts on Satan.[4] In a unanimously figurative creation, Adam and Eve provide, especially in the unique institution of marriage, the definitive metaphor for the approach to apocalyptic harmony. Through them, God sanctifies the originally Satanic ambition to ascend as well as the love of a creature for its *own* image. Thus suspended morally as well as cosmologically between hell and heaven, or between "is not" and "is," Milton's version of an essentially figurative humanity represents a metaphysically indeterminate, emphatically semiotic rendition of Man's traditional position on the Great Chain of Being.

While humankind is notable for its metaphorical balance of sameness and difference, angels enjoy greater metonymical proximity to God, as well as the material and intellectual advantages that accrue to being nearer to God than we. Chapter 8 analyzed the significant distinctions between human beings and angels and then, having completed the relative positioning of Man in Milton's cosmos, represented the Fall as the disintegration of Adam and Eve's metamorphic bias toward heaven. The infinite capacity for otherness implicit in Milton's cosmos makes the tragedy of the Fall all the more striking and inevitably leads to the question of theodicy. In its final two chapters this study turned to that question and particularly to the ramifications of God's insistence on his own glory for the justification of his ways to men.

That God should create for his glory's sake need not constitute an objection to his character. Basic to the idea of glory is the natural tendency of all being toward ostentation and signification. As Raphael's famed plant simile testifies (5, 479–82), the energy of life works toward a flowering and spiritual advancement that declares both the distinctive identity of a creature and its communal inclination to return to its source. In rational creatures, the tendency represented by the flowering of plants appears as the inborn desire to know and praise God. The universality and instinctiveness of this desire appear clearly on the last day that breaks for unfallen humanity:

> when all things that breathe
> From th' Earth's great Altar send up silent praise
> To the Creator, and his Nostrils fill
> With grateful Smell, forth came the human pair
> And join'd thir vocal Worship to the Choir
> Of Creatures wanting voice.   (9, 194–99)

In Miltonic nature, the pervasive inclination to glorify God manifests an inescapable fact of being. One does not question a flower's bloom. A creature must go against the grain of all existence, including its own nature, to neglect the praise of God. Yet even when we define creatures' praise of God as proceeding from a native tendency, latent in chaos and actualized by God's formative will, we still may ask why the categorical imperative of glorification becomes the occasion of so much evil. As chapter 9 indicated, the sacrifices required of rational creatures in order to glorify God in the moral realm raise doubts as to the kind of pleasure desired by the creator.

Chapter 10 consequently set out to examine the distinction between natural and moral glory and in so doing proposed that the second divinity manifests this distinction: as the Word he mediates the natural order, and as the Son he mediates the moral order. The exaltation of the Son thus explicitly unfolds the ethical counterpart of the metaphysical indeterminancy of Milton's cosmos. That is, given that the substance of goodness is materially equivalent to the substance of being, it must similarly be constituted by the potential for otherness. In this respect, the lightness of being is for Milton a universal principle, as logically it must be given his affirmation of free choice: a God of absolute power and definite purpose must have recourse to infinite options if Man's will is to be free. The good that we know, which derives from God's infinite essence, only illustrates or exemplifies the potential good that we know not. The Son, as the metamorphic creature par excellence, is capable of participating at all levels and in any form of created being. But he possesses no authority over the realm of possibility, which substantiates the definitively divine attributes of omniscience, omnipresence, and omnipotence. Nevertheless, no matter what circumstances develop within the finite, actual realm over which he presides, no matter how events appear to detract from God's glory, the Son is metamorphosed in a fashion that allows him to accommodate the apparent deviation to the ultimate purpose of all creation. He adapts even the fallen Satan's dynamic version of glory — "From this descent / Celestial Virtues rising, will appear / More glorious" — to divine purposes (2, 14–16).

The perfection of the Son's exaltation thus occurs only after he drops to apparently the absolute nadir of *doxa*. He takes the form of a baby born in a barn and later, spat upon and beaten, undergoes the shameful execution of an ideological criminal and religious heretic. In Jesus, Satan sees an image of his defeated self ultimately transformed into a participant with God. He is of course an image with a key difference. While Satan suffers defeat in attempting to establish his own glory apart from God, the Son suffers martyrdom in the course of his glorification of God. The perfect testimony of martyrdom represents the most genuine and costly praise that can be offered to God and, at the same time, the most certain path toward one's own glory. In the end, therefore, the strategy behind Milton's theodicy does reflect typical Reformation thought. As Luther insists, "The Christian will boast most proudly in the glory of Christ, who was born, who suffered and died," for by following the example of

Christ, "we are made illustrious and we become beautiful, as every concrete does through its abstract."[5] Satan may well stand up for that part of Man that seeks autonomy, but the Son justifies God by allowing creatures to become divine.

Yet I think it improper to claim success for Milton's theodicy simply because through the Son creatures can at some future date participate in divinity. As William Kerrigan has observed, "Theodicy arises from the threat of revulsion at this world, and insofar as the argument concludes without transforming this attitude, it goes nowhere."[6] According to the argument of this book, however, the rational success of Milton's theodicy is limited and largely negative, amounting chiefly to a defense against the charge that God intends corruption for his glory's sake. Nonetheless, even this accomplishment should not be slighted. If Milton's epic offers no solution to the problem of pain, it does reassure us that we do not live under an order intentionally designed to produce misery. In this respect, *Paradise Lost* casts the absolutely necessary foundation for what, according to Kenneth Burke, all literature attempts to provide its readers — "equipment for living."[7] In depicting Adam and Eve ultimately coping with their Fall, Milton poignantly illustrates the noble human capacity for grace under pressure. Hazlitt's classic observations on Adam and Eve, in whom "hung trembling all our hopes and fears," aptly express the metaphysical poise that Milton makes available to us through them:

> They stood awhile perfect, but they afterwards fell, and were driven out of Paradise, tasting the first fruits of bitterness as they had done of bliss. But their pangs were such as a pure spirit might feel at the sight — their tears "such as angels weep." The pathos is of that mild contemplative kind which arises from regret for the loss of unspeakable happiness, and resignation to inevitable fate. There is none of the fierceness of intemperate passion, none of the agony of mind and turbulence of action, which is the result of habitual struggles of the will with circumstances, irritated by repeated disappointment, and constantly setting its desires on that which there is an impossibility of attaining.[8]

The power of Milton's theodicy, indeed the glory of *Paradise Lost*, lies in its capacity to awaken or refresh its readers' resilience and potential for quiet dignity even in the face of tragedy.

Human equanimity under the brute consciousness that things might have happened differently is the most clearly heroic behavior in *Paradise Lost*, and such heroism, despite the claims of recent scholarship, is not so much a matter of submission and obedience as it is of contemplation and resolution. The complete vulnerability that Eve determinedly suffers in begging Adam's forgiveness is astounding in its mediatory power. And the decision to procreate, despite what could happen and despite the death that surely will, reflects a kind of heroism about which angel and devil can know little if anything. Next to them, the angels seem to me to be little more than automata — and sterile, promiscuous, monosexual automata at that.[9] Only *after* Adam and Eve's display of resolve are they given more than a mysterious hint of the triumph that will follow their decision to go on with life — and death. Their heroism appears most clearly in the last lines of the epic when they exit the Garden alone together to encounter what the world has in store. Here Milton's sense of glory is at its ripest as human sturdiness in the face of the unknown is most fully present. Although we may question the order of glory that Milton's God has established, at this moment humankind displays its own capacity for noble splendor in a fashion quite unimaginable in the prelapsarian world.

NOTES

INDEX

NOTES

Introduction

1. Throughout this study I use *apocalypse* and *apocalyptic* in a relatively limited, temporally schematic sense to indicate simply the end of time and the end of the process of glorification. I am aware that *the apocalypse* meant much more than that to a seventeenth-century Christian. For the broader implications of the apocalypse and their relevance to Milton's thought, see Leland Ryken, *The Apocalyptic Vision in Paradise Lost* (Ithaca, N.Y.: Cornell University Press, 1970); Austin C. Dobbins, *Milton and the Book of Revelation* (University, Ala.: University of Alabama Press, 1975); and Michael Fixler, *Milton and the Kingdoms of God* (London: Faber and Faber, 1964).

2. *Luther's Works*, gen. eds. Jaroslav Pelikan and Helmut T. Lehmann, 55 vols. (St. Louis, Mo., Concordia, Kans., and Philadelphia: Fortress Press, 1955–76), 26, 227. Except where otherwise noted, subsequent citations of Luther will be to this edition, hereafter abbreviated as *LW*.

3. This and all future citations of Milton's poetry refer to *John Milton: Complete Poems and Major Prose*, ed. Merritt Y. Hughes (New York: Odyssey, 1957).

4. C. S. Lewis, *The Weight of Glory* (New York: Macmillan, 1949), p. 8.

5. The scattered references to glory in Milton scholarship testify to the range of meanings associated with this concept. R. B. Jenkins, *Milton and the Theme of Fame* (The Hague: Mouton, 1973), considers glory as a synonym for fame, and Arnold Stein, *Heroic Knowledge* (Hamden, Conn.: Archon, 1965), agrees that, as in *Lycidas*, glory equals fame minus the intervening variable of fortune, the "perfect witness of all-judging Jove" (pp. 78–83). However, Joan Malory Webber, *Milton and His Epic Tradition* (Seattle: University of Washington Press, 1979), wrote that glory "has a rich biblical meaning, now lapsed into obscurity" (p. 200). Moreover, C. A. Patrides, *Milton and the Christian Tradition* (Oxford: Clarendon Press, 1966), has noted the traditional Christian assertion that "'the principal end of our Creation' is the glory of God" (p. 38), and fame surely does not adequately substitute as a synonym for glory in this case. Nor would fame serve for Merritt Y. Hughes' claim, "Mil-

ton and the Sense of Glory," *PQ* 28 (1949), pp. 107–24, that Milton understood "the historical process from the world's creation to its end as begun for the glory of God and ending in the glory of both men and God" (p. 107). Surprisingly, Hughes and Denis Saurat, *Milton: Man and Thinker* (New York: Dial Press, 1935), seem vaguely to agree on the general meaning of glory, though Saurat stressed Milton's pursuit of Milton's glory: "There is no contradiction, no inconsistency, between the two parts of Milton's life . . . they are one: the search for the glory of Milton" (p. 25). Even more surprisingly, William Empson, *Milton's God* (1961; Cambridge: Cambridge University Press, 1981), agrees with Patrides concerning Christianity's traditional assertion of the final cause of creation, but he finds a sinister and tyrannic necessity in this divine principle (p. 155). More recent scholarship has left it to the forthright Stella Purce Revard, *The War in Heaven* (Ithaca, N.Y.: Cornell University Press, 1980), to ask the obvious question, "But what is glory?" She goes on to assert that "it is a term closely connected with God and with the Son as he is the image of God" (p. 256). Aside from the insightful Revard, only Francis Blessington, *Paradise Lost and the Classical Epic* (London: Routledge and Kegan Paul, 1979), pp. 83–85, and, before him, William J. Grace, *Ideas in Milton* (South Bend, Ind.: University of Notre Dame Press, 1968), pp. 66–67, have attempted to explain what glory means beyond mere fame. Their accounts, however, are intended only as brief summaries and do not set out fully to define glory.

6. C. S. Lewis, *A Preface to Paradise Lost* (London: Oxford University Press, 1942), p. 1. Subsequent textual references are to this edition.

7. E. D. Hirsch, Jr., "Objective Interpretation," *PMLA* 75 (1960), p. 469. Like Hirsch (p. 467), I use "intention" in Husserl's sense of the term as, roughly speaking, awareness or consciousness of a given mental phenomenon – in this case, the verbal meaning of *Paradise Lost*.

8. Ibid., p. 476.

9. Although he does not identify chaos with God, W.B.C. Watkins, *An Anatomy of Milton's Verse* (Hamden, Conn.: Archon Books, 1965), does assert that "matter is to all intents and purposes the feminine aspect of God" (p. 63). The standard opinions of Milton scholarship concerning chaos are surveyed in chapter 4.

10. Hirsch "Objective Interpretation," p. 476. In attempting to assess Milton's "typical outlook," I resort first to his own works, and in matters of theology to his *Christian Doctrine* before other theological works in the Christian tradition. I am aware that this commonsense practice has been reversed by at least one interpreter concerned to defend the orthodoxy of *Paradise Lost*. See C. A. Patrides, "Milton and the Arian Controversy: Or, Some Reflexions on Contextual Settings and the Experience of Deuteroscopy," *Proceedings of the American Philosophical Society* 120 (1976), pp. 245–52.

11. Two recent studies have focused on the relations between Milton and Ovid: Louis Martz, *Poet of Exile* (New Haven, Conn.: Yale University Press, 1980); Richard J. DuRocher, *Milton and Ovid* (Ithaca, N.Y.: Cornell University Press, 1985). Martz's book touches only tangentially on the concerns of my argument. Although DuRocher's book is more directly pertinent, it appeared too recently for me to be able to take advantage of its insights.

12. Empson, *Milton's God*, p. 319.

13. Stanley E. Fish, *Surprised by Sin* (1967; Berkeley and Los Angeles: University of California Press, 1971), p. 289.

14. It could be argued that the Milton of the last twenty years is increasingly a Protestant Milton. I prefer the older, more balanced view expressed, for example, by Douglas Bush in *The Renaissance and English Humanism* (Toronto: University of Toronto Press, 1939), pp. 101–34.

15. *Luther and Erasmus: Free Will and Salvation*, ed. E. Gordon Rupp and Philip Watson (Philadelphia: Westminster Press, Library of Christian Classics, 1979), 17, 331–32. Subsequent references in the text are by page number to this volume in this edition.

16. Dennis Danielson, *Milton's Good God* (Cambridge: Cambridge University Press, 1982), forms a notable exception to the general indifference of recent scholarship to Milton's theodicy. His book sets out in detail the relation of Milton's assertion of free will to his theodicy. Though he describes this relation primarily in terms of Arminianism, he also demonstrates Milton's alignment with Erasmus and opposition to Luther and stresses the importance of the notion of prevenient or enabling grace to this position (pp. 66–69).

17. On certain occasions in this study, I find it best to use the capitalized word *Man* to express the meaning "all human beings." When I use the same term to refer to a male human being, I use the lower case.

18. Jeffrey Barnouw, "The Separation of Reason and Faith in Bacon and Hobbes, and in Leibniz's Theodicy," *Journal of the History of Ideas* 42 (1981), p. 628.

19. Fish, *Surprised by Sin*, p. 9.

20. Leopold Damrosch, Jr., *God's Plot and Man's Stories* (Chicago: University of Chicago Press, 1985), pp. 80–87, reverses Lewis and offers the novel suggestion that if Milton errs in his representation of God, he errs by not making him anthropomorphic enough.

Chapter 1. Glory in the Old Testament

1. Joseph Mead, *The Complete Works*, ed. John Worthington (London, 1677), p. 92.

2. On Milton's translations of the Psalms and his knowledge of Hebrew, see William B. Hunter, Jr., "Milton Translates the Psalms," *PQ* 40 (1961), pp. 485–94.

3. *The Holy Bible: Authorized (King James) Version* (1611; London: William Collins, 1911). All subsequent references in the text are to this edition.

4. On Milton's translation of the Psalms as indicative of his own opinions and not simply as ciphers of the tradition, see W. R. Parker, *Milton: A Life*, 2 vols. (Oxford: Clarendon Press, 1968), 1, 18; Mary Ann Radzinowicz, *Toward Samson Agonistes* (Princeton, N.J.: Princeton University Press, 1978), pp. 189–208.

5. In developing the etymology of *kabod*, I have used a number of sources, including only those points about which there is general agreement. See Klaus Thraede, "Gloria," in *Reallexikon fur Antike und Christentum*, ed. Theodor Klauser (Stuttgart, W. Germany: Anton Hiersemann, 1979), Lieferung 82, pp. 196–225; *The Interpreter's Dictionary of the Bible*, ed. George Buttrick, 4 vols. (New York: Abingdon Press, 1962), 2, 401–3; Gerhard von Rad, *Old Testament Theology*, trans. D.M.G.

Stalker, 2 vols. (New York: Harper and Row, 1962), 1, 239–41; Edmund Jacob, *Theology of the Old Testament*, trans. Arthur W. Heathcote and Philip J. Allcock (London: Hodder and Stoughton, 1958), pp. 80–81; Everett Falconer Harrison, "The Use of Doxa in Greek Literature with Special Reference to the New Testament," diss., University of Pennsylvania, 1950.

6. *LW* 6, 6.

7. Ibid.

8. *LW* 26, 20.

9. This and subsequent citations of Aristotle are from *The Basic Works of Aristotle*, ed. Richard P. McKeon (New York: Random House, 1941).

10. Subsequent references to Milton's prose appear in the text by volume and page from *The Complete Prose Works*, gen. ed. Don M. Wolfe, 8 vols. (New Haven, Conn.: Yale University Press, 1953–82), hereafter abbreviated as *CP*.

11. On Milton's use of the epic scales, see K. W. Grandsen, "*Paradise Lost* and the *Aeneid*," *EIC* 17 (1967), p. 286.

12. Obviously, the mere fact of literal weight does not make a creature good, just as literal lightness hardly indicates evil. Leviathan is weighty, after all, and flowers most light. Lightness sometimes suggests the readiness for moral ascent, and heaviness the reverse. Furthermore, it would be difficult to construct a useful rule for exactly when weight suggests good or lightness evil, though I would contend that for rational creatures authentic gravity always indicates true glory. A good synonym for authentic gravity would be moral solidity.

13. *LW* 25, 248.

14. *LW* 17, 312.

15. *LW* 26, 102.

16. On Milton and Moses, see William Kerrigan, *The Prophetic Milton* (Charlottesville: University of Virginia Press, 1974), pp. 88–90, 122–24, 128–30. Kerrigan cites James Holly Hanford's note, "That Shepherd Who First Taught the Chosen Seed," *UTQ* 8 (1939), pp. 403–19 and contends with William Madsen, who in *From Shadowy Types to Truth* (New Haven, Conn.: Yale University Press, 1968), pp. 52, 72–81, claims that Milton and Moses are not comparable because Moses possesses knowledge not available to the Hebrews. Milton, says Madsen, preaches that, under the new dispensation, knowledge of God is equally available to every Christian.

17. J. M. Evans, *Paradise Lost and the Genesis Tradition* (Oxford: Clarendon Press, 1968), p. 40.

Chapter 2.   Homeric Glory

1. On the ancient Greek's desire for everlasting fame, see C. M. Bowra, *The Greek Experience* (New York: World Publishing, 1958), pp. 20–41; Werner Jaeger, *Paideia*, trans. Gilbert Highet, 3 vols. (New York: Oxford University Press, 1945), 1, 12–14. Throughout this chapter, I am indebted to Jaeger's commentary on Homer (1, 3–56). For definitions of *kleos, timé,* and *kudos* I am also indebted to James M. Redfield, *Nature and Culture in the Iliad* (Chicago: University of Chicago Press, 1975), pp. 30–35.

2. Quotations of Homer are from Robert Fitzgerald's translations of the *Iliad*

(New York: Anchor, 1975) and the *Odyssey* (New York: Anchor, 1963). The line numbers in parenthetical citations correspond to the Greek texts.

3. Milton scholars generally have concluded with John Steadman, *Milton and the Renaissance Hero* (Oxford: Clarendon Press, 1967), p. vi, that Milton rejects "the classical conception of the hero" and instead "explores the theological preconditions and limitations of heroic virtue." Steadman goes on to claim that Milton "exposes" the "heroic pretenses of . . . traditional heroes as essentially diabolical" (p. 170). This exaggeration is a typical example of what has become a popular tenet of Milton scholarship. Witness, for example, C. M. Bowra, *From Virgil to Milton* (New York: St. Martin's Press, 1945), pp. 229-30; Stanley E. Fish, *Surprised by Sin* (1967; Berkeley and Los Angeles: University of California Press, 1971), p. 162; Dennis Burden, *The Logical Epic* (Cambridge, Mass.: Harvard University Press, 1967), p. 11; Georgia B. Christopher, *Milton and the Science of the Saints* (Princeton, N.J.: Princeton University Press, 1982), p. 77; Joan Malory Webber, *Milton and His Epic Tradition* (Seattle: University of Washington Press, 1979), pp. 119-20; Stella Purce Revard, *The War in Heaven* (Ithaca, N.Y.: Cornell University Press, 1980), pp. 266-72.

For a more balanced and accurate reading of Milton's attitude toward classical heroism as it appears in the characters and construction of *Paradise Lost,* see Davis P. Harding, *The Club of Hercules* (Urbana: University of Illinois Press, 1962), pp. 24-46, and Francis Blessington, *Paradise Lost and the Classical Epic* (London: Routledge and Kegan Paul, 1979).

4. Redfield, *Nature and Culture,* p. 33.

5. Ibid.

6. Revard, *War in Heaven,* p. 254.

7. My discussion of *areté* is particularly indebted to Jaeger's *Paideia* (1, 3-34).

8. Opposed to those who trace *areté* to *aresko* ("to please"), Jaeger remarks that "it is true that *areté* often contains an element of social recognition — its meaning then alters to 'esteem,' 'respect.' But that is a secondary sense. . . . The word must originally have been an objective description of the worth of its possessor, of a power peculiar to him, which makes him a complete man" (ibid., p. 418). Note the parallel with *kabod.*

9. Ibid., p. 9. On Homeric society as a "shame-culture," as opposed to a "guilt-culture," see E. R. Dodds, *The Greeks and the Irrational* (Berkeley and Los Angeles: University of California Press, 1951), pp. 17-18.

10. Christopher Hill details Milton's ambivalence toward the common people in *Milton and the English Revolution* (New York: Viking, 1977), pp. 69-79, 89-92, 113-14, 160-62. Hill sees in Milton a fiercer foe of the hereditary aristocracy than is justified by his writings.

11. The return to order and life celebrated in *Paradise Regain'd* and the *Odyssey* lies outside the scope of this study. For a general description of the parallels between them, see Webber, *Milton and His Epic Tradition,* pp. 167-209.

12. W. Thomas MacCary, *Childlike Achilles: Ontogeny and Phylogeny in the Iliad* (New York: Columbia University Press, 1982), pp. 17-29. Webber similarly observed that human consciousness is intimately connected to, and in part constituted by, the awareness of death. Moreover, claims Webber, "Any definition of literary

epic that will work must begin with the fact of mortality, and with the effort to deal with the sadness of this condition" (*Milton and His Epic Tradition*, p. 12).

13. MacCary, *Childlike Achilles*, p. xii.

14. William Kerrigan, "The Heretical Milton: From Assumption to Mortalism," *ELR* 5 (1975), pp. 143–44.

15. Jasper Griffen, *Homer on Life and Death* (Oxford: Clarendon Press, 1980), pp. 45–47.

16. Ibid., pp. 89–90; Redfield explains that on the battlefield man becomes to man "as predator to prey" (*Nature and Culture*, pp. 196–99). Thus not only does Akhilleus threaten to make mincemeat out of Hektor, but also Zeus says that Hera wants to "eat the Trojans raw"; Hecuba wishes she could rip out Akhilleus' liver and tear it with her teeth (4, 35–36; 24, 212–13). Appropriately, in Book XIII of his *Metamorphoses*, Ovid has Hecuba transformed into a dog, the animal Homer most often associates with the ingestion of raw meat (565ff.).

17. Kerrigan, "Heretical Milton," p. 137; as Redfield argues, the death of heroes on the battlefield becomes the occasion for an antifuneral of abuse and mutilation for the corpse (*Nature and Culture*, pp. 183–86).

18. Redfield, *Nature and Culture*, p. 34; Griffen, *Homer on Life and Death*, p. 98.

19. Bowra, *Greek Experience*, pp. 200–201.

20. Milton refers to the competition between Aias and Odysseus in *The Second Defense* (*CP* 4, i, 595).

21. Thucydides, *The Peloponnesian War*, ed. Benjamin Jowett, 2 vols. (Oxford: Clarendon Press, 1900), 1, 133.

22. C. S. Lewis, *A Preface to Paradise Lost* (London: Oxford University Press, 1942), pp. 28–30.

23. Griffen, *Homer on Life and Death*, p. 55.

24. Ibid., p. 91.

25. Ibid., p. 95.

26. Despite the recognition from the first that God sometimes relents even though his people deserve punishment and that sometimes righteous men — like Abel or Job — suffer for no apparent reason, the Deuteronomic ethic, so called for the book of the Pentateuch that states it most explicitly, remains a standard, conservative view among the Jews through the time of Christ. In the gospels, the wealthy, complacent, politically potent Saducees and, to a lesser extent, the self-righteous Pharisees, champion this ethos.

Chapter 3. Glory Revised

1. In addition to sources listed in chap. 1, n. 8, I use the following in developing the meaning of *doxa*: *Theological Dictionary of the New Testament*, ed. Gerhard Kittel, trans. G. W. Bromiley, 10 vols. (Grand Rapids, Mich.: William B. Eerdmans, 1964), 2, 223–44; L. H. Brockington, "The Greek Translator of Isaiah and His Interest in Doxa," *Vetus Testamentum* 1 (1951), pp. 27–31.

2. Plato, *Republic* 5, 478d. This and subsequent references to Plato are from *The Collected Dialogues of Plato*, ed. Edith Hamilton and Huntington Cairns (Princeton, N.J.: Princeton University Press, 1963).

3. *Dictionary of the New Testament*, 2, 238.

4. "The Migration of Abraham," *Philo*, ed. F. H. Colson and G. H. Whitaker, 10 vols. (London: William Heinemann, 1962), 4, 185.

5. Plato, *Republic* 3, 413b.

6. Ernst Cassirer, "The Subject-Object Problem in the Philosophy of the Renaissance," chap. 4 of *The Individual and the Cosmos in Renaissance Philosophy*, trans. Mario Domandi (New York: Barnes and Noble, 1963), p. 191.

7. Jaeger, *Paideia*, 1, 13.

8. George Sandys, *Ovid's Metamorphosis Englished*, ed. Karl H. Hulley and Stanley Vandersall (Lincoln: University of Nebraska Press, 1970), p. 572.

9. Northrop Frye, "Agon and Logos," in *The Prison and the Pinnacle*, ed. Balachandra Rajan (Toronto: University of Toronto Press, 1973), p. 136.

10. Ibid., p. 136.

11. Philip E. Slater, *The Glory of Hera* (Boston: Beacon Press, 1968), p. 38.

12. Ibid., p. 36.

13. Stella Purce Revard, *The War in Heaven* (Ithaca, N.Y.: Cornell University Press, 1980), pp. 254–55.

14. C. S. Lewis, *A Preface to Paradise Lost* (London: Oxford University Press, 1942), p. 36.

15. Augustine, *The City of God*, trans. John Healy (New York: E. P. Dutton, 1931), p. 219.

16. Jacob Burckhardt, *The Civilization of the Renaissance in Italy*, trans. S.G.C. Middlemore (New York: Harper, 1929), p. 151.

17. Sir Philip Sidney, *The Defence of Poesy*, in Sidney, *Selected Prose and Poetry*, 2nd ed., ed. Robert Kimbrough (Madison: University of Wisconsin Press, 1983), p. 113.

18. Ibid.

19. Ibid., p. 116.

20. John Robinson, *Essayes or Observations Divine and Morall Collected Out of Holy Scriptures, Ancient and Moderne Writers, Both Divine and Humane* (London, 1638), p. 227.

21. On Milton's intention to write an Arthuriad, see E.M.W. Tillyard, *The Miltonic Setting* (London: Chatto and Windus, 1947), pp. 168–204. Tillyard persuasively reasons that "Milton could not write an epic in praise of his country after he believed that his country had failed in its crisis" (p. 199).

22. C. M. Bowra, *The Greek Experience* (New York: World Publishing, 1958), p. 34.

23. On the impact of the Restoration on those who survived the defeat, see Christopher Hill, *The Experience of Defeat* (New York: Viking, 1984).

Chapter 4. Divine Potency

1. On the importance of weight in Aristotle's metaphysics, see D. O'Brien, "Heavy and Light in Democritus and Aristotle: Two Conceptions of Change and Identity," *Journal of Hellenic Studies* 97 (1977) pp. 64–74.

2. Treatments of Milton's use of the term *subtance* against a background com-

posed of a wide variety of thinkers—Plotinus, Cicero, Aquinas, the Stoics, Asthanius, Arius, and Ralph Cudworth, to name a few—appear in the following works: William B. Hunter, Jr., C. A. Patrides, and J. H. Adamson, *Bright Essence* (Salt Lake City: University of Utah Press, 1971), pp. 3–62; Barbara Lewalski, *Milton's Brief Epic* (Providence, R.I.: Brown University Press, 1966), pp. 137–53; Walter Clyde Curry, *Milton's Ontology, Cosmogony, and Physics* (Lexington: University of Kentucky Press, 1957).

3. For the concentration on Aristotle in the Cambridge curriculum, see Harris F. Fletcher, *The Intellectual Development of John Milton*, 2 vols. (Urbana: University of Illinois Press, 1956), 2, 67; William T. Costello, *The Scholastic Curriculum at Early Seventeenth-Century Cambridge* (Cambridge, Mass.: Harvard University Press, 1958), pp. 70–102; Kathryn A. McEuen provides a solid introduction to Milton's relationship to Aristotle in *CP* 1, 261–64 and offers a bibliography on the versions of Aristotle available to Renaissance thinkers.

4. References to Aristotle are taken mainly from Book VII of the *Metaphysics* because it contains Aristotle's "definitive discussion of substance," according to Edwin Hartman, "Aristotle on Identity," *Philosophical Review* 85 (1976), p. 548. Hartman demonstrates that Aristotle modified his early concept of substance as it appears in the *Categories*. In his mature work, Aristotle argues that in order to avoid a dependence on Platonic Universals or a slide into the sheer multiplicity of Democritus' atomism, one must present "criteria for substantiality . . . and show how material objects fit the criteria better than anything else does." The criteria he devised are that a substance must be "in a clear way knowable and definable . . . prior to the accidents it may at any time have and to the matter that may at any time constitute it" ("Aristotle on Identity," p. 548). See also Christopher Stead, *Divine Substance* (Oxford: Clarendon Press, 1977), pp. 55–88.

5. On the active/passive interaction animating all of creation in *Paradise Lost,* see Joseph H. Summers, *The Muse's Method* (Cambridge, Mass.: Harvard University Press, 1962), pp. 87–111; and especially W.B.C. Watkins, *An Anatomy of Milton's Verse* (Hamden, Conn.: Archon Books, 1965), pp. 37, 59–71.

6. William B. Hunter, Jr., "Some Problems in John Milton's Theological Vocabulary," in Hunter, Patrides, and Adamson, *Bright Essence*, p. 20. See Stead, *Divine Substance*, pp. 118–25.

7. Hunter, "Milton's Theological Vocabulary," p. 20, presents three categories of substance—individuality, specific genus, and the substratum—as if they were distinct meanings of the term and not related perspectives on the same topic.

8. "Specific character" is a decidedly Aristotelian locution. See Stead, *Divine Substance*, p. 61.

9. Lewalski, *Brief Epic*, p. 138.

10. The Greek word *kosmos* means, primarily, "ornament" or "decoration" and thence, the "material universe" in an ordered and beautiful state.

11. Compare Plato's *Philebus* 16c–e, 23c–d. On the Platonic view of substance see Stead, *Divine Substance*, pp. 42–54.

12. The term *ostentation* is sometimes used by philosophers to refer to the material manifestations of a substance. See Hartman, "Aristotle on Identity," p. 547.

13. O'Brien, "Heavy and Light," p. 74.

14. A. B. Chambers, "Chaos in *Paradise Lost,*" *JHI* 24 (1963), p. 65.

15. Ibid., pp. 65, 69.

16. O'Brien, "Heavy and Light," p. 74.

17. Ibid.

18. Ibid.

19. Charles Trinkaus, *In Our Image and Likeness,* 2 vols. (Chicago: University of Chicago Press, 1970), 1, 70.

20. *LW* 14, 114.

21. Philip Watson, *Let God be God!* (Philadelphia: Fortress Press, 1947), p. 80.

22. Watkins, *Anatomy of Milton's Verse,* p. 3.

23. C. S. Lewis admits the possibility that potentiality is essential to Milton's God in *A Preface to Paradise Lost* (London: Oxford University Press, 1942), p. 88. See also Curry, *Ontology, Cosmogony, and Physics,* p. 34.

24. Isabel MacCaffrey, *Paradise Lost as "Myth"* (Cambridge, Mass.: Harvard University Press, 1959), p. 164.

25. Ibid., pp. 164–65.

26. Ibid., p. 164.

27. Ibid.

28. Curry, *Ontology, Cosmogony, and Physics,* pp. 34–35.

29. Ibid., pp. 37, 146.

30. Ibid., p. 77.

31. I am indebted to Steve Fallon of the University of Notre Dame for this observation.

32. Curry identifies chaos with the remote secondary matter, or the "prepared" matter out of which God makes the world. It appears to me, however, that remote secondary matter would refer to the "matter unform'd and void: Darkness profound," which occurs *after* "God the Heav'n created, [and] the Earth" (*PL* 7, 232–33).

33. Georgia B. Christopher, *Milton and the Science of the Saints* (Princeton, N.J.: Princeton University Press, 1982), p. 21.

34. Despite the potential for confusion, Milton uses the term *form* to apply also to genera. He distinguished between the two varieties of form as *proper* and *common.* Common form is an intellectual convenience — the genus, "something which in thought and reason is one and the same thing common to many species." Proper form, by way of contrast, "in fact and by nature . . . occurs individually" (*CP* 8, 301). Milton thus writes that "if all things which differ in number also differ in essence, but not by reason of their matter, then they necessarily differ by reason of their forms. But this is not by reason of common forms; hence it is by reason of proper ones. Thus the rational soul is the form of man generically; the soul of Socrates is the proper form of Socrates" (*CP* 8, 233–34). In Milton's usage, form always indicates one thing as distinct from another. If we speak of common forms, we are speaking of degrees of matter — man as opposed to angel or rock, for example. Adam unites proper and common form at his creation because he is the only extant man.

35. Milton's innovation follows from his separation of the ontological and metaphysical grounds of existence. For Milton, matter is the ontological base upon which

reality rests. But even though matter is the potential or prerequisite for reality, it never itself occurs in reality. Form is the shape matter takes when it enters actual existence.

Milton's distinction between matter as the ontological prerequisite of reality and form as the metaphysical principle of reality — matter indicating what is common to all being, form what is proper to particular beings — was anticipated by earlier thinkers, particularly Ibn Gabirol (Avicebron) and to some degree by those influenced by him, such as Duns Scotus and Ficino. See Curry, *Ontology, Cosmogony and Physics*, pp. 163–71, and Trinkaus, *Image and Likeness*, 2, 504.

36. According to Ibn Gabirol, prime matter is the *"genus generalissium"*; for a brief summary of Gabirol's thought, see Etienne Gilson, *History of Christian Philosophy in the Middle Ages* (New York: Random House, 1955), pp. 226–29.

37. Ibid., p. 648.

38. By "various forms, various degrees / Of Substance" Milton probably meant Raphael to refer to genera. Thus "forms" in this context would mean "common" forms.

39. William Empson, *Milton's God* (1961; Cambridge: Cambridge University Press, 1981), pp. 147–59.

Chapter 5. The Metamorphic Epic

1. Davis P. Harding, *Milton and the Renaissance Ovid* (Urbana: University of Illinois Press, 1946), pp. 26–57.

2. Ibid., pp. 55–57.

3. John Reesing, *Milton's Poetic Art* (Cambridge, Mass.: Harvard University Press, 1968), p. 5.

4. Harding, *Milton and Ovid*, p. 57.

5. Edward Tayler, *Milton's Poetry: Its Development in Time* (Pittsburgh, Pa.: Duquesne University Press, 1979), p. 205.

6. George Huntston Williams, *The Radical Reformation* (Philadelphia: Westminster Press, 1962), p. 259.

7. Christopher Hill, *Milton and the English Revolution* (New York: Viking, 1977), p. 259. For a lucid exposition of the worldview that Hill claims has already disintegrated by Milton's time, see C. S. Lewis, *The Discarded Image* (London: Cambridge University Press, 1964).

8. Works of interest for an appreciation of the intellectual history of the seventeenth century are Paolo Rossi, *Francis Bacon, From Magic to Science*, trans. Sacha Rabinovitch (Chicago: University of Chicago Press, 1968); Francis A. Yates, *The Rosicrucian Enlightenment* (Boulder, Colo.: Shambala, 1978); Charles Webster, *The Great Instauration: Science, Medicine, and Reform, 1626–1660* (New York: Holmes and Meier, 1975); and D. P. Walker, *The Ancient Theology* (Ithaca, N.Y.: Cornell University Press, 1972).

9. John Worthington, "The Author's Life," in Joseph Mead, *The Works*, ed. Worthington (London, 1677), p. i; Hill, *Milton and the English Revolution*, pp. 33–34; James W. Davidson, *The Logic of Millennial Thought* (New Haven, Conn.: Yale University Press, 1977), pp. 45–47; Thomas Fuller, *The History of the Worthies of*

England, 3 vols. (London, 1840), 1, 519-20; B. G. Cooper, "The Academic Redis-covery of Apocalyptic Ideas in the Seventeenth Century," *Baptist Quarterly* 19 (1961-62), pp. 29-34.

10. Davidson, *Millennial Thought,* pp. 5-6, 12, 57, 61, 169, 222, 230, discusses the millennial speculations of the great scientists.

11. See Edmund Gosse, *Father and Son* (London: Heinemann, 1907).

12. The folktalelike opening of *Lear* led Tolstoy to claim that Shakespeare's ver-sion was actually inferior to its source, but George Orwell suggested other reasons for Tolstoy's perversity; see Frank Kermode, ed. *Four Centuries of Shakespearian Criticism* (New York: Avon, 1965), pp. 513-31.

13. W. H. Auden, "A Joker in the Pack," *The Dyer's Hand* (New York: Random House, 1962), argued that Iago resembles a "practical joker, a parabolic figure for the autonomous pursuit of scientific knowledge through experiment" (p. 270).

14. Lucretius, *De rerum natura,* 3d ed., trans. W. H. D. Rouse (Cambridge, Mass.: Harvard University Press, Loeb Classical Library, 1937), 1, 150, 216.

15. Werner Jaeger, *The Theology of the Early Greek Philosophers* (Oxford: Clar-endon Press, 1947), pp. 7-11.

16. For recent studies of Anaxagoras, see Michael C. Stokes, *One and Many in Presocratic Philosophy* (Cambridge, Mass.: Harvard University Press, 1971), pp. 43-48, 238; Sven-Tage Teodorsson, *Anaxagoras' Theory of Matter* (Goteborg, Sweden: Acta Universitatis Gothoburgensis, 1982); and Malcolm Schofield, *An Essay on Anaxagoras* (Cambridge: Cambridge University Press, 1980).

17. *Plutarch's Lives,* trans. Bernadette Perrin, 10 vols. (New York: Putnam, 1915), 3, 13.

18. Ibid., 3, 11; Plato, in the *Phaedrus,* 270a, and *Epistle II,* 311a, also notes and praises the relationship between Anaxagoras and Pericles.

19. *Plutarch's Lives,* 3, 15.

20. Plato, *Greater Hippias,* 283a; Plato, *Laws XII,* 967b.

21. Plato, *Phaedo* 97b, renders Socrates' account of his study of Anaxagoras.

22. The quotation is from a summary of Anaxagoras' system by Friedrich Nietz-sche, *Early Greek Philosophy and Other Essays,* trans. Maximilian A. Mugge, *The Complete Works of Friedrich Nietzsche,* ed. Oscar Levy, 18 vols. (New York: Russell and Russell, 1964), 2, 147.

23. John Reidy, Introduction to Thomas Norton, *Ordinal of Alchemy* (Oxford: Oxford University Press, 1975), p. lxxiv; William Empson, *Milton's God* (1961; Cam-bridge: Cambridge University Press, 1981), pp. 169-72, first heard the echoes of Para-celsian alchemy in Milton's use of digestion to convey the substantial unity of matter and spirit.

24. Norton, *Ordinal,* p. 7.

25. William Kerrigan, *The Sacred Complex* (Cambridge, Mass.: Harvard Univer-sity Press, 1983), pp. 219-20.

26. On the religious aspects of alchemy, see Arthur E. Waite, *Alchemists Through the Ages* (New York: Rudolph Steiner, 1970), pp. 11, 140; and Lee Stavenhangen, ed., *A Testament of Alchemy* (Hanover, N.H.: University Press of New England, 1974), pp. 64-67. Religious, mystical science — an anatomy and physiology of being,

as it were—flowered in the late Renaissance as an elaboration, at once arcane and exploratory, of the familiar faith in analogical correspondence between God, Man, and the rest of creation. If one understood the correspondences, one presumably could purify one's own being, just as one could make gold out of baser metals. Note that this process is epistemological (or *gnostic*) in its premises. Whatever the practice of transformation might involve, metamorphosis depends first upon knowledge. Consider these words of Robert Fludd in praise of medicine: "More than a simple description of diseases and the workings of the human body, it is the very basis on which natural philosophy must rest. Our knowledge of the microcosm will teach us of the great world, and this in turn will lead us to our Creator. Similarly, as we progress in our understanding of the universe, the more we will be rewarded with a perfect knowledge of ourselves." This quotation appears in Allen G. Debus, *The Chemical Philosophy*, 2 vols. (New York: Neale Watson, 1977), 1, 216. Debus takes it from Fludd, *Tractatus Apologeticus* (Leiden, 1617), pp. 91–93.

27. Reidy, Introduction to Norton, *Ordinal*, p. lxvi.

28. Nietzsche, *Greek Philosophy*, p. 145.

29. John Milton, *Paradise Lost, Books I and II*, ed. F. T. Prince (Oxford: Oxford University Press, 1962), note to 2, 890–916.

30. References to Ovid, *Metamorphoses*, are abbreviated as *Met.* and are by book and line number of the Latin text. The English translation is by George Sandys, *Ovid's Metamorphosis Englished*, ed. Karl H. Hulley and Stanley Vandersall (Lincoln: University of Nebraska Press, 1970). Quotations of Sandys' commentary are by page number from this edition. Milton would have known Sandys' work. Mead lists "Sands Metamorpho" in his book-buying accounts as early as 1622. Harris F. Fletcher, *The Intellectual Development of John Milton*, 2 vols. (Urbana: University of Illinois Press, 1956), 2, 605, points out that Sandys was used by educators as "a standard of excellence of rendering against which the efforts of boys were measured." Chances are, therefore, that Milton would have had access to Sandys even before he left grammar school.

31. Merritt Y. Hughes, "Milton and the Sense of Glory," *PQ* 28 (1949), p. 114.

32. Irving Massey, *The Gaping Pig: Literature and Metamorphosis* (Berkeley and Los Angeles: University of California Press, 1976), p. 19.

33. *LW* 11, 447.

34. Joseph A. Fitzmyer, S.J., "Glory Reflected on the Face of Christ (2 Cor. 3:7–4:6) and a Palestinian Jewish Motif," *Theological Studies* 42 (1981), p. 632.

35. Ibid., p. 639.

Chapter 6. Withered Glory

1. Northrop Frye, *Five Essays on Milton's Epics* (London: Routledge and Kegan Paul, 1966), p. 53.

2. On the apocalyptic implications of the War in Heaven, see William Madsen, *From Shadowy Types to Truth* (New Haven, Conn.: Yale University Press, 1968), pp. 111–13; J. H. Adamson, "The War in Heaven: The Merkabah," in William B. Hunter, Jr., C. A. Patrides, and J. H. Adamson, *Bright Essence* (Salt Lake City: Uni-

versity of Utah Press, 1971), pp. 103–14; William B. Hunter, Jr., "The War in Heaven: The Exaltation of the Son," in ibid., pp. 115–30.

3. J. B. Broadbent, *Some Graver Subject* (London: Chatto and Windus, 1960), pp. 74, 84f.

4. Robert Burton, *The Anatomy of Melancholy*, ed. Floyd Dell and Paul Jordan-Smith (New York: Tudor Publishing, 1955), p. 946. That the inhabitants of hell undergo the same physical processes that characterize their environment testifies to the deep significance of Isabel MacCaffrey's insight into the organic unity of Milton's "mythic" cosmos. See *Paradise Lost as "Myth"* (Cambridge, Mass.: Harvard University Press, 1959), pp. 144–78. The notion that the universe was "comparable to a gigantic living being" was also advanced by Cyrano de Bergerac. See Paolo Rossi, "Nobility of Man and Plurality of Worlds," in *Science, Medicine, and Society in the Renaissance*, ed. Allen G. Debus, 2 vols. (London: Heinemann, 1972), 2, 151.

5. Hughes' note to *PL* 4, 115–20 cites Timothy Bright, *Treatise of Melancholy* (London, 1586), p. 88, on the belief that a perturbation like anger or fear causes "a boyling of heat" near the heart due to a concentration of vital spirits. See also Thomas Wright, *The Passions of the Mind in General* (London, 1604), pp. 27–33; Robert Burton cites Bright, Wright, Agrippa, Cardan, Lemnius, and Suarez on this point, in *Melancholy*, p. 219.

6. On sulphur as the principle of fire, see Henry Alan Skinner, *Medical Terms*, 2d ed. (Baltimore, Md.: Williams and Wilkins, 1961), p. 392; Allen G. Debus, *The Chemical Philosophy*, 2 vols. (New York: Neale Watson, 1977), 1, 80–83.

7. Although according to Debus, *Chemical Philosophy*, 1, 79–80, "Chemical philosophers were turning in increasing numbers to the three principles as a means of explanation," they also "felt free to utilize the four elements . . . as they saw fit." The four elements would have been associated with Galenic medicine, the three principles with Paracelsian. Opposition between these two groups of medical practitioners has been "overly simplified in the past." "A substantial number of physicians believed that compromise was possible between the two camps," says Debus ("Guintherius, Libavius and Sennert: The Chemical Compromise in Early Modern Medicine," in *Science, Medicine and Society*, 1, 151). On Milton's acquaintance with the medical controversies of this period, see William Kerrigan, *The Sacred Complex* (Cambridge, Mass.: Harvard University Press, 1983), pp. 199–200. On Milton and sulphur, see Kester Svendsen, *Milton and Science* (Cambridge, Mass.: Harvard University Press, 1956), p. 123.

8. Joseph Duchesne, *A breefe answere of Joseph Quercetanus Armeniacus, Doctor of Phisick, to the exposition of Iacobus Aubertus Vindonis, concerning the original and Causes of Mettales, Set foorth against the Chimists* (London, 1591), p. 15.

9. Ibid., pp. 8–11.

10. Ibid., p. 9.

11. Ibid. Aside from serving as a theoretical variable for the convenience of seventeenth-century thinkers in fields as diverse as chemistry and ethics, the physical-spiritual phenomenon of spirit was a mainstay of the hermetic and Neoplatonic conviction that no meaningful distinction could be made between animate and inani-

mate. See William Empson, *Milton's God* (1961; Cambridge: Cambridge University Press, 1981), pp. 169–72.

12. Technically, the fire suffered by the demons would be entitled *"ignis corrodens,"* which reverses the progress of a material toward its perfect form. See Thomas Norton, *Ordinal of Alchemy,* ed. John Reidy (Oxford: Oxford University Press, 1975), l. 3037; see also Debus, *Chemical Philosophy,* 1, 81–83.

13. Duchesne, *A breefe answere,* p. 15.

14. Harold Skulsky, *Metamorphosis: The Mind in Exile* (Cambridge, Mass.: Harvard University Press, 1981), pp. 28–29.

15. Ibid., p. 36.

16. Ibid.

17. In *The Civilization of the Renaissance in Italy,* trans. S.G.C. Middlemore (New York: Harper, 1929), p. 152, Jacob Burckhardt comments on the desire of Dante's damned for fame, citing *Inferno* 6, 89; 13, 53; 16, 85; and 31, 127.

18. Skulsky, *Metamorphosis,* p. 32.

19. I follow the usage of Francis Blessington, *Paradise Lost and the Classical Epic* (London: Routledge and Kegan Paul, 1979), p. xiii, wherein he defines *retractio* as "the reworking of a specific scene from an earlier epic" and *contaminatio* as "the conflation of several such scenes."

20. See Kerrigan, *Sacred Complex,* pp. 169–70, on Satan's narcissism.

21. Andrew Marvell, *The Complete Poems,* ed. Elizabeth Story Donno (New York: Penguin, 1972), pp. 49–50. All subsequent references are to this edition.

22. Marjorie Nicolson cites Masson's remark, "Milton and the Telescope," *ELH* 2 (1935), p. 18.

23. Sigmund Freud, "Instincts and Their Vicissitudes," trans. Cecil M. Baines, Essay 4 in *General Psychological Theory,* ed. Philip Rieff (New York: Macmillan, 1963), pp. 83–103. Empson, *Milton's God,* pp. 245–47, argues that the Christian God is a sadist.

Chapter 7. Marriage and Metamorphosis

1. According to J. M. Evans, *Paradise Lost and the Genesis Tradition* (Oxford: Clarendon Press, 1968), pp. 32, 40, some Jewish commentators maintained that Man was created in the image of the good angels as well as of God. This belief softened the polytheistic implications of "in our image." My point, however, is that Man as created appears more closely related, as an image, to the *fallen* angels than to any other creature. On the repopulation of heaven as a traditional motivation for the creation of Man, see C. A. Patrides, *Milton and the Christian Tradition* (Oxford: Clarendon Press, 1966), pp. 37–38.

2. William Kerrigan, *The Sacred Complex* (Cambridge, Mass.: Harvard University Press, 1983), pp. 138–43.

3. For the best-known rendition of the Saussurean distinction between synchrony and diachrony, and its controversial correspondence to the distinction between metaphor and metonymy, see Roman Jakobson, "The Metaphoric and Metonymic Poles," Chapter 5 of Roman Jakobson and Morris Halle, *Fundamentals of Language* (The Hague: Mouton, 1956).

4. As cited by Charles Trinkaus, *In Our Image and Likeness*, 2 vols. (Chicago: University of Chicago Press, 1970), 1, 63.

5. Roland M. Frye, *God, Man, and Satan* (Princeton: N.J.: Princeton University Press, 1960), pp. 9–10. See John Calvin, *Institutes of the Christian Religion*, trans. Ford Lewis Battles; ed. John T. McNeill, 2 vols. (Philadelphia: The Westminster Press, Library of Christian Classics, 1960), 1, 225ff.

6. Calvin, *Institutes*, 1, 225ff.

7. The passage in question is Genesis 6:6.

8. On metaphorical structure in *Paradise Lost*, see Jackson I. Cope, *The Metaphorical Epic* (Baltimore, Md.: Johns Hopkins Press, 1962). Cope stresses the "radical interdependence of metaphor and paradox" (p. 6). Cope's definition of *Paradise Lost* as metaphorical balances Isabel MacCaffrey's argument on behalf of the mythical character of Milton's epic in *Paradise Lost as "Myth"* (Cambridge, Mass.: Harvard University Press, 1959). MacCaffrey's own argument may be seen as a reaction to the tendency of modern Milton scholars to study *Paradise Lost* piecemeal rather than to explore its coherence.

9. Paul Ricoeur, *The Rule of Metaphor*, trans. Robert Czerny with Kathleen McLaughlin and John Costello (Toronto: University of Toronto Press, 1977), p. 196.

10. Ibid.

11. Ricoeur cites Aristotle's *Poetics:* "'To metaphorize well,' said Aristotle, 'implies an intuitive perception of the similarity in dissimilars'" (ibid., p. 6; see also p. 192).

12. John Halkett, *Milton and the Idea of Matrimony* (New Haven, Conn.: Yale University Press, 1970), pp. 57, 67–68.

13. Ricoeur, *Rule of Metaphor*, p. 196.

14. Halkett, *Idea of Matrimony*, p. 104, offers a reading of the "sweet reluctant amorous delay" passage that amplifies what I have said.

15. Ibid., p. 47.

16. Kerrigan, *Sacred Complex*, pp. 198–207, explains Raphael's traditional role as an authority on health; Alistair Fowler, in his edition of *Paradise Lost* (London: Longmans, 1971), notes to 5, 221–23 and 4, 166–71, remarks that Raphael is the "appropriate archangel to choose for a mission that involves marital relations," citing his role in the apocryphal Book of Tobit. The connection that Kerrigan draws between Raphael and medical concerns, however, was the more prominent one in the seventeenth century. Robert Fludd, for example, in a diagram found in *Integrum Laborum Mysterium*, shows Raphael with Gabriel, Michael, and Uriel guarding man in his castle of health. Allen G. Debus, *The Chemical Philosophy*, 2 vols. (New York: Neale Watson, 1977) 1, 251, reprints this diagram. Fowler himself mentions that Raphael's name means "Health of God," and the strategy in Tobit, by which Tobias is able to defeat the devil and win his bride, depends on a folk chemical warfare that demonstrates Raphael's scientific genius rather than his skill as a marriage counselor.

17. Joseph Mead, *The Complete Works*, ed. John Worthington (London, 1677), p. 192.

18. Evans, *Paradise Lost and the Genesis Tradition*, explains Milton's emphasis on the love between Adam and Eve in the narration of the Fall as a derivation of the allegorical tradition in which Adam and Eve represent different faculties of the

psyche (pp. 266–68). Whether or not Milton had the allegorical tradition in mind when he constructed the episodes leading to the Fall, however, the relationship between Adam and Eve must be seen to transcend whatever allegories may inform it. The most persuasive and influential writers on the Fall have rightly focused on Adam and Eve as characters, not faculties, and on the responsibilities to each other that their love and marriage properly include or exclude. See, for example, E. M. W. Tillyard, *Studies in Milton* (London: Chatto and Windus, 1951), pp. 8–52; A. J. A. Waldock, *Paradise Lost and Its Critics* (Cambridge: Cambridge University Press, 1947), pp. 25–64.

19. In first establishing Adam's life outside of the Garden, Milton exploits the sequence of events in the biblical narrative of Man's creation. In Genesis 3:7, God creates Man; in 3:8 he plants the Garden and then places Man it it. I have not been able to find any literary precedents in the hexameral tradition detailing the unfallen Adam's experiences outside of the Garden. Evans, *Paradise Lost and the Genesis Tradition*, p. 258, remarks that "nothing quite like this had been written since Dracontius's *Carmen de Deo*." But Evans refers only to a scene where "Adam also wakes up, tests his voice, and gazes around him in wonder at the green fields and the creatures grazing in them." Dracontius does not place the scene outside the Garden, nor does Evans remark specifically on the location of Milton's version of the scene. Nevertheless, Evans perceptively notes that, in Milton's handling, the scene is something of an intelligence test, and that Adam's "destiny lies in the garden." Milton probably knew of commentaries that inferred from Adam's creation outside the Garden that Paradise was an extra gift to humankind and not a place that Adam deserves according to his original nature. See Arnold Williams, *The Common Expositor* (Chapel Hill: University of North Carolina Press, 1948), p. 67.

20. In describing the torments of despair, Robert Burton, *The Anatomy of Melancholy*, eds. Floyd Dell and Paul Jordan-Smith (New York: Tudor Publishing, 1955), p. 946, says that those who suffer it "can neither eat, drink, nor sleep."

21. The correspondence between knowledge of Man and knowledge of God was a commonplace of medieval and renaissance thought based on the belief that Man was created in the image of God. See Trinkaus, *Image and Likeness*. Of reformed theologians, Calvin was the most thorough and consistent in applying the principle of correspondence between God and Man. For Calvin, as Edward Dowey comments in *The Knowledge of God in Calvin's Theology* (New York: Columbia University Press, 1952), p. 20, "every theological statement has an anthropological correlate and vice versa." On the matter of images in *Paradise Lost* and creatures' choices as images of God, see Michael McCanles, *Dialectical Criticism and Renaissance Literature* (Berkeley and Los Angeles: University of California Press, 1975), pp. 124–54.

22. In proportional terms, one could say that nature is to God as Eve is to Adam. Diagrams in Robert Fludd's *Utrusque Cosmi Maiores Scilecit Minores Metaphysica*, 2d ed., 2 vols. (Oppenheim, 1617–21), 1, tract. i, 4–5, picture a cosmos in which God holds the hand of a female figure, representing nature, who holds the hands of a male figure, representing Man. Given the importance of grasping by the hand in Book VIII of *Paradise Lost*, and the analogical resemblance of the relation between Adam and Eve to the relation between God and nature, these diagrams suggest the relevance of Fludd's work to Milton's.

23. In the first image of Donne's sonnet, God is known simply as the Creator, the artisan who must break and remake a spoiled piece. In the second image, God appears as a king who must retake a city that owes him allegiance. In the third, God is described as a betrayed lover who must ravish a resistant beloved. Although all three metaphors in Donne's sonnet are matched by Adam's narration of his creation, Donne's depiction of the relations between Man and God is considerably more violent, as befits, I suppose, life in a fallen world.

24. Pierre de La Primaudaye, *The French Academy* (London, 1589), p. 133.

25. Mead, *Works*, p. 225.

26. W. R. Parker, *Milton: A Life*, 2 vols. (Oxford: Clarendon Press, 1968), 1, 71–72.

27. On the cross as a symbol of triumph and not of defeat, and on Milton's probable awareness of that tradition, particularly with reference to *Paradise Regain'd*, see Charles A. Huttar, "The Passion of Christ in *Paradise Regained*," *English Language Notes* 19 (1982), pp. 236–60.

Chapter 8. A Triumph of Difference

1. See Jacques Derrida, "Differance," and "Form and Meaning: A Note on the Phenomenology of Language," in *Speech and Phenomena and Other Essays on Husserl's Theory of Signs*, trans. D. B. Allison, (Evanston, Ill.: Northwestern University Press, 1973), pp. 107–60.

2. One fault in Fish's compelling analysis of the Fall is that he does not discriminate between men and angels. It is not enough to say, with Dennis Burden, for example, that angels and men are alike in that God tests their obedience by issuing apparently pointless edicts (*The Logical Epic* [Cambridge, Mass.: Harvard University Press, 1967], p. 125). And although one might agree with Northrop Frye that the exaltation of the Son is the angelic equivalent of the forbidden fruit, one should also question why the fruit is the appropriate test for Man, and the Son for the angels (*Five Essays on Milton's Epics* [London: Routledge and Kegan Paul, 1966], p. 34). Stanley E. Fish remarks that the obedient acts of the angels have no significance except insofar as they manifest the unfallen attitudes of the angels, their unfailing ability to "stand" even when, for example, they have been blasted off their feet *Surprised by Sin* (1967; Berkeley and Los Angeles: University of California Press, 1971), pp. 184–86. The mock heroics of the War in Heaven, claims Fish, underscore Milton's conviction that conventional heroics, battlefield or otherwise, are at best tangential and in fact irrelevant to the true heroism of unwavering faith regardless of the circumstances. Fish's emphasis on faith and obedience reduces the range of possible significance of any given action to two alternatives: 1) what God wants; 2) against what God wants. Consequently, the story, as Fish himself concludes, is designed to consume itself along with all suggestion of subtlety and complexity.

I would argue, however, that the war is mock heroic not because Milton wishes to satirize physical heroism as being irrelevant to the criterion of obedience. At least for the good angels, the war is mock heroic for the same reason that playing poker for buttons is mock gambling — it does not hurt when you lose. The frivolity of the immortals relative to humankind is something Milton borrowed from Homer. Where it might not make any difference to a good angel in what situation he displays his faith, humans are prone by nature to take circumstances more seriously. The either-or of the angelic realm simply does not suit human experience, and God himself implicitly recognizes this difference when considering the Fall of Man (3, 93–134); indeed, the exercise of mercy generally depends on the interpretive weight allowed to circumstance.

3. Mead describes the three heavens as the Empyreal or the "heaven of Glory," the Ethereal or "starry heaven," and the air of "Sublunary heaven." Each heaven has its own proper inhabitants, the angels for Empyreal heaven, the stars for Ethereal heaven, and "the Fowls of heaven" for the air. See Joseph Mead, *The Complete Works*, ed. John Worthington (London, 1677), p. 614.

4. Frye, *Five Essays*, p. 68. As John Halkett, *Milton and the Idea of Matrimony* (New Haven, Conn.: Yale University Press, 1970), p. 122, argues, "Adam loves in Eve precisely what the angel tells him to," and "it is exactly the perfection of his marriage with Eve which acts upon Adam as the greatest incentive to succumb to the temptation to disobey."

5. Burden, *Logical Epic*, pp. 86ff., is particularly persuasive in his analysis of the dispute.

6. John Austin would describe Adam and Eve's linguistic practices during their dispute as "perlocutionary." In *How to Do Things with Words* (Oxford: Clarendon Press, 1970), p. 108, Austin defines "perlocutionary" practices as "what we bring about or achieve *by* saying something, such as convincing, persuading, deterring, and even, say, surprising or misleading."

7. I am here indebted to E.M.W. Tillyard's reading of the conversation between Adam and Eve (*Studies in Milton* [London: Routledge and Kegan Paul, 1951], pp. 117–19). I obviously read the separation scene as being significant for our understanding of why the Fall occurs. In my view, Eve represents at this point a regressive tendency within humankind. Similarly, if Adam were more secure or mature, less vulnerable to narcissistic injury, he, paradoxically, would have felt free to exercise his authority over Eve more wisely. Neither is guilty of evil here, but both act immaturely, and that, in this context, means regressively. This sets the stage for the metamorphic catastrophe. For a recent, contrary view of the separation scene, see Diane Kelsey McColley, *Milton's Eve* (Urbana: University of Illinois Press, 1983), pp. 140–86.

8. John Milton, *Paradise Lost*, ed. Alistair Fowler (London: Longmans, 1971), note to 9, 393–96.

9. J. M. Evans, *Paradise Lost and the Genesis Tradition* (Oxford: Clarendon Press, 1968), pp. 250–51, traces the image of the elm and the vine as an expression of wedded love to Catullus' *Epithalamium*. He comments that Milton took advantage of a long poetic tradition in drawing an "equation between the garden and the marriage of the first pair."

10. To persuade Pomona to relent, Vertumnus describes the tragic effects of the maiden Anaxarete's disdain for her suitor (Ovid, *Met.* 14, 690ff.).

11. See Fish's analysis of the serpent's rhetorical strategy, in *Surprised by Sin*, pp. 247–54. I have also been influenced by C. S. Lewis' commentary on the temptation and Fall, *A Preface to Paradise Lost* (London: Oxford University Press, 1942), pp. 121–22.

12. Various allegorical interpretations of the Fall were available to Milton, beginning, probably, with Philo's in *De Opificio Mundi*. Depending on the interpreter, Adam and Eve could be cast in a variety of roles. I have followed Fowler's nomenclature in associating Eve with *ratio* and Adam with *intellectus* or *mens* (Fowler, ed., *Paradise Lost*, note to 9, 360–61 and 370–75). For a history of the allegorical treatments, see Evans, *Paradise Lost and the Genesis Tradition*, pp. 69–77, 266–68. One need not rely on allegorical titles or strictly associate Adam and Eve with particular faculties in order to see that Eve represents an aspect of Man that requires the guidance of moral wisdom. See Russell E. Smith, Jr., "Adam's Fall," *ELH* 34 (1968), pp. 527–39.

13. Smith, "Adam's Fall," p. 539, maintains that Eve represents Adam's desire for angelic knowledge. While I agree with Smith that we may see Adam and Eve as parts of a whole, I do not think that either one of them falls out of desire for angelic knowledge per se. Eve sees the fruit as a quick way to achieve superior status, and she desires angelic status, not the knowledge that goes with it.

14. Irving Massey, *The Gaping Pig: Literature and Metamorphosis* (Berkeley and Los Angeles: University of California Press, 1976), p. 99.

15. Frye, for example, remarks that "When Eve . . . comes to Adam and urges him to fall with her, that is the point at which Adam should have 'divorced' Eve" (*Five Essays*, p. 69). Burden, *Logical Epic*, p. 171, agrees.

Chapter 9. The Necessity of Glory

1. William Empson, *Milton's God* (1961; Cambridge: Cambridge University Press, 1981), p. 9.

2. Lester A. Beaurline, ed., *Epicoene* (Lincoln: University of Nebraska Press, 1966), p. xii.

3. Stanley E. Fish, *Surprised by Sin* (1967; Berkeley and Los Angeles: University of California Press, 1971), p. 350.

4. Ibid., p. 289.

5. Empson, *Milton's God*, p. 10.

6. Ibid., pp. 11, 272–73.

7. Ibid., p. 241.

8. Ibid., pp. 244–77.

9. C. S. Lewis, *A Preface to Paradise Lost* (London: Oxford University Press, 1942), p. 93; see also Northrop Frye, *Five Essays on Milton's Epics* (London: Routledge and Kegan Paul, 1966), p. 99.

10. John Smith, "The Excellency and Nobleness of True Religion," in *The Cambridge Platonists*, ed. C. A. Patrides (Cambridge, Mass.: Harvard University Press, 1970), p. 170. Subsequent references will be given by page number in the text.

11. Sir Thomas Browne, *The Major Works*, ed. C. A. Patrides (New York: Penguin, 1977), pp. 104–5.

12. Frye, *Five Essays*, p. 7.

13. Arthur O. Lovejoy, "Milton and the Paradox of the Fortunate Fall," *ELH* 4 (1937), p. 178.

14. John Robinson, *Essayes or Observations Divine and Morall Collected Out*

of Holy Scriptures, Ancient and Moderne Writers, Both Divine and Humane (London, 1638), p. 37.

15. Jacob Burckhardt, *The Civilization of the Renaissance in Italy*, trans. S.G.C. Middlemore (New York: Harper, 1929), p. 431.

16. Dennis Burden, *The Logical Epic* (Cambridge, Mass.: Harvard University Press, 1967), p. 37.

Chapter 10. The Genealogy of Moral Glory

1. J. M. Evans, *Paradise Lost and the Genesis Tradition* (Oxford: Clarendon Press, 1968), p. 224.

2. Stella Purce Revard, *The War in Heaven* (Ithaca, N.Y.: Cornell University Press, 1980), pp. 23–25, most recently has stressed that we can learn much about Satan's motivation and Milton's theology from the rebellion; William Empson, *Milton's God* (1961; Cambridge: Cambridge University Press, 1981), pp. 71–90, argues brilliantly regarding the ramifications of this episode; William B. Hunter, Jr., agrees with Evans that "the exaltation of the Son has never been related to Satan in this way by any Christian tradition" ("The War in Heaven: The Exaltation of the Son," in William B. Hunter, Jr., C. A. Patrides, and J. H. Adamson, *Bright Essence* [Salt Lake City: University of Utah Press, 1971] p. 118).

3. As the *OED* indicates, *Duns* came to mean, by the sixteenth century, "one whose study of books has left him dull and stupid, . . . a dull pedant" or "one who shows no capacity for learning." William T. Costello, *The Scholastic Curriculum at Early Seventeenth-Century Cambridge* (Cambridge, Mass.: Harvard University Press, 1958), remarks that "Scotus seems always to head the litany of the damned among the medieval scholastics" (p. 170). See also McEuen's notes to Prolusion 3 (*CP* 1, 241–48). Nevertheless, Costello again reports, "early seventeenth-century Cambridge held with, and understood, the scholastics, even if some of them were proscribed" (*Scholastic Curriculum*, p. 121). He cites the advice of an older theologian to a young divine, advice that recommends Scotus as "most iudicious as well as subtile" and also recommends a list of commentators on Scotus (p. 122). For an indication of the availability of Scotus at Cambridge, see Herbert M. Adams, *Catalogue of Books Printed on the Continent of Europe, 1501–1600, in Cambridge Libraries*, 2 vols. (Cambridge: Cambridge University Press, 1967).

4. For summaries of Duns Scotus' metaphysics, and particularly of his concept of being, see Etienne Gilson, *History of Christian Philosophy in the Middle Ages* (New York: Random House, 1955), pp. 454–65; F. C. Coplestone, *A History of Medieval Philosophy* (New York: Harper and Row, 1972), pp. 213–29; Allan B. Wolter, "Duns Scotus," *Encyclopedia of Philosophy*, 8 vols. (New York: MacMillan, 1967), 2, 427–36; C[harles] Balic, "Duns Scotus," *New Catholic Encyclopedia* (New York: Mac-Graw Hill, 1967). John K. Ryan and Bernardine M. Bonansea edited a collection of essays on Scotus' philosophy entitled *John Duns Scotus, 1265–1965*, vol. 3 of *Studies in Philosophy and the History of Philosophy* (Washington, D.C.: Catholic University of America Press, 1965).

5. Milton's clearest expression of God as the indispensable conservator of crea-

tion occurs during Raphael's discourse on food (5, 398–433). Scotus' position parallels Milton's: "a creature . . . is at all times equally dependent upon God for its being, for it always has the same being from him through the same divine volition. . . . In similar fashion, although the being of a creature is permanent, nevertheless as regards God it is always in a quasi state of becoming, that is to say, it is being and it is never . . . actual apart from and independent of everything else" (*God and Creatures: The Quodlibetal Questions*, trans. Felix Alluntis and Allan B. Wolter [Princeton, N.J.: Princeton University Press, 1975], p. 275).

6. On the link between Scotus and Avicenna, see Wolter, "Duns Scotus," and Balic, "Duns Scotus."

7. John Smith, "The Excellency and Nobleness of True Religion," in *The Cambridge Platonists*, ed. C. A. Patrides (Cambridge, Mass.: Harvard University Press, 1970), p. 160.

8. Gordon Leff, *The Dissolution of the Medieval Outlook* (New York: New York University Press, 1976), pp. 13–14; Gilson, *History of Christian Philosophy*, pp. 447–71. On the renewed emphasis on absolute versus ordained power, with particular attention to its historical effects, see Edward Grant, "The Condemnation of 1277, God's Absolute Power, and Physical Thought in the Late Middle Ages," *Viator: Medieval and Renaissance Studies* 10 (Berkeley and Los Angeles: University of California Press, 1979), pp. 211–44.

9. John Duns Scotus, *Opera Omnia*, ed. Luke Wadding, 12 vols. (Lyons, 1639), V, 1368 (*Libri Primi Sententiarum*, Dist. XLIV, quest. i, n. 2). Translation mine.

10. Duns Scotus, *Quodlibetal Questions*, p. 391.

11. Grant, "Condemnation of 1277," pp. 226–29.

12. Leff, *Dissolution*, p. 18.

13. Ibid., p. 52, maintains that Scotus' insistence on "God's freedom to do whatever is logically possible, i.e., noncontradictory . . . inaugurated a theological development that continued in an unbroken line to Luther."

14. The first excerpt is from Duns Scotus, *Philosophical Writings*, ed. and trans. Allan Wolter (London: Thomas Nelson and Sons, 1962), p. 173; the second from Duns Scotus, *Quodlibetal Questions*, p. 378.

15. Dennis Danielson, *Milton's Good God* (Cambridge: Cambridge University Press, 1982), pp. 149–54. The proposed unity of God's will and his essential goodness would seem to render the term *good* meaningless "because," as Empson argues, such a God "includes all value in himself" (*Milton's God*, p. 156). Although the notoriously obscure Scotus is almost impossible to pin down on this subject, it seems that his notion of the formal distinction provides a possible answer to the paradox posed by Empson. Briefly put, the formal distinction allows Scotus both to affirm the unity of the divine character and to distinguish the attributes that constitute it (see *CP* 6, 138–49). Thus Scotus can claim that God's essential goodness is logically prior to his will, thereby subjecting the divine volition to the good. Scotus' opinion in *Quodlibetal Questions*, one of his very latest works, seems to me definitive: "As for the divine will at least this seems certain: it is simply necessitated to love its own goodness" (p. 376). On Scotus' voluntarism and the formal distinction, see Gilson, *History of Christian Philosophy*, pp. 459–61.

16. The quotation is from Ludwig Wittgenstein, *Notebooks 1914–1916*, ed. G. H. von Wright and G. E. M. Anscombe (New York: Harper and Brothers, 1961), p. 78e (cf. prop. 6.422 of Wittgenstein's *Tractatus Logico-Philosophicus*, trans. D. F. Pears and B. F. McGuiness [London: Routledge and Kegan Paul, 1961], pp. 71–72). Allan B. Wolter mentions Wittgenstein's resemblance to Scotus in his essay, "The Formal Distinction," in *Scotus, 1265–1965*, ed. Ryan and Bonansea, p. 59; and especially in the introduction to John Duns Scotus, *A Treatise on God as First Principle*, trans. Allan B. Wolter (Chicago: Franciscan Herald Press, 1966), p. xxi. Here Wolter notes the parallel between Scotus' God as the source of all possibility and the role of simple objects in Wittgenstein's *Tractatus*.

17. Wittgenstein, *Notebooks*, p. 77e, 73e; cf. Wittgenstein, *Tractatus*, prop. 6.43 (p. 72).

18. On Milton's angels see Robert H. West, *Milton and the Angels* (Athens: University of Georgia Press, 1955).

19. Duns Scotus, *Quodlibetal Questions*, p. 406.

20. John Milton, *Paradise Lost*, ed. Alistair Fowler (London: Longmans, 1971), note to 5, 594–96.

21. Duns Scotus, *Quodlibetal Questions*, pp. 389, 402.

22. Scotus, as Gilson remarks in *History of Christian Philosophy*, argued that God "is free to create or not, and to act through secondary causes or not; that he is omnipresent to all creatures and free to set up any moral code he pleases as long as it deals with rules of human conduct whose relations to his own essence are not necessary ones. Nothing of what depends on the free decisions of this absolutely free God is philosophically deducible" (p. 464).

23. Duns Scotus, *Quodlibetal Questions*, pp. 403–4.

24. This limitation on divine power appears most clearly in the irreversibility of damnation once it has occurred. Scotus argues that God can save one who, he foresees, will die in mortal sin — "possibile est Deum salvare aliquem, qui tamen morietur in peccato mortali finaliter" — but that once a creature, say, Judas Iscariot, has been doomed to perdition, not even God can alter his fate — "non autem conceditur ipsum posse salvare Iudam iam damnatur" (*Opera Omnia,* V, 1369 [*Libri Primi Sententiarum*, Dist. XLIV, quest. i, n. 3]). Similarly, Milton's God in Book III looks down from heaven, sees the already damned Satan, and reaffirms his damnation. At the same time, God foresees that man will fall into deadly sin and yet determines to save him. While Judas conventionally typifies the lost soul for Scotus, Satan fills the same role for Milton.

25. Empson, *Milton's God*, p. 77. Fowler's reply (Fowler, ed., *Paradise Lost*, note to 5, 756) argues beside the point.

26. C. S. Lewis, *A Preface to Paradise Lost* (London: Oxford University Press, 1942), pp. 27–39.

27. Hunter, "The Exaltation of the Son," p. 118.

28. The argument for Milton's Arianism, defined according to Nicene terms, has been set forth in formidable detail by Michael Bauman, *Milton's Arianism* (Frankfurt, W. Germany: Verlag Peter Lang, 1987).

29. Wolter, "Duns Scotus," *Encyclopedia of Philosophy*, 2, 435.

30. If Man had only a natural will, he would be incapable of sin, but subject to

errors in judgment. Scotus marks the difference between "the will with respect to its natural inclination and the will as free" (Wolter, "Duns Scotus," pp. 434-35). Creatures do not fall from God's favor simply because of an error in judgment. Abdiel, hoping that Satan is guilty only of such an error, recommends repentance after explaining that God's actions are consistent with right reason.

31. As Fowler's note to 5, 601 (Fowler, ed., *Paradise Lost*) indicates, the "sonorous roll-call of titles" alludes to Col. 1:16, "a proof text for Christ's agency in the creation of angels." Fowler does not mention, however, that Milton also uses this passage, with others, to "preclude the possibility" of the Son's "being co-essential, and of his generation from eternity" (*CP* 6, 211).

32. Hunter, "The Exaltation of the Son," pp. 126-29.

33. Danielson, *Milton's Good God*, pp. 214-24, claims that Milton's view of the Son's place in creation parallels Scotus'. Scotus argues that God predestines the Incarnation from all eternity, and that it occurs independently of any foreknowledge of Man's Fall. Scotus maintains this position in order to distinguish the good of the Incarnation from any dependence on sin. Danielson presents God's exaltation of the Son over the angels in *Paradise Lost* as an analogue to Scotus' doctrine. We are led to conclude, therefore, that even if Man had not fallen, the "goodness immense" that results from the Incarnation would have occurred.

But Milton does link God's foreknowledge of the Fall with the Son's offer to become Man and inextricably involves the Incarnation with Redemption: "Thou therefore, whom thou only canst redeem, / Their nature also to thy nature join" (*PL* 3, 281-82). Why would the Son take on human nature when unfallen Man would eventually assume angelic status and thus be incorporated under the Son's headship? If we keep unfallen Man's upward mobility in mind, therefore, the comparison between Scotus' and Milton's doctrines of the Son's role in creation becomes more exact, if less apt. In *Paradise Lost* God uses the Incarnation to reconstitute the intended goodness of union between Earth and heaven that Man has jeopardized through his sin. For Milton and Scotus both, sin means a deficiency in what *ought* to have been (*CP* 6, 391; cf. Duns Scotus, *Quodlibetal Questions*, p. 414).

34. Scotus' reasoning about the equality of the Father and the Son depends upon their sharing the same divine nature: "Equality is a necessary consequent of distinct supposita in the divine nature" (*Quodlibetal Questions*, p. 157). Milton, however, insisted that dual subsistence in the same essence was impossible because contradictory (*CP* 6, 209-13). Scotus gets around such objections by distinguishing between God's essential unity and the relative distinctions between the persons of the Trinity: "What is predicated according to substance is common (to all three persons)," but "incommunicable or hypostatic being is distinctive for each person there" (*Quodlibetal Questions*, p. 107). Milton calls such distinctions as those between substance, essence, and hypostasis tricks "to dazzle the eyes of freshmen" (*CP* 6, 224).

35. Duns Scotus, *Quodlibetal Questions*, p. 43.

36. Given the accuracy of the Son's analysis of the foreseen Fall (3, 144-66), I would argue that the Father's decision to show mercy — though arguably made freely — is necessary according to the divine goodness. If so, this is an example of "compatibilism" between necessity and freedom in the divine will. If God dooms Man to perdition, allowing Satan to win the battle — or even if he simply annihilates the

offenders – he will have acted in a fashion contrary to his "goodness" and "greatness" (3, 165). If the only choice consistent with previous decrees and with God's essential character is some form of mercy toward Man, then God *must* freely choose to show mercy. Accordingly, the Father's decision to offer redemption to Man, along with the details of Milton's doctrine of salvation, are prior to the Son's willingness to expiate Man's sin (3, 129–34, 173–202, 227–65). So also, in *Christian Doctrine*, the chapters on divine decree and on predestination precede the chapter on the Son. The resolution to save Man is first and necessary; the means – the Incarnate Son – is secondary and contingent, that is, part of the ordained order.

37. Hunter, "Milton's Arianism Reconsidered," in *Bright Essence*, pp. 38–41.

Conclusion

1. Leo Tolstoy, *War and Peace*, trans. Louise and Aylmer Maude; ed. George Gibian (New York: Norton, 1966), p. 1339.

2. Simone Weil, *The Iliad or The Poem of Force* (Wallingford, Pa,: Pendle Hill, 1945), p. 13.

3. Milan Kundera, *The Unbearable Lightness of Being*, trans. Michael Heim (New York: Harper and Row, 1984), p. 6. Subsequent references in the text are to this edition.

4. Linda Gregerson, "The Limbs of Truth: Milton's Use of Simile in *Paradise Lost*," *Milton Studies* 14 (1980), p. 136.

5. *LW* 17, 10; 11, 376.

6. William Kerrigan, *The Sacred Complex* (Cambridge, Mass.: Harvard University Press, 1983), pp. 279–80.

7. Kenneth Burke, "Literature as Equipment for Living," in *The Philosophy of Literary Form* (1941, 1967; Berkeley and Los Angeles: University of California Press, 1973), pp. 293–304. I am indebted to Warwick Wadlington, *Reading Faulknerian Tragedy* (Ithaca, N.Y.: Cornell University Press, 1987), for introducing me to the rich interpretive tradition associated with Kenneth Burke and Clifford Geertz.

8. William Hazlitt, "*Lecture on Shakespeare and Milton*," chap. 2 of *Milton: Poetry and Prose*, ed. A.M.D. Hughes (Oxford: Clarendon Press, 1920), p. 42.

9. The narrator informs us that "Spirits . . . / Can either Sex assume" (*PL* 1, 423–24; but see 10, 890). The ability to assume either sex, however, does not mean that the angels are hermaphrodites. Milton consistently depicts the angels as essentially masculine, though they possess what for Milton is a feminine capacity to submit and yield. Furthermore, by calling the angels promiscuous, I intend an allusion to Raphael's description of their effortless lovemaking, not an implication of immoral lack of discrimination. Milton never suggests that angels have particular marriage partners; he did not even advocate monogamy within human marriage. Finally, by describing the angels as sterile, I simply reiterate the most significant sexual difference between humans and angels, one that Raphael neglects in his paean to the superiority of spiritual lovemaking: angels do not breed. C. S. Lewis, *A Preface to Paradise Lost* (London: Oxford University Press, 1942), pp. 112–15, addresses these same concerns and , I think rightly, attributes the details of Milton's depiction to the views of contemporary scientific thought. But he also judges Milton imprudent, I think wrongly, for having raised the matter.

INDEX